D1727954

Contributions to Management Science

More information about this series at http://www.springer.com/series/1505

Robert C. Gericke

Corporate Governance and Risk Management in Financial Institutions

An International Comparison Between Brazil and Germany

Für Hilko,
mit herzlichem Dank
für Deine Freundschaft!

Robert.

Springer

Robert C. Gericke
Frankfurt am Main, Germany

ISSN 1431-1941   ISSN 2197-716X   (electronic)
Contributions to Management Science
ISBN 978-3-319-67310-3   ISBN 978-3-319-67311-0   (eBook)
https://doi.org/10.1007/978-3-319-67311-0

Library of Congress Control Number: 2018932418

Printed on acid-free paper

This Springer imprint is published by the registered company Springer International Publishing AG part of
Springer Nature.
The registered company address is: Gewerbestrasse 11, 6330 Cham, Switzerland

I'd like to thank my mother Ingeborg, who from early on planted and nourished the idea in me of one day writing a doctoral thesis. For this and a thousand other reasons, this monograph is dedicated to her.

Preface

In this monograph, we have discussed various aspects of corporate governance and risk management from an international viewpoint and with a special focus on Brazil and Germany as well as banking, taking into account the developments since the beginning of the latest financial crisis in 2007/2008 and until 2013/2014.

Clearly, Brazil and Germany are quite different countries—culturally and economically. Still, there are some similarities, reflected for instance in total market capitalization of listed companies or the Open Budget Index.

In terms of corporate governance, we could confirm that the general impression is still that of clear differences, but when looking deeper into the different topics, we found that differences are diminishing as Brazil is improving in these areas, while Germany appears to progress quite slowly.

With regard to risk management, differences are perceived to be strong overall but appear to be muted in the area of financial services, certainly due to strict and similar or even identical regulation (e.g., Basel III).

Our analysis of data from surveys used for this study shows that there have been moderate increases in perceived quality, regulation, and importance of both risk management and corporate governance. This is largely true for both countries; still we found that especially regarding corporate governance, such increases have been lower or even nonexistent in Germany.

The reason might be that the Brazilian society feels a stronger necessity to improve in those areas than that of Germany, which might have started from a higher level. Still, the crises (financial and European sovereign) have had more impact—although still moderate—on Germany than on Brazil.

The hypotheses that corporate governance and risk management had become more important over the 2007–2013 period could however not be fully confirmed, given that results of the analysis of annual reports did not produce consistent results.

Agreement existed among participants in our survey that risk management is a part of corporate governance, although also here, affirmation from participants covering Germany was weaker than that from respondents working in Brazil.

Consequently, we believe that risk management should be included as a section in its own right in those corporate governance codes where this is not yet the case. This would also help to further strengthen the conceptual integration of risk management as part of corporate governance and might support the advancement of both.

Furthermore, the establishment of risk, advisory, and remuneration committees (where not already in place) and family councils for family-owned businesses might be helpful to instill more discipline and achieve a higher internal independence.

In summary, no major changes have been perceived to have taken place in the areas of corporate governance and risk management since the beginning of the financial crisis, while it is evident that a number of (regulatory) developments have occurred during that period. They may however have been relatively constant and were therefore, subjectively, less noted, or expectations had been higher so that the actions taken appear weak in the perception of our respondents.

Keywords: Corporate governance, Risk management, Financial institutions, Brazil and Germany

Frankfurt, Germany   Robert C. Gericke
Summer 2017

Acknowledgments

I would like to thank everyone who supported me before and during the elaboration of this document. Without their support, the realization of this dream would not have been possible for me. Despite all the valuable contributions received, all remaining errors or omissions are entirely mine.

While it would be almost impossible to name everyone to whom I am deeply grateful in relation to this monograph, I'd like to mention a few.

First and foremost, I am highly indebted to my doctoral advisor, Professor Doutor Renato Pereira, who somehow managed to push me into the right direction all along—and finally over the finish line just before the deadline.

Furthermore, I am grateful to all professors and lecturers of the doctoral course preceding the elaboration of this paper—their input has been very helpful in forming a basis for this study, particularly in showing the width and depth of the faculty of economics. The same is true for the colleagues in that course who shared their know-how and passion for academic work with me.

Also, I'd like to thank everyone who responded to my queries, be it in libraries, universities, publishers, or associations in Brazil, Germany, or Portugal. A special *"obrigado"* goes out to those employees of organizations who forwarded the links to the questionnaires to their members and colleagues.

Most of the hypotheses presented here could not have been tested without the time and energy 282 respondents put into answering my survey, and the results of the same would not have become that clear to me without the dedication and hard work of Magdalena Kwiatkowska whom I am deeply grateful for her analytical support.

Independently from this thesis, I am forever indebted to those gentlemen I am lucky enough to consider my mentors and who, together with many others, instilled in me the curiosity, endurance, and attitude needed to joyfully embrace every project—no matter how challenging—just like they do: Hans-Jürgen Albrecht, Markus Enders, and Erfried Seidl.

Last but certainly not least, I'd like to express my heartfelt gratitude to my wife Michelle, who endured years during which this project stood between us and many other things we could have done while I was reading or writing—we shall do them now! *Te amo pra sempre.*

Contents

List of Abbreviations

3BL	Triple Bottom Line (also: TBL)
AG	*Aktiengesellschaft* (German Stock Corporation)
AIFM	Alternative Investment Fund Managers Directive
AktG	*Aktiengesetz* (German Stock Companies Act)
ANBIMA	*Associação Brasileira das Entidades dos Mercados Financeiro e de Capitais* (Brazilian Association of Financial and Capital Market Entities)
APE	*Associações de Poupança e Empréstimo* (Brazilian savings and loan associations)
AQR	Asset Quality Review
AR	Annual Report
BaFin	*Bundesanstalt für Finanzdienstleistungsaufsicht* (German Banking Supervisory Authority)
BB	Banco do Brasil
BCB	*Banco Central do Brasil* (Central Bank of Brazil)
BCBS	Basel Committee on Banking Supervision
BCGI	Brazilian Corporate Governance Index
BIITS	Brazil, India, Indonesia, Turkey, and South Africa
BilMoG	*Bilanzmodernisierungsgesetz* (German Act regarding the modernization of accounting rules)
BilReG	*Bilanzrechtsreformgesetz* (Act for the reform of accounting laws)
BIS	Bank for International Settlements
BPB	*Bundeszentrale für politische Bildung* (Federal Agency for Political Education)
BR	Brazil/Brazilian
BRIC	Brazil, Russia, India, and China
BRL	Brazilian Real
BSP	Board Service Provider
CA	Corporate Accountability
CAM	Câmara de Arbitragem do Mercado (Brazilian Arbitration Panel)
CBRM	Change-Based Risk Management

CC	Corporate Citizenship
CEC	Corporate Environmental Citizenship
CEE	Central and Eastern Europe
CEO	Chief Executive Officer
CER	Corporate Environmental Responsibility
CIRS	Critical Incident Reporting System
CFO	Chief Financial Officer
CFP	Corporate Financial Performance
CG	Corporate Governance
CMN	*Conselho Monetário Nacional* (Brazilian National Monetary Council)
COO	Chief Operating Officer
COSO	Committee of Sponsoring Organizations of the Treadway Commission
COSY	Company Oriented Sustainability
CP	Corporate Philanthropy
CR	Corporate Responsibility
CRD	Capital Requirements Directive
CRO	Chief Risk Officer
CS	Corporate Sustainability
CSP	Corporate Social Performance
CSR	Corporate Social Responsibility (also: RSC)
CVM	*Comissão de Valores Mobiliários* (Brazilian Securities and Exchanges Commission)
DAX	*Deutscher Aktienindex* (German Stock Market Index)
DB	Deutsche Bank
DE	Germany/German
D&O	Directors' and officers' liability insurance
DZB	DZ Bank
EC	European Commission
ECB	European Central Bank
ecoDa	European Confederation of Directors' Associations
E-KPI	Environmental Key Performance Indicator
EL	Expected Loss
ELC	Expected Loss Class
E P&L	Environmental Profit and Loss Statement
EN	English
ERM	Enterprise Risk Management
ERP	Enterprise Resource Planning
ESG	Environmental, Social and Governance
EU	European Union
EUR	Euro
FDI	Foreign Direct Investment
FKAG	Finanzkonglomerate-Aufsichtsgesetz (German Financial Conglomerates Supervisory Act)
FMEA	Failure Mode and Effects Analysis

FMT	Financial Market Trends
FTE	Full Time Equivalent
FVC	Financial Vehicle Corporation
GAAP	Generally Accepted Accounting Principles
GARP	Global Association of Risk Professionals
GCC	Global Corporate Citizenship
GCGC	German Corporate Governance Code (*Deutscher Corporate Governance Kodex*)
GDP	Gross Domestic Product
GEC	Group Executive Committee
GmbH	*Gesellschaft mit beschränkter Haftung* (German Limited Liability Company)
GRC	Governance, Risk, and Compliance
GRCo	Global Risk Committee
GRI	Global Reporting Initiative
H	Hypothesis
HACCP	Hazard Analysis and Critical Control Points
HAZOP	Hazard and Operability Study
HGB	*Handelsgesetzbuch* (German Commercial Code)
HR	Human Resources
HVB	HypoVereinsbank AG/UniCredit
IBGC	*Instituto Brasileiro de Governança Corporativa* (Brazilian Institute of Corporate Governance)
IBGE	*Instituto Brasileiro de Geografia e Estatística* (Brazilian Institute of Geography and Statistics)
ICAAP	Internal Capital Adequacy Assessment Process
ICGN	International Corporate Governance Network
ICS	Internal Control System
IF	Investment Fund
IFRS	International Financial Reporting Standards
IGC	*Índice de Governança Corporativa* (Brazilian Corporate Governance Index)
ILO	International Labour Organization
IMF	International Monetary Fund
IPCA	*Índice Nacional de Preços ao Consumidor Amplo* (Brazilian Extended National Consumer Price Index)
IPCG	*Insituto Português de Corporate Governance* (Portuguese Corporate Governance Institute)
IPO	Initial Public Offering
ISE	*Índice de Sustentabilidade Empresarial* (Sustainability Index of BM&FBovespa)
IT	Information Technology
KAGB	*Kapitalanlagegesetzbuch* (German Capital Investment Act)

KonTraG	*Gesetz zur Kontrolle und Transparenz im Unternehmensbereich* (German Transparency and Control Act)
KPI	Key Performance Indicator
KRI	Key Risk Indicator
KWG	*Kreditwesengesetz* (German Banking Act)
LC	Local currency
LCR	Liquidity Coverage Ratio
LCT	Local currency in thousands
LGD	Loss Given Default
LTI	Long term incentive
LTIP	Long-term incentive plan
M&A	Mergers and Acquisitions
MaRisk	*Mindestanforderungen an das Risikomanagement* (German Minimum Requirements for Risk Management)
MFI	Monetary Financial Institution
MMF	Money Market Fund
MP	Member of Parliament
MR	Management Report
MRC	Management Risk Controlling
N/A	Not applicable/not available
NGO	Non-governmental Organization
NSFR	Net Stable Funding Ratio
NYSE	New York Stock Exchange
OECD	Organization for Economic Cooperation and Development
OCB	Organizational Citizenship Behavior
OTC	Over the Counter
PCGC	Portuguese Corporate Governance Code (*Código de Governo das Sociedades do IPCG*)
PCGK	Public Corporate Governance Kodex (German Public Corporate Governance Code)
PDCA	Plan-Do-Control-Act
PDSA	Plan-Do-Study-Act
PEVC	Private Equity and Venture Capital
PD	Probability of Default
PPP	Purchase Power Parity
PRI	Principles for Responsible Investment
PT	Portugal/Portuguese
Q	Question(s)
RM	Risk Management
RMR	Risk Management Report
ROA	Return on Assets
RSC	*Responsabilidade Social Corporativa* (Corporate Social Responsibility (also: CSR))
RWA	Risk-Weighted Assets

SE	*Societas Europaea* (European Company)
SEC	Securities and Exchange Commission
SD	Sustainable Development
SME	Small and Medium-Sized Enterprises
SoFFin	*Sonderfonds Finanzmarktstabilisierung* (German State fund for financial market stabilization)
SPSS	Statistical Package for the Social Sciences (IBM software)
SRI	Socially Responsible Investment
SRM	Single Resolution Mechanism
STI	Short-term incentive
TAA	Total Adjusted Asset
TBL	Triple Bottom Line (also: 3BL)
TBRL	Brazilian Reais in thousands
TEUR	Euros in thousands
TransPuG	*Gesetz zur weiteren Reform des Aktien- und Bilanzrechts, zur Transparenz und Publizität* (German Act for further reform of the stock and accounting rules, for transparency and publicity)
UK	United Kingdom
UN	United Nations
UNO	United Nations Organization
UNEP	United Nations Environment Programme
UNEP FI	United Nations Environment Program Finance Initiative
US	United States (of America) (also: USA)
USA	United States of America (also: US)
USD	United States Dollar
VaR	Value at Risk
VorstOG	*Vorstandsvergütungs-Offenlegungsgesetz* (German Act regarding the disclosure of management board's compensation)
ZCG	*Zeitschrift für Corporate Governance* (German Review of Corporate Governance)

List of Figures

List of Tables

Chapter 1
Introduction

1.1 Corporate Governance, Risk Management, and the Latest Financial Crisis

In the early 2000s, a number of—mostly developed—economies enacted corporate governance codes which usually apply to publicly traded companies in the respective jurisdictions. Following the 2007–2009 financial crisis, some of those rules have been amended with regards to processes and responsibilities regarding risk management. Even before the Sarbanes-Oxley Act of 2002[1]—which in its Sections 404 and 409 also deals with questions of risk management—a Transparency and Control Act (*Gesetz zur Kontrolle und Transparenz im Unternehmensbereich*—KonTraG) in Germany in 1998 (Brown et al. 2009:548f.) and changes of the Brazilian Act of Corporations (*Lei das Sociedades por Acções; Lei n° 10.303/2001*) in 2001 (Silveira 2010:179) have been introduced in Germany and Brazil respectively, along with non-compulsory industry standards (e.g. *Deutscher Corporate Governance Kodex*, Germany, 2002; *Código das Melhores Práticas de Governança Corporativa*, Brazil, 1999). Since then, and partly during the time frame for implementation and adaptation, one of the most severe financial crises has affected the world economy, whereas both Germany and Brazil have been affected to a lesser extent than many other economies so far, whilst Germany has felt the impact on many of its financial institutions, some of which had to be bailed out.[2] The externalities of banking towards the end of 2009 are shown in Table 1.1.

Together with their predominant economic and political weight in their respective regions and their different, yet comparable legal-economic environments, this

---

[1]The introduction of the Sarbanes-Oxley-Act "*raised hackles around the globe for its perceived 'unilateralism' and lack of statutory exemptions—in short, its apparent eagerness to impose U.S. style governance everywhere*". (Hollister 2005:464, cfr. Klonoski 2012).

[2]E.g. Commerzbank/Dresdner Bank; EuroHypo; HypoRealEstate/Depfa. For details, cfr. 3.5.

© Springer International Publishing AG, part of Springer Nature 2018   1
R. C. Gericke, *Corporate Governance and Risk Management in Financial Institutions*, Contributions to Management Science,
https://doi.org/10.1007/978-3-319-67311-0_1

Table 1.1 Externalities of banking in Brazil, Germany, and the US

Externalities of banking in USD billion			
Country	Capital injection and facilities	Asset purchases, guarantees and facilities	Debt guarantees and facilities
Brazil	0	0	1
Germany	119	711	667
USA	806	3.322	2.300

Source: Blundell-Wignall et al. (2009:24); October 2009 OECD data (estimates)

appears to make those two countries apt objects of a detailed analysis regarding corporate governance and risk management developments between 2007 and 2013, with a special focus on major banks.

This leads us to propose the following set of research questions as a basis for an empirical study in form of a doctoral thesis:

1. What is the current state of corporate governance and risk management in Germany and Brazil?
2. How have these changed since the start of the latest financial crisis?
3. What impact (if any) has this had on corporate governance and risk management structures, reporting and responsibilities of the five major financial institutions of those two countries?

1.2   Rationale

This study is a multi-disciplinary one, combining questions of Economics and Management (Risk Management) with those of Laws (Corporate Law and Social Regulation—Corporate Governance, Transparency), Social Science and Culture, meant to shed light on an area of great importance, which has recently undergone significant changes in a number of economies, in order to draw conclusions for potential future regulations in different jurisdictions.

Studies on corporate governance have so far focused more on questions such as board composition, conflicts of interest regarding positions held on both, management board and supervisory board or, in one-tier board structures, the joint position of Chairman and CEO, diverging interests between shareholders and management (principal-agent-theory) as well as on ownership structures, legal changes, corporate governance and performance, and cross-listings etc.,[3] rather than on the specific question of risk management as a main aspect of corporate governance, being both a current topic and a fundamental one. As such, research on recent developments and findings for future application shall provide useful and unique results.

---

[3]For an overview of studies on several topics with a focus on emerging markets, cfr. Claessens and Yurtoglu (2012).

1.3 Hypotheses

In order to answer the above-mentioned set of questions, an empirical study shall be conducted, checking the validity of the following hypotheses:

1. There have been major changes in risk management since the beginning of the latest financial crisis both in Brazil and Germany

   a. Risk management quality increased since the beginning of the latest financial crisis both in Brazil and Germany
   b. Risk management regulation increased since the beginning of the latest financial crisis both in Brazil and Germany
   c. Risk management importance increased since the beginning of the latest financial crisis both in Brazil and Germany

2. There have been major changes in corporate governance since the beginning of the latest financial crisis both in Brazil and Germany

   a. Corporate governance quality increased since the beginning of the latest financial crisis both in Brazil and Germany
   b. Corporate governance regulation increased since the beginning of the latest financial crisis both in Brazil and Germany
   c. Corporate governance importance increased since the beginning of the latest financial crisis both in Brazil and Germany

3. Corporate governance is significantly different between Brazil and Germany
4. Risk management is significantly different between Brazil and Germany
5. Financial institutions differ significantly between Brazil and Germany
6. Remuneration is now more closely linked to risk management/capped than before the latest financial crisis
7. Risk management is being perceived as more important in financial institutions than in other businesses
8. Corporate Governance being perceived as more important in financial institutions than in other businesses
9. Risk management is not generally understood as part of corporate governance
10. The importance of risk management as part of corporate governance has increased since the latest financial crisis
11. The importance of corporate governance in financial institutions in Brazil and Germany has increased significantly since the beginning of the latest financial crisis

    Indicators would be, in banks' annual reports since 2007:

    a. Corporate governance introduced as an own section
    b. An increased corporate governance word count
    c. An increased crisis word count
    d. An increase in Corporate governance highlighted
    e. An increase in CSR highlighted

12. The importance of risk management in financial institutions in Brazil and Germany has increased significantly since the beginning of the latest financial crisis

    Indicators would be, in banks' annual reports since 2007:

    a. Risk management introduced as an own section
    b. An increased risk management word count
    c. An increased word count referring to risk
    d. An increase in risk management highlighted

1.4   Structure

In order to test and evaluate above-mentioned hypotheses, we propose the following course of research:

1. Inventory of literature (*"state of the art"*) regarding the following topics:

    a. Corporate governance;
    b. Risk management;
    c. Financial institutions;
    d. The latest financial crisis.

2. Overview of the institutional background:

    a. Overview of relevant banking regulation;
    b. Inventory of corporate governance frameworks;
    c. Regulation regarding risk management on an international basis;
    d. Descriptive analysis of major banks in Brazil and Germany.

3. Description of the research design applied in this thesis.
4. Empirical analysis of data.
5. Conclusions: How have risk management and corporate governance issues changed over the 2007–2013 period and how different are Brazil and Germany?

As such, the proposed study shall determine which corporate governance rules/ best practices are suitable to improve risk management.

The remainder of this study is structured as follows: Chapter 2 provides an overview of relevant literature, Chap. 3 shall give an introduction to the institutional background in both countries, including an analysis of the largest banks by assets, Chap. 4 lays out the research design, and finally, Chap. 5 provides for discussion of the findings and conclusions, including the identification of limitations and suggestions for further research.

Chapter 2
Literature Review

Although the topic of corporate governance, understood as *"the system by which companies are directed and controlled"* (Cadbury 1992:topic 2.5)[1] is as old as corporations themselves, academic research on this issue has increased substantially over the past 20 years or so (cfr. i.a. Adiloglu and Vuran 2012:543), i.e. since the early 1990s, namely the publication of the Cadbury Report in 1992. Corporate Governance has received particular attention during an episode of financial crises in Russia, Asia, and Brazil in 1998 (Claessens and Yurtoglu 2012:2) and following a wave of corporate scandals in both the US and Europe in the early 2000s which brought corporate governance issues into the public focus and has since been an area of constant interest, both in academic research and in the public domain. The latest financial crisis (culminating in 2008–2009) has served to increase that interest and triggered a number of new and revised guidelines/codes on several aspects of corporate governance. *"[T]he most recent financial crisis has seen its share of corporate governance failures in financial institutions and corporations, leading to systemic consequences."* (Claessens and Yurtoglu 2012:2)

The main body of literature relates to *"household"* questions of corporate governance, such as composition, structure and independence of boards, remuneration of top managers, information disclosure, auditing, shareholder involvement and ownership structure (cfr. Filatotchev et al. 2006, cit per Aguilera et al. 2011:380), *"mostly rooted in agency theory, assuming that by managing the principal-agency problem between shareholders and managers, firms will operate more efficiently and perform better"* (Aguilera et al. 2011:380).

Another related issue at stake is the increasing complexity of the financial system and the growing sophistication of its participants who act either as providers, users or intermediaries of corporate financing. The *"private, market-based investment*

---

[1]For alternative definitions, cfr. below in this and further sections.

© Springer International Publishing AG, part of Springer Nature 2018
R. C. Gericke, *Corporate Governance and Risk Management in Financial Institutions*, Contributions to Management Science,
https://doi.org/10.1007/978-3-319-67311-0_2

process is much more important for most economies than it used to be, and that process needs to be underpinned by good corporate governance" (Claessens and Yurtoglu 2012:2). The increasing significance of corporate governance topics over the past decades thus not only broadened the spectrum of areas covered, but also started to expand the spotlight from the United States to other markets, including important, consolidated economies such as the UK and Germany, as well as emerging markets like Russia, India, China and Brazil—the so-called BRIC countries (O'Neill 2001[2]).

Given the *"internationalization and globalization in trade and finance"* (Claessens and Yurtoglu 2012:5) and its impact on corporate governance, several studies with a focus on international comparison have been carried out, mostly however taking the US as main point of reference (e.g., Klonoski 2012, comparing German and US attitudes towards universal guidelines) or indeed Germany as the European anchor of corporate governance issues (e.g. Bordean and Pop 2012, who consider the German corporate governance model to be *"inspirational"* (p. 27)). The wealth of literature on comparative corporate governance appears to be strongly biased towards North America, Europe, and Asia with few studies taking a closer look at South American or even African countries (Claessens and Yurtoglu 2012).

Far less literature is available on the topic of risk management as an element of corporate governance. This is so much so that one may wonder whether risk management does actually form part of the canon of corporate governance topics. A look at several corporate governance guidelines, such as the Portuguese Corporate Governance Code (2014), section VI, however confirms this understanding, while position in order and extension of the relevant chapters imply a reduced focus on risk-related matters, although under the agency theory, the main topic of corporate governance actually is the mitigation of managers' self-serving behaviour (Aguilera et al. 2011:380, referring to Shleifer and Vishny 1997).

The present study therefore aims at extending corporate governance research by comparing the corporate governance systems of two comparable, but (not only culturally) different countries—Brazil and Germany—while taking a particular interest in the risk management issues at stake and how—if at all—they have changed during the latest financial crisis.

In this section, we shall give a general overview on definitions in corporate governance literature, in order to cut down, subsequently, on the systems in Brazil and Germany and the focus questions of comparative analysis, corporate governance in banks, risk management, and the relevant implications of the latest financial crisis.

At times, comparisons to the United States of America (US) will be drawn—not only to put the systems of Brazil and Germany in relation to each other by use of a third, *"external"*, point of reference, but because with a total market capitalization of

---

[2]O'Neill was head of global economic research at the time of that article's publication and has meanwhile retired as chairman of Goldman Sachs Asset Management.

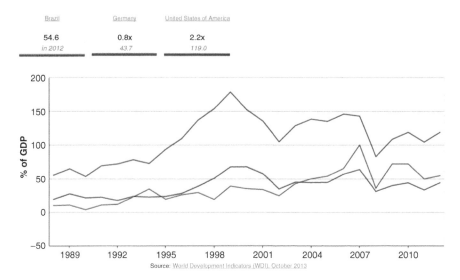

Fig. 2.1 Market capitalization of Brazil, Germany, USA as % of GDP. Source: knoema.com (license CC BY-ND 4.0; 03.09.2014)

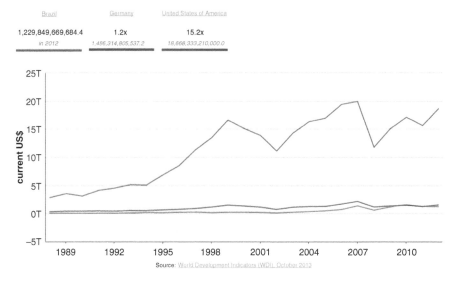

Fig. 2.2 Market capitalization of Brazil, Germany, USA in current US$. Source: knoema.com (license CC BY-ND 4.0; 03.09.2014)

about 18.67 trillion US$ at the end of 2012, the US capital market is approximately seven times bigger than those of Germany (1.49 trillion US$) and Brazil (1.23 trillion US$) combined (cfr. Figs. 2.1 and 2.2)—and as such, by far the biggest

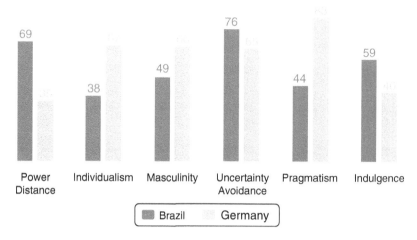

Fig. 2.3   Hofstede's cultural dimensions BR-DE. Source: Hofstede

market on Earth (followed by China with ca. 3.7 trillion and Great Britain with around 3 trillion. (data.worldbank.org)).

Apart from economic differences, there clearly are cultural differences between Brazil and Germany. These can be identified by Hofstede's cultural dimensions, as used by Klonoski in his comparative analysis (Klonoski 2012), illustrated by Fig. 2.3.

Interestingly, the only comparable dimension is "Uncertainty Avoidance", a core topic of risk management.

2.1   Corporate Governance

> *"Corporate governance, a phrase that a decade or two ago meant little to all but a handful of scholars and shareholders, has become a mainstream concern—a staple of discussion in corporate boardrooms, academic meetings, and policy circles around the globe."* (Claessens and Yurtoglu 2012:2)

The interest in corporate governance has been increasing exponentially since sometime around the year 2000. While the total of academic articles on the subject of corporate governance had increased constantly from one in 1975 to a total of 2761 in 2000, already in 2005, that number stood at 9690 and has since continued to grow rapidly. (Rodrigues 2009:83)

2.1.1   Definitions

"One problem in describing corporate governance is that it is multi-faceted—one can drown in details." (Black et al. 2012:3) Consequently, a large number of

definitions can be found in the literature of corporate governance, and the following examples are by no means an extensive overview, but are rather intended at giving an overview of definitions at different times and in various circumstances and contexts.

In footnote 2 on page 31 of the *Financial Market Trends* issue no. 62, December 1995 (FMT), we find the following definition: *"Corporate governance may be succinctly defined as the interaction between owners, managers and other stakeholders in directing and controlling a limited liability company, as a separate legal entity, characterised by limited liability, transferability of shares of its equity and an indefinite life."* By stressing the limited liability of the corporation, the author alludes to—and in the subsequent passage further underlines—the (possible) separation between ownership and management of those companies which is the starting point of the principal-agent problem. It should be remembered that this applies only in those cases in which ownership and management are really separate, e.g. not in fully owner-managed firms and at best to a limited extend in those corporations which are controlled by a majority/main shareholder with a significant representation on the board etc.

Shleifer and Vishny (1997:737), in their *"seminal"* (Claessens and Yurtoglu 2012:4) review state that *"Corporate governance deals with the ways in which suppliers of finance to corporations assure themselves of getting a return on their investment"*, which thus mentions as relevant players the corporations as such as well as equity and debt providers, such as shareholders, bondholders, and banks. It should be noted however that any other stakeholders (e.g. employees as far as they are not shareholders who actually put in money; suppliers as far as they do not extend financing in any form, etc.) are excluded.

According to Aguilera et al. (2011:380), Aoki (2001) refers to corporate governance as the *"structure of rights and responsibilities among the parties with a stake in the firm"*.

Adiloglu and Vuran (2012:544) add: *"Corporate governance refers to the quality, transparency, and dependability of the relationships between the shareholders, board of directors, management, and employees that define the authority and responsibility of each in delivering sustainable value to all the stakeholders"* and describe it thus as *"the system by which organizations are governed and controlled. It is concerned with the ways in which corporations are governed generally and in particular with the relationship between the management of an organization and its shareholders"*. Thus, these authors introduce the element of transparency, and therewith implicitly, the reference to relevant corporate governance related issues in corporate statements, be it as a part of the annual report/financial reports, or in the form of a dedicated corporate governance report.

The German Corporate Governance Code (May 2013) *"contains internationally and nationally recognized standards for good and responsible Governance"* (GCGC—Foreword).

The European Commission (EC) adopts the OECD (1999) definition of corporate governance as *"a set of relationships between a company's management, its board, its shareholders and other stakeholders. Corporate Governance also provides the structure through which the objectives of the company are set, and the means of attaining those objectives and monitoring performance are determined"* (European Commission 2001:24).

Corporate Social Responsibility (CSR), is a sub-section of corporate governance (cfr. Claessens and Yurtoglu 2012:4) and seen as a responsibility of companies, as described by Hart (2007) as follows: *"The major challenge—and opportunity—of our time is to create a form of commerce that uplifts the entire human community of 6.5 billion and does so in a way that respects both natural and cultural diversity. Indeed, that is the only realistic and viable pathway to a sustainable world. And business can—and must—lead the way."* (Jacob 2012:260).

Professor Ludo van der Heyden, Professor for Corporate Governance and Strategy at INSEAD, referred to it in a lecture given in Lisbon on 02/04/2013 as a system of *"checks and balances"* meant to ensure *"responsible business"* and aiming at *"value preservation"*, sometimes at *"value creation"*, but trying to avoid *"ups and downs"*. He further described the Canadian corporate governance system as the *"probably leading"* one while now the *"probably best discussion"* on the topic was in the UK. Furthermore, the advanced role of Brazil was mentioned both regarding the *"Novo Mercado"* and the licensing of directors.

Anne Shehan, the head of corporate governance for Calstrs, the California state teachers' pension fund sees *"a strong interest in making sure companies perform better over the long haul"* (TIME, December 16, 2013, p. 35).

The classification by Claessens and Yurtoglu (2012:3f.) can be pictured as in Fig. 2.4.

Claessens and Yurtoglu (2012:3) distinguish between two types of definitions regarding corporate governance: On the one hand, those related to behavioural patterns, and on the other, the definitions regarding normative frameworks.

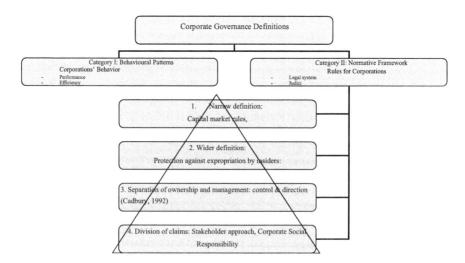

Fig. 2.4 Categorization of Corporate Governance Definitions. Source: own illustration

While category I (behavioural patterns) is deemed suitable for studies of individual jurisdictions or firms within a specific country, the second set of definitions which deals with the normative framework however is best suited, according to the authors, for comparative studies. According to Claessens and Yurtoglu (2012:3), it *"investigates how differences in the normative framework affect the behavioural patterns of firms, investors, and others"*.

For this second set, a sub-division into a narrow and a wider definition has been proposed by those authors, according to which corporate governance in a limited perspective (1) would only cover the rules regarding equity investments in publicly listed firms, such as capital market listing requirements, limitations for insider dealing, arrangements regarding the publication of annual accounts and the protection of minorities.

Another definition of corporate governance more closely focussing on the financing aspect (2) would be close to the one offered by Shleifer and Vishny (1997:737) which reads: *"Corporate governance deals with the ways in which suppliers of finance to corporations assure themselves of getting a return on their investment"* and include the strengthening of minority and creditor rights—e.g. an adequate legal environment including comprehensive rules on collaterals (mortgages and other liens), bankruptcy, law suits (including class action), executive remuneration, etc. Claessens and Yurtoglu (2012:4) propose to expand afore-mentioned definition *"to define corporate governance as being concerned with the resolution of collective action problems among dispersed investors and the reconciliation of conflicts of interest between various corporate claimholders"* (Claessens and Yurtoglu 2012:4).

The *"standard"* definition offered by Sir Adrian Cadbury in Sect. 2.5 of the Report of the Committee on the Financial Aspects of Corporate Governance, the so-called Cadbury Report of December 1st, 1992, is somewhat broader, focussing on the separation between ownership and management, and reads as follows:

"Corporate governance is the system by which companies are directed and controlled. Boards of directors are responsible for the governance of their companies. The shareholders' role in governance is to appoint the directors and the auditors and to satisfy themselves that an appropriate governance structure is in place. The responsibilities of the board include setting the company's strategic aims, providing the leadership to put them into effect, supervising the management of the business and reporting to shareholders on their stewardship. The board's actions are subject to laws, regulations and the shareholders in general meeting." (Cadbury 1992:Sect. 2.5)

The Cadbury Report will be discussed in more detail below (2.1.6.1).

Finally, the broadest definitions concentrate on the division of a corporation's profits, the so-called *"division of claims"* (Claessens and Yurtoglu 2012:4) and cover the expectations of all types of shareholders (majority/minority, with and without voting rights and/or (direct) influence on the management etc.). Understood in this way, corporate governance has been defined by Zingales (1998:499) as *"the complex set of constraints that shape the ex post bargaining over the quasi rents generated by the firm"*, which Claessens and Yurtoglu (2012:4) propose to expand into *"the complex set of constraints that determine the quasi-rents (profits) generated by the firm in the course of relationships with stakeholders and shape the ex post bargaining over them"*. In their explanation, they refer to *"value-added by firms and the allocation of it among stakeholders"*, thus apparently using *"quasi-rents"*, *"profits"*, and *"value-added"* as synonyms, and add that their definition may be understood as referring to a set of rules as well as to institutions. The use of a concept based on *"profits"* may be somewhat misleading as it seems to refer to the economic result, or earnings, of a corporation after deduction of its costs. This would, however, certainly not be a helpful interpretation as—interestingly and strangely as it appears—the actual economic result or performance of a firm is rarely a main feature of corporate governance discussion (unless as a measure for behavioral patterns, for instance).

The use of the expression *"value-added"* points in that direction as it seems to focus more on the non-economic or perceived value arising from the company's activity or attributed to it by the stakeholders, rather than (only) on pecuniary gains. Such *"advantages"* may indeed rather be called *"benefits"* or even *"perceived benefits"* as their value lies effectively in the perception of the relevant stakeholder. An employee, for example, might regard their job as extremely valuable to them personally for the meaning it gives to their lives, while from an economic/management/shareholder standpoint it might appear obsolete, neutral, or even detrimental for the company's financial results. Consequently, the use of an expression such as *"benefits"*—particularly when assessing it from the relevant stakeholder's angle—appears more adequate to describe the subject of the afore-mentioned bargaining process.

This leads us to the inclusion of a variety of different stakeholders into the bargaining process, away from the isolated view of owners and managers in their principal-agent-dilemma towards a multi-facetted competition between different groups and/or individuals, jointly and separately described as—and acting as—stakeholders, in which each of them pursues the maximization of their own benefit from the entity's activity, irrespectively of the question whether or not any (perceived) benefit may be regarded as a benefit by others. The dynamic[3] of that bargaining process may at times lead to severe conflicts which may manifest themselves in the protests of neighbors, NGOs or other private or public entities or individuals, and at times may produce win-win-situations where one or several stakeholders concede an item perceived by them as neutral, non-beneficial or detrimental, while another stakeholders attributes a positive value to that item.

Freeman (1984:46) defines a stakeholder as *"any group or individual who can affect, or is affected by, the achievement of the organization's objectives"*.

A dynamic process has also been identified regarding the corporate governance rules and institutions themselves and their evolution over time, affected by their time and regional location as well as the reciprocal impact each of them (institutions and rules) has on the other, shaping and being shaped by *"the political economy process"*. (Claessens and Yurtoglu 2012:4)

---

[3]For a detailed analysis of dynamics in economic science, cfr. Pereira, Renato (Org.), A Dinâmica nas Ciências Económicas e Empresariais—Contributos para uma Visão Abrangente, Lisbon, 2010.

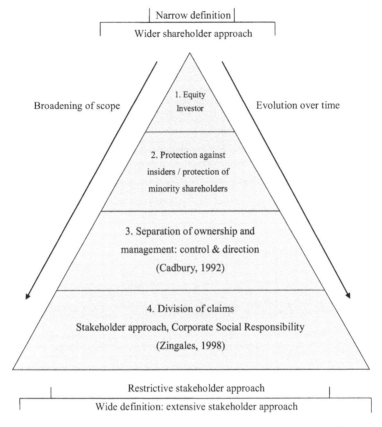

Fig. 2.5 Pyramid and Levels of Corporate Governance Definitions. Source: own illustration

This concept has already been expressed by Shleifer and Vishny (1997:738) when they claimed that *"Corporate governance mechanisms are economic and legal institutions that can be altered through political process."*

According to Claessens and Yurtoglu (2012:4), *"This dynamic aspect is very relevant in a cross-country review, but has received attention from researchers only lately."* It shall therefore be part of the subsequent comparison of corporate governance frameworks in Brazil and Germany. The classification by Claessens and Yurtoglu (2012:3f.) can be illustrated as in Fig. 2.5.

The different levels can also be labeled as core, owner, manager, and stakeholder perspectives, respectively.

The *"Initiative Corporate Governance within the German Real Estate Industry"* identifies as the aims of (good) corporate governance:

- To safeguard the interests of all stakeholders;
- To ensure sustainability;
- To provide control mechanisms for senior management; and
- To minimize risks.

It is understood as:

- A tool to (re)gain trust, particularly in times of crisis and in international business;
- A sign of the social responsibility of companies
- A competitive advantage inside and outside the corporation's business segment
- Risk reduction for the corporation
- A possibility for auto-regulation as opposed to state regulation
- A means for improvement of the perception as a value-oriented employer vis-á-vis the company's employees
- An opportunity to increase customer satisfaction
- A financial benefit, given that it avoids damages related to non-compliance, fines, and reputational losses.

(Initiative Corporate Governance der deutschen Immobilienwirtschaft, http://www.immo-initiative.de/)

However, "[a] generally accepted definition of corporate governance has not yet evolved" (Mülbert 2010:4). Although this affirmation is from 2010, it still seems to hold true.

2.1.2 Questions Regarding Definitions

As indicated above, some questions arise when looking at those definitions, namely:

1. Why would the broadest—or indeed, any—definition only relate to the ex-post bargaining?
2. Does a merely, or at least principally, financial perspective correspond to the reality of companies and, in particular, corporations, even when considering specifically financial institutions?
3. Should the term corporate governance only relate to corporations in the more narrow sense of publicly listed companies, or may it, as the wording *"companies"* in the Cadbury Report suggests, include all kind of companies?

Regarding question (1) above, it would appear to us that good corporate governance should, from an ex-ante perspective, regulate the bargaining over *"resources"* of a company in a fair and transparent way, such that both any ex-ante and ex-post bargaining shall occur within the limitations and under the rules thereby defined. Rather than focusing only on *"profits"* or *"quasi-rents"*, all resources should be taken into account with a view to the benefits they provide to individual participants. Thus, *"benefits"* might replace the notions of *"profits"* or *"quasi-rents"* when it comes to the bargaining which should occur within the boundaries drawn by corporate governance. This clearly makes the concept more complex and its definition, implementation and surveillance more difficult, at the same time however this seems to be best suited to adapt to a complex reality in order to produce *"fair"* results in a real world (Cfr. Claessens and Yurtoglu 2012).

The same might be said about a (self-imposed) restriction or limitation on the financial perspective under question (2) above, through which corporate governance might be viewed, particularly regarding capital markets regulations. This clearly is a central element good corporate governance needs to take care of, but—as above-mentioned broader definitions suggest—should not be the only one, in order not to lose (all) other important benefits (and potential risks) of the operation of a company out of sight, such as its importance for—and impact on—its market(s) (e.g. the (global) financial markets in the case of financial institutions when it comes to their products as opposed to their equity structure), the relevance of its other *"factors of production"*[4] such as employees (including executives) for society and other resources or *"benefits"* which might actually reduce the company's profits, but be at least potentially beneficial to some or all of its stakeholders as might be the case with investments in culture and environment. While this, as evidenced already by the broadest definitions quoted above, strongly widens the concept of corporate governance, this appears to be necessary in order to being able to take into account all *"benefits"* each shareholder might harvest from their relationship with the company throughout the whole life and/or investment circle of that specific institution.

The same rationale appears to apply to question (3) whether only corporations (understood as publicly listed companies (cfr. Cadbury 1992:chapter 1.5), and, in some cases, public institutions) should be covered by corporate governance frameworks—as the term *"corporate"* in the expression *"corporate governance"* suggests—or if it would also make sense to include other organizations, namely smaller private companies, into the definition of that term.

Clearly, the more narrow definitions of corporate governance, as they (almost) exclusively focus on matters of capital markets control mechanisms, stock-inherent voting rights etc., are not extensible to smaller and/or non-listed entities. As such, the present question shall only be considered assuming wider definitions, particularly those which take into account several or all stakeholders of an organization rather than only effective shareholders of a corporation.

Under those conditions, however, an inclusion of other, i.e. non-listed, institutions and firms might be beneficial to both the framework and all covered entities regarding those areas of corporate governance which are not exclusive to stock-market listed firms. Even in family-run and other owner-managed firms, most basic or general rules of corporate governance may conceivably be useful if applied relative to the organization's size and structure. To that end, however, the rules would need to be sufficiently abstract so that they may be applied. For instance, transparency requirements increase with firm size in Germany independently from the type of company or capital structure (cfr. below 3.2.3) by requiring larger firms to provide more extensive financial reporting, and independent directorships, a dedicated risk organization (to avoid the term *"committee"* which might appear exaggerated for many companies) etc. could be particularly useful for larger family-run types of business of the so-called German *"Mittelstand"* for example.

Given however, that this paper is concentrating on financial institutions, this need not be discussed in more detail, as most of those entities are listed anyway and in any

---

[4]Cfr. Adam Smith (1776), David Ricardo (1817).

case subject to specific regulation which, under a subsidiarity rule, would overrule general corporate governance provisions.

Apart from considering the immediate business partners of a company, the broader *"stakeholder"* approach also should take into account the socio-cultural relationships of the firm with its environment, especially when it comes to international activities, where the respect of local legislation and consideration of rules based on the local culture are necessary in order to achieve its aims.

Taking all this into account, a more general description of good corporate governance might be '*the framework/system of internal and external, voluntary and compulsory rules and institutions which shape the dynamic interaction between a private or public entity and its economic, social and cultural environment in order to maximize the benefits for all parties involved*'.

Clearly, this is a very wide and general definition which does not necessarily facilitate the investigation of specific fields, countries or industries within the corporate governance domain. Especially the number and complexity of rules and institutions relevant to corporate governance issues is so vast, that a full assessment would constitute an aeonian task. A more feasible approach would be a functional one, especially when focusing on a particular industry. (Cfr. Claessens and Yurtoglu 2012:4f.) For the financial services industry, Bodie and Merton (1995) presented a *"unifying conceptual framework"* in a certain analogy to the work in the economics literature of Schumpeter (1911), Williamson (1985), and North (1994). This concept is comparable to the functional approach adopted in sociology by Robert K. Merton (1957) and by others, particularly in the area of financial innovation such as Black and Scholes (1974) and Ross (1976).[5]

As a *"conceptual 'anchor'"* for that framework, they use functions instead of institutions and call it the *"functional perspective"*, based on the following two basic assumptions:

- *"Financial functions are more stable than financial institutions—that is, functions change less over time and vary less across borders.*
- *Institutional form follows function—that is, innovation and competition among institutions ultimately result in greater efficiency in the performance of financial system functions."*

(Bodie and Merton 1995:4)

2.1.3 What Is Corporate Governance?

"While the general importance of corporate governance has been established, knowledge on specific issues or channels is still weak." (Claessens and Yurtoglu 2012:30)

---

[5]For a more detailed list on authors adopting a functional approach, please refer to Bodie and Merton (1995:4), footnotes 1–3.

Corporate Governance focuses on the interaction between acting bodies and individuals of corporations regarding their structures and processes (cfr. Plamper 2010:123). Special attention is being paid to the potential conflicts between executives (*"agents"*) and the owners (shareholders) of a corporation or their representatives (*"principals"*). This Principal-Agent-Conflict is to be discussed later (2.1.11 below).

But corporate governance is more than just about the relationship between executives and shareholders. It is about good management.

Corporate governance is about corporate culture, about oversight executed by supervisory board members as well as board members, but also about active shareholders. It is more than good corporate behaviour, although this might just be the catchiest way to put it. It is about the inclusion of all stakeholders' interest into the decision-taking process within a company—in short: good corporate management. And it is about ethics. For Kurt Eichenwald (2005), the collapse of Enron was due to a collapse of ethical standards, breaking a company's own code of conduct. As such, corporate governance is about responsible ethics (*"Verantwortungsethik"* (*cfr. Weber* 1988:*551f.*)[6]; Middelhoff 2007).

In essence, corporate governance can be understood as a system which is designed to avoid fraud and unethical behaviour in a corporation. This system must define the principles, processes and tools it takes to manage a company in accordance with best practices and thus not only adheres to ethical principles, but also boosts the firm's performance (Middelhoff 2007).

Corporate governance also covers the participation of certain groups on boards, such as women. According to a TIME article, ca. 18% of executive officers and managers in the securities, investment-banking and commodities industries in the US are women, as well as 17% of Fortune-500 companies' board-of-director seats are occupied by women. The average return for a company with at least one woman on its board is said to be around 16% compared to 12% without a woman (*TIME*, March 13, 2014:29).

The Sarbanes-Oxley Act of 2005 was incepted in the wake of afore-mentioned scandals at Enron and Worldcom and aimed at re-establishing the confidence of the public in the financial reporting of companies. Its sponsors, Senators Paul S. Sarbanes, a Republican, and Michael Oxley, a Democrat, launched this project in order to regulate by law what before had been largely left in the US to the self-regulating mechanisms of companies and professional bodies. It increased the demands on financial reporting, obliges CEOs and CFOs to sign off on them, confirming that they may commit a crime by giving false confirmation and requires detailed information about internal controls and risk management procedures as well as a complaints management system. Not least importantly, very specific rules

---

[6]The expression of *"Verantwortungsethik"* was introduced by Max Weber in his 1919 speech *"Politik als Beruf"* in differentiation to the expression *"Gesinnungsethik"* (ethics of conviction or dispositional ethics), following Max Scheler's differentiation between *"Gesinnungsethik"* and *"Erfolgsethik"* (ethics of success).

regarding the establishment of an Audit Committee and the qualification of its members were codified.

In contrast to this US-model, we find a system of corporate governance still to a large extend auto-regulated by their self-imposed codes of corporate governance in Brazil and Germany, although obviously, many aspects are being regulated by law, namely the laws on publicly listed companies.

Another important difference, particularly between Germany and the US, is the two-tier board consisting of the Board of Directors (*"Vorstand"*) and the Supervisory Board (*"Aufsichtsrat"*), while the US boards usually consist of both the executives and the *"supervisors"*, sometimes even in one person, as is often the case with the uni-personal role of CEO and Chairman of the Board.

Yet another relevant discrepancy is the employee participation or 'codetermination' (*"Mitbestimmung"*) in German companies which in the case of large companies means that there are as many representatives of employees on the Board as there are representatives of the shareholders (*"paritätische Mitbestimmung"*). Where and when it works as designed, this *"balance of power"* actually serves the concept of corporate governance as it provides for another level of *"checks and balances"*[7] within the corporate structure, particularly as members go into board meetings with a notion of their power but also their responsibility, being prepared for the controversies they might expect by having evaluated the possibilities and limits of compromises which might have to be found for the sake of the company as a whole.

This is extremely difficult to grasp from a US—or, more generally, Anglo-Saxon[8]—point of view and clearly, there are examples of cases in which this setup has been (ab)used to serve for collective bargaining rather than for corporate governance purposes as described above (Middelhoff 2007).

The Brazilian system is quite similar to the American one and therefore many of the differences between Germany and the US can be found between Brazil and Germany, as for example the predominance of a single board structure in Brazil (cfr. 2.1.20 below; Esperança et al. 2011:247). Still, a number of important differences can be found between the US and Brazil, as for example the ownership structure with a predominance of free float in the US while Brazilian companies are mostly characterized by a single controlling shareholder (Silveira 2010:12f.).

---

[7]The system of "checks and balances" was first used by the U.S. Constitutional Convention in Philadelphia which met between May and September of 1787. The model of government chosen relied upon a series of checks and balances by dividing federal authority between the Legislative, the Judicial, and the Executive branches of government. (U.S. Department of State, Office of the Historian, https://history.state.gov/milestones/1784-1800/convention-and-ratification)

[8]According to Aguilera et al. (2011:391 ff.), Millar et al. (2005), *"classify three different systems: (a) the Anglo-Saxon (i.e., market-based system), (b) the Communitarian system, which includes Continental European countries (i.e., stakeholder-based system), and (c) the Emerging Market system that comprises the East European countries, Asian countries such as China, Malaysia, Thailand, Indonesia, the Philippines, and some of the Latin American countries such as Mexico, Chile, and Brazil."*

2.1.4   The Role of Boards

"Board structures and the distributions of power on boards vary substantially both among OECD member countries and within individual countries. [...] A general observation is that boards' capability to hold management accountable has declined over decades." (FMT 1995:22)

In Anglo-Saxon countries, direct representation on boards is available to shareholders only, and their role in conflict resolution or effective management control has historically been limited: *"It is generally conceded that in major English-speaking countries boards had great difficulty in fulfilling the oversight function in a meaningful way, because they have traditionally worked on a collegial basis under the dominance of senior management. Until recently one-tier boards have, more often than not, tended to ratify strategic decisions of management."* (FMT 1995:22) Whereas the implied tendency towards a stronger oversight has certainly continued since the publication of that article, it still remains very different from the system of two-tier boards, particularly with the codetermination element of the German system, in which the supervisory board is clearly in a much better position to contribute to control and conflict resolution, both between shareholders and management and between different groups of shareholders (FMT 1995:23). The *"direct representation of particular interest groups on boards"* has reduced the need for major investor relations departments or shareholder committees, but reduced the ability of boards to take quick decisions in reaction to market movements etc.

Corporate governance recommendations for company boards include for example the provision that *"the functions of Chief Executive Officer and Chair of the Board of Directors in unitary boards are separated. When a dual board structure exists, the head of the management board should not become chair of the supervisory board upon retirement. In both cases, some form of "comply or explain" and associated transparency is necessary to preserve flexibility for companies in special situations"* (OECD 2009:10).

For board members, "fit and proper person tests" as applied by regulators in specific lines of business, such as banking (e.g. section 33 par. 1, sentence 1, No. 4; par. 2 KWG for financial institutions in Germany), could become part of general corporate governance rules or best practices and be extended to include *"general governance and risk management skills"* (Cfr. OECD 2009:10).

Lipton et al. (2011:793) focus on the *"risk oversight function of the board of directors"* which they see at the core of a re-assessment of the political and regulatory environment following the financial crisis, as shall be discussed further below. They propose that "[g]iven the challenging and complicated current risk environment, a board may also want to consider a director's background and experience in determining the composition of any committees charged with risk management oversight and with respect to the composition of the board as a whole" (Lipton et al. 2011:798).

2.1.5 The Growing Role of Institutional Investors

Another aspect is the *"growing role of institutional investors"* as shareholders in corporations and for corporate governance: *"[I]ncentives for institutional investors to engage in corporate governance activities are at best mixed. The main objective of an institutional investor is to obtain good financial results rather than to become actively involved in corporate governance."* One factor is the *"growing sophistication of investment management"*, leading to a *"'commoditisation' of equity markets"* (FMT 1995:24).

According to Aguilera et al. (2011:387), *"[i]nstitutional investors are mutual funds, pension funds, hedge funds, insurance companies, and other non-banking organizations that invest their members' capital in shares and bonds. The main goal of institutional investors is to maximize the financial gains from a portfolio of investments, which makes them more concerned about maximizing shareholder value and liquidity"*.

The differentiation between market-based countries, bank-based countries and other countries (cfr. 2.1.22 below) helps to identify differences. In Anglo-Saxon countries, institutional investors rarely show much activity in corporate governance-related issues, while this has a long-standing tradition in Germany, for instance, while in France, corporate governance activity by investors has been increasing for decades now. (Cfr. FMT 1995:26)

A partly different, but still comparable and related group, *"international investors still mainly consider shares to be financial assets and have been relatively slow to assert their ownership rights"* (FMT 1995:30).

Estrin and Prevezer (2010:51) describe the negative consequences of poor governance as *"considerable legal uncertainty and an overhang of non-voting shares and poor company performance"*.

2.1.6 Key Sources of Corporate Governance

2.1.6.1 The Cadbury Report

In the Report of the Committee on the Financial Aspects of Corporate Governance (The Cadbury Report), Sir Adrian Cadbury states that *"[boards] must be free to drive their companies forward, but exercise that freedom within a framework of effective accountability. This is the essence of any system of good corporate governance."* (Cadbury 1992:1.1)

Apart from mentioning *"effective accountability"* as the cornerstone of corporate governance, this paragraph introduces the adjective *"good"*, thus clarifying that the main purpose of the report and its recommendations (*"Code of Best Practices"*) is to provide guidelines for *good* corporate governance.

In chapter 1.2 we find the Committee's focus *"on the control and reporting functions of boards, and on the role of auditors."* The Cadbury Report refers in chapter 1.3 to *"a Code of Best Practice designed to achieve the necessary high standards of corporate behaviour"*. Corporate behavior clearly refers to corporations, understood as *"listed companies"* (chapter 1.5), but in chapter 3.1 a differentiation is made as follows: *"The Code of Best Practice [. . .] is directed to the boards of directors of all listed companies registered in the UK, but we would encourage as many other companies as possible to aim at meeting its requirements."* Chapter 1.6 deals with the responsibilities of directors, shareholders and auditors, while chapter 1.8 stipulates the *"unitary board system"* as a basis. A limitation to corporate governance is identified in chapter 1.9 which states that *"no system of control can eliminate the risk of fraud without so shackling companies as to impede their ability to compete in the market place."*

Interestingly, chapter 1.10 expresses the Commission's belief that *"compliance with a voluntary code coupled with disclosure, will prove more effective than a statutory code"*.

As *"underlying factors"* for corporate scandals in the past, the authors identify *"the looseness of accounting standards, the absence of a clear framework for ensuring that directors kept under review the controls in their business, and competitive pressures both on companies and on auditors which made it difficult for auditors to stand up to demanding boards"* (chapter 2.1).

We find the central definition of corporate governance in chapter 2.5: *"Corporate governance is the system by which companies are directed and controlled. Boards of directors are responsible for the governance of their companies. The shareholders' role in governance is to appoint the directors and the auditors and to satisfy themselves that an appropriate governance structure is in place. The responsibilities of the board include setting the company's strategic aims, providing the leadership to put them into effect, supervising the management of the business and reporting to shareholders on their stewardship. The board's actions are subject to laws, regulations and the shareholders in general meeting."* Two aspects shall be pointed out here: (i) the mere reference to laws and regulations indicates a (limited) *"compliance attitude"* adopted in the Report, and (ii) the repeated reference to shareholders without mentioning of other stakeholders is an indication of the shareholder approach adopted by the Commission (cfr. also chapter 6.1 ff.), however mitigated by a reference in chapter 3.2 to other stakeholders, demanding *"[. . .] confidence which needs to exist between business and all those who have a stake in its success"*.

Chapter 2.7 describes the role of auditors, which is further elaborated in chapters 5.1 ff.—In an apparent deviation from chapter 1.9, chapter 5.20 (a) warns of potential negative effects of auditors' statements: *"There must be a risk that any qualification about the company's financial viability, however it is expressed, will precipitate the company's collapse. There is a fine balance to be drawn between drawing proper attention to the conditions on which continuation of the business depends, and not thereby bringing the business down."*

Chapter 3.2 refers in relation to a Code of Conduct to the *"principles on which the Code is based"* as *"openness, integrity and accountability. They go together."*

Chapter 3.7 establishes the *"Comply or Explain"* rule and provides for further flexibility by establishing in chapter 3.10 that *"[t]he Code is to be followed by individuals and companies in the light of their own particular circumstances"*.

The Report then goes on (3.14) to state that *"[t]he responsibility for putting the Code into practice lies directly with the boards of directors"* and continues to deal with the Board in chapters 4.1 ff. (Board Effectiveness) and 4.40 ff. (Board Remuneration).

In chapter 2.6 the Report refers specifically to the *"financial aspects of corporate governance (the Committee's remit)"* and the only reference to risk management as such in the Cadbury Report appears in chapter 4.24, while the remainder refers to specific risks, mainly the risk of fraud (chapters 4.31; 7.2).

2.1.6.2 OECD Principles of Corporate Governance, 1999 and 2004

The OECD Principles of Corporate Governance were first released in 1999 (OECD 1999) and underwent a first revision in 2004. Another review was initiated in 2014 in order to update the Principles with relevant and useful developments in capital markets and the corporate sector.

They are one of twelve key standards of the Financial Stability Board and together with the other standards aim at ensuring financial stability on an international basis, forming the basis for the corporate governance component of the Report on the Observance of Standards and Codes of the World Bank Group.

The OECD Principles are meant to serve as a benchmark for "an effective corporate governance framework" and thus benefit regulators and other rule-making bodies, based on "a high level of transparency, accountability, board oversight, and respect for the rights of shareholders and role of key stakeholders".

(http://www.oecd.org/corporate/oecdprinciplesofcorporategovernance.htm)

There are six succinct Principles of Corporate Governance being addressed by the OECD which are briefly presented and summarized in the first part of their publication, followed by a second part with annotations on each of them. Those Principles are:

1. Ensuring the Basis for an Effective Corporate Governance Framework;
2. The Rights of Shareholders and Key Ownership Functions;
3. The Equitable Treatment of Shareholders;
4. The Role of Stakeholders in Corporate Governance;
5. Disclosure and Transparency;
6. The Responsibilities of the Board.

(OECD 2004)

2.1.6.3 ISO 26000 and ISO 38500

There are two international standards regarding corporate governance. One is ISO 26000 on Corporate Social Responsibility (CSR—see 2.1.9 below), the other is entitled *"Corporate governance of information technology"*—ISO/IEC 38500. While both do not fully—or rather *"purely"*—apply for corporate governance, we believe it is worthwhile taking a look at both of them.

The fact that there is no *"technical"* standard on corporate governance in its own right seems to underline the difficulty in clearly defining this area and in giving clear advice as to how to correctly fill this expression with a clear meaning. Far more technical and *"definable"* seems to be everything related to information technology, thus possibly explaining the existence of an international standard as restrictively defined as *"Corporate governance of information technology"*.

Standard ISO/IEC 38500 is still valid in its first edition dated June 1st, 2008 under reference number ISO/IEC 38500.2008(E). It was prepared by Standards Australia (as AS8015:2005) and was adopted, under a *"fast-track procedure"*, by Joint Technical Committee ISO/IEC JTC 1, Information Technology, in parallel with its approval by national bodies of ISO and IEC.

Further on in its foreword, ISO/IEC 38500 is described as *"a high level, principles based advisory standard. In addition to providing broad guidance on the role of a governing body, it encourages organizations to use appropriate standards to unterpin their governance of IT."*

The standard is organized in three parts dealing with (i) scope, application and objectives, (ii) a framework for good corporate governance of IT, and (iii) guidance for the corporate governance of IT.

2.1.7 Corporate Governance, Financial Performance and the Cost of Equity

When relating corporate governance to the positive effects it is supposed to have on companies and their surroundings in general, several issues arise.

Firstly, the measurement of corporate governance itself is difficult. A number of indices have been proposed, including the GIM index presented by Gompers, Ischii, and Metrick (Gompers et al. 2003), which however only measures the quality of *"external"* governance without taking *"internal"* governance factors into account (Cremers and Nair 2003).

Bhagat et al. (2008:1803) describe corporate governance indices as *"highly imperfect instruments"* and suggest *"caution in attempting to draw inferences regarding a firm's quality or future stock market performance from its ranking on any particular corporate governance measure"*.

Secondly, it is hard to establish a link between good corporate governance practices and their effects on such parameters as economic and financial performance. One of those difficulties is the potentially long time lag, as those practices take time to take effect rather than showing results immediately (Regalli and Soana 2012). Probably also for this reason, studies on the relationship between corporate governance and financial performance have been largely inconclusive (Dalton et al. 1999; Donker and Zahir 2008).

Quaresma (2011) however found *"some statistical evidences"* to confirm a positive relationship *"between the best corporate governance practices and the financial performance"* of international listed banks. Klapper and Love (2002) show that *"better corporate governance is highly correlated with better operating performance and market valuation"*.

Regalli and Soana (2012:2) describe it as *"conceivable that the effect of good governance is to lengthen company life and stabilize certain financial results, rather than improve them"*.

The authors therefore propose to investigate *"indirect"* benefits—rather than direct ones—such as stakeholder's perception of the company, by measuring the cost of capital, both equity and debt. They argue that good corporate governance requires recognition as such, given that its mere existence is insufficient. Furthermore, they believe that such recognition often comes before the effects can be measured in terms of economic and financial results (Regalli and Soana 2012:3).

The confirmation of a positive relationship between a perception of good corporate governance practices in a firm by its lenders and equity providers would then indicate that a lower risk is associated with such a firm, i.e. that better corporate governance implies lower risk (Regalli and Soana 2012:3).

Regalli and Soana (2012:9) find however that the cost of equity increases the better the governance of companies, rather than to decrease. They wonder why the supposed decrease in risk triggered by higher corporate governance standards does not translate into lower risk premiums.

2.1.8 Corporate Governance and Transparency

"In the longer run good corporate governance requires transparent and material information, so that the discipline of the market applies to management at all stages of the asset cycle" (Blundell-Wignall et al. 2009:26)

Adiloglu and Vuran (2012) study transparency levels of financial information disclosure in Turkey and compare them to the financial ratios of 57 companies, which are grouped into *"most transparent"*, *"transparent"* and *"least transparent"* ones.

They argue that European scandals such as those of Ahold, Vivendi, and Cable & Wireless show that corporate governance, control issues and transparency are important topics not only for the United States or emerging markets, but also for Europe (Adiloglu and Vuran 2012:544).

2.1.9 Sustainability and Corporate Social Responsibility

Although the concept of Corporate Social Responsibility (CSR) is said to be older than that of Sustainability, it appears that since around 2005 there has been a tendency, at least in Germany, to focus more on CSR measures and CSR reporting, while sustainability continues to be a catch-phrase in almost all areas of economic and social life. (Grothe 2010:183)

In its early days, around 1960, the first phase of CSR—CSR_1—concentrated mainly on social topics and a company's responsibility towards society (Loew et al. 2004:10). CSR_2, which appeared in the mid-1970s started to bring measurability into focus, concentrating on corporate social performance or CSP. Corporate Social Rectitude became the headline of the CSR_3 phase in the 1980s. It then also included environmental issues as part of an *"esoteric"* view (Cosmos, Science and Religion—CSR_4) during the 1990s (Loew et al. 2004:10), while sustainability has come to grow out of its environmental protection origins and nowadays encompasses a whole variety of social, ecological, ethical and economic aspects which are hard to define and thus give the whole concept a somewhat blurred image (Grothe 2010:187).

This might be the main reason for corporations to embrace the concept of CSR instead of sustainability as *"it is easy for companies to be well-regarded for their good deeds. This is different for the extremely cumbersome and complex approach of sustainability"* (Grothe 2010:184). Leitschuh (2008:46) even refers to CSR as a *"light version of sustainability"*, fearing that CSR takes steam out of the discussion around sustainable management. On the other hand this author concedes that any form of dialogue about the social and ecological responsibility of corporations is welcome.

In summary, it might be stated that the concepts of CSR and Sustainability have both grown towards each other, ending up merging both in terms of issues covered and terminology, serving partly as synonyms for each other as illustrated in Fig. 2.6.

Today, the European Commission defines corporate social responsibility (CSR) as *"the voluntary integration of social and environmental objectives into the commercial activities of enterprises and into their relationships with their partners"*.

(http://europa.eu/legislation_summaries/external_trade/c00019_en.htm)

Despite of aforementioned harmonization, CSR as well as Corporate Citizenship (CC), with their Anglo-Saxon origins, are being interpreted and defined in quite

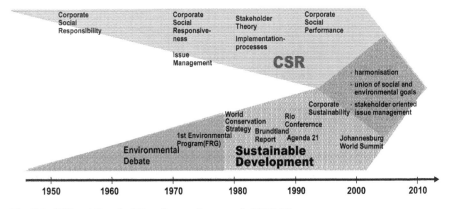

Fig. 2.6 CSR and Sustainability. Source: Loew et al. (2004:12)

Fig. 2.7 The intersections with sustainable business performance. Source: Wieser (2005:44)

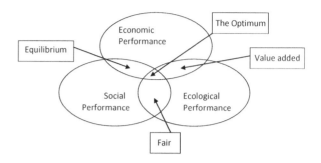

different ways on an international, European, and German level. While internationally, CSR tends to deal with ecological and social challenges, the German *"discussion on sustainability"* (now used as a synonym to CSR discussions) includes three *"dimensions of sustainability"* (Grothe 2010:187): in addition to the social and ecological levels, also the economic contributions of a corporation to a macrosocial sustainability. Consequently, Grothe demands that *"[s]ocial responsibility has to be further developed within the economic dimension of sustainability. To this end, a discussion has to take place about what society as a whole desires and which contribution the corporate level can and should make."* (Grothe 2010:187)

The relationship between those three dimensions of sustainability can be illustrated by Fig. 2.7.

Table 2.1 proposes a number of definitions relation to CSR.

Oftentimes, different concepts are mixed, both in terminology and definition, including social corporate responsibility, corporate citizenship, business ethics, sustainable development, reputation management, environmental management, corporate social performance, corporate volunteerism, and corporate governance (cfr. Schuch 2011:1).

Since June 2004, when the technical steering committee of ISO decided to start a normation procedure for CSR, resulting in DIN ISO 26000 as described and discussed below, this concept has indeed become quite specific and tangible.

One may thus consider CSR as a more precisely defined and thus operational version of the wider concept of sustainability which shall help by relevant measures and reportings to turn companies into *"good corporate citizens"* (Grothe 2010:184).

In Brazil, too, CSR started out in the 1960s rather as a matter of philanthropy, but then also evolved into efforts undertaken by corporations to achieve *"sustained effects"*. (http://www.csr-weltweit.de/en/laenderprofile/profil/brasilien/index.html)

"Corporate social responsibility can make a positive contribution to the strategic goal decided by the Lisbon European Council: for the European Union "to become the most competitive and dynamic knowledge-based economy in the world"." (EU Green Paper on corporate social responsibility—http://europa.eu/legislation_summaries/employment_ and_social_policy/employment_rights_and_work_organi sation/n26039_en.htm)

In 1998, *Instituto Ethos* was created in Brazil in order to further implement CSR in Brazil, following a trend of ethically (rather than religiously, as in the 1960s)

Table 2.1 Terms relating to sustainability and CSR

Term	Definition	Level	Definition generally accepted	Comments
Sustainable development	Sustainable development is, "a form of development that meets the needs of the present without compromising the ability of future generations to meet their own needs" (Hauff 1987:46).	Society as a whole	Yes	
Sustainable management	Sustainable corporate governance is a model of corporate governance designed systematically to optimise the company's efforts to achieve social, ecological and economic sustainability objectives. Measures necessary to further this aim are implemented on both the strategic and the operational levels.	Company	No	The authors have derived this definition from the sustainability principle.
Corporate Social Responsibility (CSR)	CSR is, "a concept whereby companies integrate social and environmental concerns in their business operations and in their interaction with their stakeholders on a voluntary basis". (European Commission 2001a:5)	Company	Europe: yes International: no	The EU clarified its position further in its Communication of 2002: being socially responsible, "means going beyond compliance and investing more in human capital, the environment and relations with stakeholders" (European Commission 2002b: 3). Ensuring compliance with statutory provisions thus constitutes one of the necessary conditions for CSR.
Corporate Citizenship (CC)	Corporate citizenship relates to the company's commitment to solving social problems in its local environment and around its sites above and beyond its actual business activities. Corporate citizenship activities include donation and sponsorship	Company	No	Original definition formulated reference to Westebbe and Logan (1995) and Mutz and Korfmacher (2003).

(continued)

Table 2.1 (continued)

Term	Definition	Level	Definition generally accepted	Comments
	(corporate giving), the creation of benevolent company institutions (corporate foundations) and the direct involvement of company staff in social projects and undertakings (corporate volunteering). Activities with no direct benefit to the company and activities that generate some form of economic return can both fall under the concept of corporate citizenship.			

Source: Loew et al. (2004:14)

motivated efforts aiming at the "*humanization of business and their integration with society*" (Schuch 2011:14). Measures have so far focused on São Paulo and Rio de Janeiro regions, thus further increasing the already existing disparities within the country, leading Schuch to suggest promoting CSR more in other regions (Schuch 2011:17f.).

According to Carroll and Buchholtz, the four levels of CSR depicted in form of a pyramid mount from a basic level ("Economic Responsibilities")—to be profitable—via "Legal Responsibilites"—to obey the law—and "Ethical Responsibilities" to a philanthropic or charitable one of *"Maximum Wealth"* (Loew et al. 2004:21). That top level is being described as *"desired"* while the compliance with ethical responsibilities is being regarded as *"expected"*. The bottom two layers of the pyramid however are both considered *"required"* by Loew et al. (2004:21). Thus, this pyramid is quite comparable to Maslow's hierarchy of needs (Maslow 1943).

The different shades of the green ellipses for Corporate Citizenship (CC), Corporate Social Responsibility (CSR), and Corporate Sustainability (SD) in Fig. 2.8 are meant to demonstrate that the ecological aspect gains importance from left to right, while at the same time, the importance of the social component diminishes. The relevance of Corporate Sustainability (CS) becomes evident by its role in linking the micro-economic level to the macro-level of SD.

However, and despite their differences and separate evolutionary history (Lorson et al. 2014b:54), CS and CSR have been converging and a part of the literature (cfr. Lorson et al. 2014b:54; Montiel 2008:245 ff.) predicts that this will continue, or as Lorson et al. (2014b:54) put it, that *"CS and CSR only differ by* the letter 'R'".

Lorson et al. (2014a, 2014b) have very recently tried to structure the different concepts and definitions related to sustainable development (SD) which as Loew et al. (2004:15) showed, expresses a macro-economic perspective, while corporate

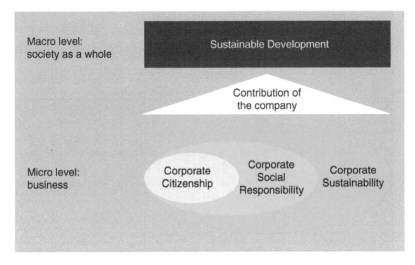

Fig. 2.8 The relationship between CSR, CC and SCG and sustainable development. Source: Loew et al. (2004:13)

sustainability (CS), corporate social responsibility (CSR) and corporate citizenship (CC) are part of the company level, i.e. a micro-economic perspective, cfr. Table 2.2.

Goldmann et al. (2010) compared corporate social responsibility in Germany and Brazil and found improvements in the area of corporate governance, environment and regarding employees in German companies. In particular they state that most companies now do have answers to questions regarding sustainability, particularly in form of CSR reports. They did find however that their quality differs widely and suggest that establishing general (minimum) standards would take the CSR topic on a company-wide level. Deficiencies were observed in the areas of client relationship, relations to stakeholders, assumption of social responsibility and social cultural action (Goldmann et al. 2010:192).

With regards to financial institutions in particular, the European Commission stated in their 2001 Green Paper that *"[f]inancial institutions are making increasing use of social and environmental checklists to evaluate the risks of loans to, and investments in companies. Similarly, being recognised as a socially responsible enterprise, for example through listing in an ethical stock market index, can support the rating of a company and therefore entails concrete financial advantages."* (European Commission 2001:7)

As for publicly listed companies, the European Commission noted at the time already that *"[s]tock market social indexes are useful benchmarks for demonstrating the positive impact of social screening on financial performance: the Domini 400 Social Index has outperformed the S&P 500 by more than 1% on a [n] annualised total return basis and on a riskadjusted basis since its inception in May 1990 while the Dow Jones Sustainable Index has grown by 180% since 1993 compared to 125% for the Dow Jones Global Index over the same period."* (European Commission 2001:7)

Table 2.2 Concepts and definitions related to sustainable development

		Sustainable Development (SD)	Corporate Sustainability (CS)	Corporate Social Responsibility (CSR)	Corporate Citizenship (CC)
Origin		Europe	Europe / USA	USA	USA
Time of Apperance		1987 (first mentioned 1713 in Germany)	1990s	1953	1990s
Cience		Business Ethics			
Level of Application		Society/ macro-economic	Company/micro-economic		
Regional Association		Global	Global thinking—mainly local and regional action		Mainly local
Type of management		Normative: political model	**Normative** and strategic: corporate philosophy and strategies	Normative, **strategic**, and operative: corporate philosophy, strategies, and activities	Strategic and operative: corporate strategies and activities
Part of Core Business		N/a	N/a	Yes	No (additional activities)
Aim		Enabling of a sustainable development; maintenance or—if possible—improvement of the quality of life of current and future generations			
Weighting of sustainablility dimensions:	Ecology	**1**	2	2	3
	Economy	1	1	3	1
	Social	1	2	**1**	1
Synonyms		Sustainability	CSR, Sustainability, SD, Ecological Sustainability, COSY	CC, CR, COSY	CSR, CR
Overlap		CS and CSR	SD and CSR	SD, CS, and CC	CSR
Ranking by Number of Publications		2nd	4th	1st	3rd

(continued)

Table 2.2 (continued)

		Sustainable Development (SD)	Corporate Sustainability (CS)	Corporate Social Responsibility (CSR)	Corporate Citizenship (CC)
Related concepts		TBL/3BL	TBL/3BL	CSP, CFP, CER, CA, CP, CR	CEC, GCC, OCB, CP
Official definition		Yes:	No	(Yes), for Europe only:	No
		"Sustainable development is a development which takes into account the necessities of current generations without jeopardizing the possibilities for future generations to pursue their own necessities" (WECD, Our common future, 1987:54 as quoted in German by Lorson et al. 2014b:55)		"a concept which serves as a basis for companies to integrate social and environmental issues into their business and the interaction with their stakeholders on a voluntary basis." (EC 2001:5)	
Definition proposed by Lorson et al. (2014)		"Sustainable development can be described as enhancing quailty of life and tus allowing people to live in a healty environment and improve social, economic and environmental conditions for present and future generations." (Ortiz et al. 2009:29)	"Corporate sustainability is a strategic approach of management by which companies try to optimize their contributions to the social, ecological and economic challenges of sustainability in a systematic way, based on stakeholder interests." (Lorson et al. 2014a:18)	"CSR is a concept with process traits by which companies assume responsitbility for the environment and social issues on a voluntary basis, i.e. beyond their own interest and legal obligations, in line with the interests of their stakeolders." (Lorson et al. 2014a:15)	"Corporate citizenship is part of company strategy and as such covers company activities which are primarily aimed at achieving (economic) advantages for the company, taking into account stakeholder interests." (Lorson et al. 2014a:17)

Source: Lorson et al. (2014b:55); own adaptation and translations

Ten years later, the EC in its 2011 *"renewed EU strategy 2011–14 for Corporate Social Responsibility"* expressed its intention to *"[c]onsider a requirement on all investment funds and financial institutions to inform all their clients (citizens, enterprises, public authorities etc.) about any ethical or responsible investment criteria they apply or any standards and codes to which they adhere."* (European Commission 2011:11) This shall further facilitate the EC's desire to make *"asset managers and asset owners, especially pension funds"* take CSR more into consideration when choosing their investments, stressing that *"public authorities have a particular responsibility to promote CSR in enterprises which they own or in which they invest"* (European Commission 2011:11). In this context, the EC makes specific reference to both the UN Principles for Responsible Investment[9] and the UN Guiding Principles on Business and Human Rights. The latter rest on three pillars:

1. The State's duty to respect human rights;
2. The corporate responsibility to respect human rights; and
3. The need for access to effective remedy.

Thus, the EC goes beyond the European borders and engages in promoting CSR through its external policies. (European Commission 2011:14)

The *"Principles for Responsible Investment"* (PRI), as part of the United Nations UNEP Finance Initiative /UN Global Compact help investors to identify and recognize the relevance of environmental, social and governance (ESG) factors, which are understood to contribute to *"the long-term health and stability of the market as a whole"* (http://www.unpri.org/introducing-responsible-investment/).

There is a catalogue of six principles for responsible investment:

1. To incorporate ESG issues into investment analysis and decision-making process, including the development of ESG-related tools, metrics and analyses as well as the obligation of investment service providers to also integrate ESG factors into evolving research and analysis.
2. To be active owners and incorporate ESG issues into ownership policies and practices. This principle also covers the disclosure of ownership policies which are in line with the PRI, exercise and compliance with voting rights as well as the active engagement in ESG initiatives.
3. To seek appropriate disclosure on ESG issues by participated entities; i.e. (standardized) reporting by companies within the investment portfolio on ESG issues, their integration into annual reports etc.
4. To promote acceptance and implementation of the PRI within the investment industry, by communicating ESG expectations to service providers, particularly as part of requests for proposals.

---

[9]Viviers et al. (2008:23) claimed that responsible investing, understood as the act of *"considering environmental, social and corporate governance issues in making investment decisions, is more consistent with a deontological construct than a utilitarian one"*. (Klonoski 2012).

5. To cooperate with PRI partners to enhance the effectiveness of implementing the Principles, by supporting initiatives such as information platforms and networks on PRI issues.
6. To report on the company's own progress with the implementation of PRIs, which not only includes reporting, but also trying to determine the impact of the Principles. (http://www.unpri.org/introducing-responsible-investment/).

By referring to pension funds, the EC also makes implicit reference to its 2001 strategy to promote socially responsible investment (SRI), where it stated that *"SRI funds invest in companies complying with specific social and environmental criteria"* (European Commission 2001:14). It clarifies that those criteria can be positive or negative. As examples for negative criteria serve alcohol, tobacco and armament industries, while positive criteria *"include[e] socially and environmentally proactive companies"* (European Commission 2001:14). Clearly, it is difficult to determine when a company is *"socially and environmentally proactive"* or not.

Interestingly, the EC explicitly promotes shareholder activism (cfr. 2.1.16 below) when it says that *"[a]nother important option for investors is to engage in shareholder activism to induce company management to adopt socially responsible practices. Shareholder activism is expected to increase together with the importance of corporate governance issues and the development of pension funds"*. (European Commission 2001:14)

ISO 26000 establishes seven principles which should be adhered to by companies:

1. Accountability

    An organization should be responsible for the implications of its decisions and activities regarding society, economy, and environment and be held accountable by providing information on it.
2. Transparency

    An organization should act transparently especially when its decisions and activities have an impact on environment or society. This implies trustworthy, open, comprehensive communication and reporting regarding the purpose, type and localization of the organization's activities.
3. Ethical behavior

    The actions of an organization should rest on the values of honesty, fairness, and accountability.
4. Respect regarding stakeholders

    An organization should know its (relevant) stakeholders and know and respect their interests.
5. Respect for the Rule of Law

    Each organization should absolutely abide by Law and Order.
6. Respect for international standards of behavior

    Organizations should act in accordance with international standards of conducting business. This includes international common law, generally accepted international rules or treaties and conventions. Standards of behavior such as the UN Human Rights Convention or the international labor standards of ILO shall serve as a guideline in situations in which the organization does not find adequate national social and environmental standards, as might be the case in international operations.

7. Respect for Human Rights

Each organization should acknowledge the basic human rights, their significance and general applicability. This should happen independently from location, cultural background or specific situations. (Bundesministerium für Arbeit und Soziales[10])

ISO 26000, as its name implies, is however a guideline rather than a technical standard and as such not certifiable as a management system norm (such as ISO 9001 or ISO 14001) (Cfr. Statement (*"Stellungnahme"*) jointly issued by the German Federal Government and several business associations[11]).

2.1.9.1   The Environmental Profit & Loss Statement (E P&L)

Apart from the primary resources (Land, Labor, Capital), companies obviously also use social and environmental (natural) resources within their chain of value-creation. These are however rarely identified or even accounted for. Reportedly as the first company to do so worldwide, Puma started a program under former CEO Jochen Zeitz to identify and quantify ecological effects of Puma's business in monetary terms.

To this end, they defined and analysed a set of Environmental Key Performance Indicators (E-KPIs) within the company and its suppliers. Regarding CO_2-Emissions, the so-called *"social costs of carbon"* were used, and the regeneration of natural water sources was equally analysed with the aim of identifying costs and risks stemming from the limited availability of water, which in itself differs between regions and over time.

The results of that analysis allow the management to steer the company also with regards to environmental risks and in a more environmentally conscious way, thus identifying risks earlier and being able to respond better to an increasingly vigilant public. (http://www.pwc.de/de/nachhaltigkeit/puma-mit-pwc-zur-oekologischen-gewinn-und-verlustrechnung.jhtml)

The total *"external cost"* identified by Puma is said to reach around € 150m p.a.

Internal and external dimensions of CSR according to the EU greenbook are summarized by Table 2.3 (Goldmann et al. 2010:188; Loew et al. 2004:27).

---

[10]Die DIN ISO 26000 – Leitfaden zur gesellschaftlichen Verantwortung von Organisationen" – Ein Überblick, in: http://www.bmas.de/SharedDocs/Downloads/DE/PDF-Publikationen/a395-csr-din-26000.pdf?__blob=publicationFile

[11]http://www.arbeitgeber.de/www/arbeitgeber.nsf/res/Stn-spitzenverb-iso26000.pdf/$file/Stn-spitzenverb-iso26000.pdf

Table 2.3 Internal and external dimension of CSR

Internal dimension of CSR	External dimension of CSR
Human resources management (employees) Life-long learning, non-discrimination, gender equality, participation in equity and returns.	**Local community** Integration of companies into the local fabric, tax payments, employment, environmental impact, voluntary contributions: partnerships, sponsoring, …
Occupational safety Several issues already solved by legal regulation, new challenges by outsourcing, external providers. Taking occupational safety issues into account during procurement and sub-contracting	**Business partners, suppliers, customers** "Social" responsibility also for suppliers and their staff, dependence of suppliers on fair pricing, suppliers' compliance. Price not the only criterium for supplier selection. Adaptation of demand, quality, product and service safety, reliability, design for all.
Socially acceptable restructuring of companies Mergers & Acqusitions, rationalizations, restructuring may result in a reduction of headcount, mass lay-offs, and closure of subsidiaries. Consideration of economic and social consequences for relevant region. Consideration of employees' interests. Mitigate negative consequences.	**Human Rights** Global supply chains, international business: relevant rules include OECD Guidelines for Multinational Companies, ILO Declaration on basic principles and rights of labor. Code of conduct for countries in which human rights are often neglected. Cotonou treaty against corruption. Voluntary company codes of conduct, Demand for a European code of conduct.
Management of environmental impact and use of resources Win-win-potential through efficient use of resources, support of companies with compliance, incentives for exemplary companies.	**Global Environmental Protection** Cross-border consequences, use of resources. Improve environmental impact throughout supply chain, investments in other countries, OECD guidelines, Global Compact, codes of conduct.

Source: Loew (2004:27); own translation

Further to the publication of the EU Green Book on CSR, the European Commission (EC) in March 2006 stressed its desire to make *"Europe a pole of excellence on corporate social responsibility"* and stipulates what follows:

"In the context of increased global competition and an ageing population, the EU must stimulate the production of enterprises which respect their social responsibilities. CSR may contribute to:

- *the inclusion of disadvantaged groups in the labour market;*
- *an increase in investment in skills development, lifelong learning and the employability of employees;*
- *improvements in public health, for example by means of voluntary labelling of foodstuffs and non-toxic chemicals;*
- *innovation on social and environmental matters;*
- *reduced levels of pollution and a more rational use of natural resources [...];*
- *the respect for European values and standards on human rights, environmental protection and employment;*
- *the Millennium Development Goals".*

Equally, Porter and Kramer (2006) see a competitive advantage in CSR, particularly due to the publicity it attracts via numerous CSR-rankings of companies, some of which have been listed by Grothe (2010:188 ff.).

Although their methodologies are *"sometimes questionable"* (Porter and Kramer 2006:78), they help to better define and segment the individual elements today believed to constitute corporate social governance. The most common of CSR-relevant criteria are (cfr. Grothe 2010:190 ff.):

1. Business Ethics;
2. Corporate Governance;
3. Community/Society;
4. Customers;
5. Employees;
6. Financial Strength/Performance;
7. Transparency;
8. Environment;
9. Product.

The fact that at least points 1 through 7 are basic elements of corporate governance (points 3 through 5 commonly referred to as part of the *"stakeholders"* group in its wider definition) as will be discussed in more detail below, shows the proximity of the two concepts of CSR and corporate governance and one may hypothesize that as both concepts open up to related topics, they too might overlap ever more and finally merge.

As a general finding of different ratings, Grothe (2010:192) affirms that progress has been made by companies in the areas of corporate governance, environment, and employees. She regards the German Corporate Governance Code as well as environmental management certifications of large corporations and good employee-relationships as the main driving forces. Significant deficits were identified in relation to clients, certain stakeholder groups, social responsibility and socio-cultural action.

In response, Porter and Kramer (2006:84) demand *"an affirmative corporate social agenda"* which *"moves from mitigating harm to reinforcing corporate strategy through social progress"*.

As a main critic of CSR, Milton Friedman (1962:112) is often quoted stating *"there is one and only one social responsibility of business: to use its resources and engage in activities designed to increase its profits so long as it stays within the rules of the game, which is to say, engages in open and free competition, without deception or fraud"*. He also posed the question *"[w]hat does it mean to say that "business" has responsibilities?"* and went on to answer that *"[o]nly people have responsibilities. A corporation is an artificial person and in this sense may have artificial responsibilities [...]"*. (Friedman 1970)

Corporate governance, however, is only one field within the spectrum of Governance-related topics. Another, at times closely linked, aspect is that of Public Governance which itself is composed of two branches: Societal Governance and Organizational Governance (Plamper 2010:123). In order to cover all aspects of

Fig. 2.9 Global Governance (*Also "Public Corporate Governance"*). Source: own illustration

society, one might add *"Private Governance"* as the interaction between participants in private structures and their processes or, as Rudder refers to Private Governance: *"policy making activities of private groups"* (Rudder 2008:899) or the influence of private stakeholders on global governance, generating transnational rules and regulations (Schaller 2007). This leads us to the structure chart in Fig. 2.9, trying to systemize Governance, or *"Global Governance"* (Hall 2002).

Societal Governance covers the *"interaction (structures and processes) between protagonists of society including the State, but also private companies and the so-called Third Sector"* (Plamper 2010:123).

Currently, Societal Governance finds itself in the focus of Public Governance discussions, reflecting the erosion of a sharp separation between public and private governance topics towards a more generalistic approach as a result of the practical and theoretical discussions over the past decade or so. As such, it has approached and invaded the sphere of our topic, evolving ever more towards close *"interaction and cooperation of different stakeholders, from companies and associations to public and semi-public institutions, from a local up to a global level"* (Plamper 2010:129). As a reason for this, Plamper identifies the difficulty individual organizations face in trying to achieve those aims and therefore change from an individual approach to a cooperative one.

Organizational Governance refers to the *"structures and processes of public institutions"* (Plamper 2010:123), and includes the term Public Corporate Governance which only covers public companies such as public railways, banks, or public utilities. Beyond that more limited scope, Organizational Governance also includes the public bodies on a local, regional, and national level.

Two main differences between organizational governance and societal governance have been identified by Plamper who refers to Kooiman's (2003:211) assumption that interactions, interdependence and inter-penetrations are elementary ingredients of governance:

- The consensual approach of the participants of society in the sense of *"division of work"* rather than the pursuit of common aims; and
- The possibility to *"exit"* (Hirschman 1970:21 ff. as quoted by Plamper 2010:129) quickly and at any moment those interactions—also described as *"voting by feet"* (Plamper 2010:129).

This leads him to the following conclusions regarding risk management and compliance:

- The participants of society have to trust one another[12];
- Each stakeholder will limit their invested resources in order not to waste significant amounts of time or money;
- Compliance is being accepted as a 'natural' precondition of societal governance, waiving the need for further sanctions (Plamper 2010:129f.).

2.1.10 Stakeholder Management

As mentioned before, the shareholder approach of the 1980s and 1990s has gradually widened to include other *"stakeholders"* of companies such as employees, clients, suppliers, and the community to name but a few. Leßner and Lis (2014:107) affirm that a working and credible corporate governance system reduces the *"apparent discrepancy between shareholder value and stakeholder value"*.

Carroll and Buchholtz (2012:10) group stakeholders into five categories:

- Government (local, state, federal),
- Employees (including Unions),
- Consumers,
- Owners, and
- Commuity

It is interesting to note that suppliers are not shown in this list, although they do constitute a very important part of the stakeholder universe, cfr. also Table 2.3 (right column, 2nd box).

Just as each (group of) shareholder(s)—cfr. Fig. 2.10—presents a set of challenges to the top management, the inclusion of other stakeholders only adds to the complexity and therefore requires an even more sophisticated *"stakeholder management"* approach. Neßler and Lis (2014:107) even state that *"good governance accordingly is rather a question of stakeholder management"*.

2.1.11 Principal-Agent-Conflict (Agency Theory)

"In a free-enterprise, private-property system, a corporate executive is an employee of the owners of the business. He has direct responsibility to his employers. [. . .] [T]he key point is that, in his capacity as a corporate executive, the manager is the agent of the individuals who own the corporation [. . .], and his primary responsibility is to them." (Friedman 1970)

---

[12]Plamper (2010:129f.) distinguishes between confidence and trust, which according to him can both be necessary for a working relationship under those terms. Confidence is described as experience from earlier interaction with the other party while trust is a forward-looking "act of faith" in someone who is as yet not known to the partner.

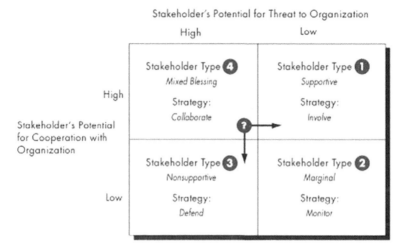

Fig. 2.10 Diagnostic Typology of Organizational Stakeholders. Source: Savage et al. (1991:65)

Agency theory—or, as Shleifer and Vishny put it, the *Agency Problem* (Shleifer and Vishny 1997:740)—is based on the assumption that there are inherent conflicts of interest between the owners (principals) and managers (directors/agents) of companies. Those conflicts depend on both the type of the owner and the agent, as the shareholders might be interested in a long-term growth of their investments—which may include a relatively low cost basis—particularly in the case of a family ownership or institutional property structure, while the executives might be tempted to pursue short term gains, e.g. in order to achieve a higher compensation quicker, leading them to assume higher risks. But the opposite might also be true as short-term investors might eye fast returns while managers might pursue a long-term strategy. In any case, the modern-world separation of ownership and management of companies—prominent in larger companies as opposed to small and medium-sized ones—often leads to mismatches between the interests of the managers and those of the shareholders—or, in broader terms, stakeholders—which the agency theory seeks to identify, describe and mitigate. In order to cut down on the *"self-serving behavior"* of managers (Shleifer and Vishny 1997), several tools of corporate governance can be used such as an active supervisory board, closer shareholder and stakeholder involvement, information disclosure, auditing, and executive remuneration (Filatotchev et al. 2006).

Still, the relationship between corporate governance and an overall better performance, including reduced principal-agent-conflicts, is largely inconclusive (cfr. 2.1.7 above).

Aguilera et al. (2011) propose to use the theory of complementarity as a basis to study the interdependence of various elements of structure, strategy, and processes of an organization (Aoki 2001; Milgrom and Roberts 1990, 1995).

Rediker and Seth (1995) introduced the idea of a *"bundle of governance mech-anisms"* as part of a cost-benefit-analysis testing substitution effects of internal and external monitoring as well as incentivation of managers, arguing that the combina-tion of those mechanisms rather than each one individually define the measures' effectiveness.

Given the high concentration of shareholdings and the usual presence of a controlling shareholder in Brazil, the main agency conflict in that country is *"between controlling and minority shareholders"*, which consequently has been the main topic of corporate governance discussion in Brazil, although the share of listed companies with a controlling shareholder decreased from 100% to around 90% between 2005 and 2009 (Silveira 2010:182f.) According to Claessens and Yurtoglu (2012:9), *"the principal-agent problems in most countries around the world will be less management-versus-owner and more minority-versus-controlling shareholder"* ('principal-principal-problem').

Mülbert (2010:16 ff.) analyses agency conflicts in banks and finds that the particularities lie in the business and the structure of banks, leading to an exacerba-tion of *"the multiple agency conflicts present within banks and to reduce the effectiveness of some of the mechanisms for mitigating these conflicts. The overall effect is for banks to take on more risk than a generic firm would do"* (p. 19).

2.1.12 Compensation/Remuneration

The main focus of discussions around compensation within corporate governance is on the *"optimal contracting framework"* to minimize agency costs between man-agers and shareholders (Rossi 2012a:33).[13] At the same time, there appears to be a strong link between remuneration and risk management which shall be covered in this section. The relevant literature mainly suggests that weak corporate governance increases the influence managers have on their own remuneration packages (Cfr. Oliva and de Albuquerque 2006). A necessary measure to control, motivate and satisfy would be reward management, based on findings of HR metrics, for instance (Armstrong et al. 2006; Wolf 2009; cfr. especially on the relationship between compensation, work motivation and job satisfaction: Igalens and Roussel 1999).

Other academic work covers executive compensation and corporate social responsibility (Mahoney and Thorn 2006) as well as executive compensation in socially responsible firms (Frye et al. 2006), and particularly the adequateness of compensation (Schütte 2009) and its elements (Krieg 2010; Beblo et al. 2005).

According to Rossi (2012a:38), *"lax corporate governance practices enabled management teams to set incentive compensation arrangements that did not appro-priately take risk into consideration"*.

---

[13]Chernenko et al. (2012) show that if equity is overvalued, mispricing offsets agency costs.

He assumes that cognitive biases of bank managers compounded these problems and led to *"an explosion in exotic mortgage products and synthetic derivative products with limited historical experience to form sound risk views"*.

The OECD (2009:7f.) argues that remuneration systems as a *"key aspect of corporate governance"* have often failed because *"negotiations and decisions are not carried out at arm's length"* as *"[m]anagers and others have too much influence over the [...] conditions"* and *"the use of company stock price as a single measure [...] does not allow to benchmark firm specific performance against an industry or market average"*. According to the OECD, *"transparency needs to be improved beyond disclosure"* and remuneration has to be adjusted for *"related risks"*, while *"legal limits such as caps should be limited to specific and temporary circumstances"* (OECD 2009:8).

Current discussions and legislative initiatives around remuneration, particularly in the German-speaking economies, focus on the adequateness of management board remuneration in relation to a reference salary. The basic questions are (i) what the relevant reference remuneration shall be and (ii) what the maximum multiplier of that remuneration should be. A Swiss referendum in November 2013 on a proposed bill therefore asked if management board members' remuneration should be capped at twelve times the salary of the worst paid employee in their company. The Swiss voters answered with *"no"* and thus voted against a fixed limit of executive remuneration.

So far, public discussion has been less specific than that by focusing on the absolute amount of individual managers' compensation and frowning at exaggerated payment of bonuses, for instance. This appears to be changing as differentiations are being made between the individual elements of compensation, with some proposing a more Anglo-Saxon approach also for Germany, asking for a 50/50 split between total compensation and stock (options), with total compensation consisting of base salary, bonus, and a long-term incentive plan (LTIP). (*Immobilien Zeitung*, 07/11/2013:6)

The focus seems to shift more towards the relationship between managers' and workers' compensation, as intensive media reaction on a study by the Hans-Böckler-Stiftung on the so-called *"Manager to Worker Pay Ratio"* shows, which was published in November 2013. According to that study, the median multiplier for members of management boards of the DAX-30-corporations was 53 times the average employee's salary (Preen et al. 2014:101).

In this case, the reference for the so-called *"Manager to Worker Pay Ratio"* (Preen et al. 2014:102) was the average salary, rather than the lowest salary as in Switzerland. This points to a major difficulty in determining adequate board compensation in relation to employees' salaries: the question which salary shall be used as reference (*"vertical appropriateness of Executive Board compensation"*). The European Commission published a proposal to amend the shareholder directive on April 9, 2014, to include the relation between the average board member's compensation to the average full-time-employee compensation in the reporting obligations of listed companies (http://europa.eu/rapid/press-release_IP-14-396_en.htm?locale=en).

Preen et al. (2014:101 ff.) argue that even the average compensation of full-time employees is neither a sufficient, nor a fair reference for all companies, as significant differences exist both between companies of the same branch—for instance, due to their level of internationalization—and between corporations in different business areas. But even the mere relation to any (average) salary reference could incentivize top management to increase company-wide (or rather, reference-group) compensation to the detriment of shareholders (thus constituting yet another aspect of the principal-agent-conflict discussed before).

Another aspect of the definition of possible reference groups is the question whether or not trainees and employees in a protected working relationship should be included, or indeed salaries of part-time or seasonal employees be annualized to full time equivalents (FTEs). The same applies for employees of multi-national corporations which work abroad. If they were to be included, corrections for purchase power parity (PPP) including foreign exchange rate fluctuations, for instance, would need to be established (Preen et al. 2014:102).

A very clear and detailed definition of a formula for remuneration relations needs to be found, taking the above-mentioned factors into consideration, in order to provide for a fair and transparent comparison. This has also become evident in the US, where the Dodd-Frank-Act of 2010 requires companies to publish the relation between the median income of all employees to that of board members. While the aim there is not so much to limit manager compensation but rather to provide for more transparency, a vivid debate has emerged as to how to define *"all employees"* (Preen et al. 2014:102).

Finally, even if such a clear definition existed and were widely accepted, any comparison would still be unequal for companies in different businesses: While some industries like transportation and retail employ a very high number of low-qualified part-time employees relative to their total staff and thus show a relatively low median income, other businesses such as financial institutions with highly qualified, usually full-time employees would provide, in comparison, for a higher level of income. This is also true for the difference between smaller and large companies, particularly if company benefits are included in the equation, given that they tend to be higher and more common in larger institutions (Preen et al. 2014:102).

The authors describe two ways of establishing vertical appropriateness of Executive Board compensation in practice. One is to split employees into hierarchical groups and compare board compensation to each of the groups; another approach would be to take the *"core group of employees"* as reference, meaning the group of employees most numerous in the company, assuming that they are of particular relevance for the success of the entity.

Once the reference group has been established, one still needs to define the compensation of the board. This might be base salary or annual remuneration including bonuses. Stock options, extra benefits etc. might also enter the formula (Cfr. Archer 2003 and Chhabra 2008).

Preen et al. (2014:103) argue that variable compensation of members of the board basically remunerates them for the entrepreneurial risk they are taking, while ordinary employees do not usually take such kinds of risk. Consequently, vertical appropriateness of Executive Board compensation should be restricted to the comparison of base salaries (Preen et al. 2014:103).

While this argumentation makes a lot of sense regarding comparability, it seems to exclude the aspect of performance-related compensation, and indeed any additional compensation over and above the base salary from the equation. This might be called into question if the aim of vertical comparison is the determination of the appropriateness of executive compensation, particularly in an environment where variable compensation might exceed base salary manyfold and public discussion concentrates on total board members' remuneration's appropriateness rather than on their base salaries.

Should only base salary be taken into consideration for the definition of board members' remuneration, the same should apply for the definition of the remuneration of the reference group within the company's employees (and vice versa including additional remuneration) (Preen et al. 2014:103).

Their study groups companies into three size clusters based on the number of employees as well as by sector (insurance, commerce, chemical, and metal & automotive). They find significant differences both within and between the sectors when it comes to the multiple of board remuneration versus that of the *"relevant staff"*, ranging from 1:8 in small metal&automotive sector companies to 1:37 for commerce (90%-percentile, base salary) or from 1:12 in small chemical industrial companies to 1:68 in the same sector for large corporations or even to 1:104 in commerce, when comparing total remuneration (again, 90%-percentile) (Preen et al. 2014:104f.; cfr. Schütte 2009:18f.).

In summary, regulation on board compensation would need to clearly define groups and their compensation in a way to be comparable and fair, take differences of company size and industry sector into account and should even consider international differences. It would appear that this is extremely hard to achieve and one might be inclined to leave restrictions to the *"market forces"*, including public opinion.

A softer alternative would be to make the establishment and maintenance of a remuneration committee compulsory (as already happened in Brazil, cfr. 3.1.2 below and recommended by Anderson 2009:9).

2.1.12.1 Incentives/Risk Management

Rossi (2012a) builds on two strands of research in designing a model to describe the relationship between incentives and the effectiveness of risk management functions within corporate structures. On the one hand, he uses literature on executive compensation, incentives and risk-taking, and combines this with behavioral economics on the other hand.

He notes that *"Risk management at financial institutions differs in large measure from that of nonfinancial companies in that risk is a primary ingredient in their development of products and services. For purposes of exposition, a distinction is made up front between risk management and business management."* Rossi

(2012a:33) explains that the business manager is responsible for profitability, while the risk manager's task is to identify and measure risk as well as proposing and/or taking actions of mitigation. Their responsibility includes *"quantifying uncertainty"* and mitigating risks outside the company's risk appetite, while risk management has evolved into a *"highly analytic-focused discipline"*, with two main features—*"a deeply rooted connection between risk and product [on the one hand] and uncertainty [on the other]"*.

Rossi describes it as *"natural"* that *"business management will take an active interest in participating in risk discussions"*, and explains that *"the fundamental drivers shaping risk-taking are rooted in more subtle behavioral characteristics"* (Rossi 2012a:33).

He further refers to the marginalization of risk managers during discussions of strategic business issues in major institutions such as Lehman Brothers and Washington Mutual as part of *"risk management breakdowns"* which have been identified by a number of congressional inquiries following the financial crisis (e.g. Valukas 2010:12).

Such behavioral patterns *"can lead to significant breakdowns in risk management, potentially jeopardizing the health of the firm"* (Rossi 2012a:33).

Rossi (2012a:37) claims that weak governance and risk infrastructure amplifies risk-taking behavior, cfr. Fig. 2.12. The formula used by the author is

$$A_t = f\left(D_t|S_t, M_t|S_t, \frac{E_t}{E_{t+n}}|S_t\right)$$

where D_t stands for the quality of the firm's risk data warehouse, M_t represents the accuracy of the analytics and models deployed to estimate risk, and E_t/E_{t+n} symbolizes the degree to which forward-looking estimates of risk (E_{t+n}) deviate from effective historical risk outcomes (E_t). By this relationship, the degree to which risk management estimates of future risk outcomes differ from previous experience shall be captured.

In summary, Rossi's scenarios illustrate *"that in the presence of cognitive biases and poor governance, risk management can be marginalized and suboptimal outcomes realized"* and show *"how weak governance and incentive contracts can set in motion a series of behaviors predicated on certain strongly held views toward risk-taking"*. Among those are confirmation biases which cause management to weight specific results more to correspond to a specific view. Those effects include:

- A house-money effect, where previous performance influences management loss-aversion (cfr. Fig. 2.11);
- a herd effect, by which management follows competitor actions based on imperfect information; and
- ambiguity bias that leads management toward outcomes having greater certainty.

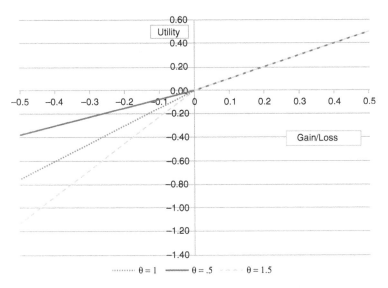

Fig. 2.11 Management cognitive bias influences loss aversion. Source: Rossi (2012b:11)

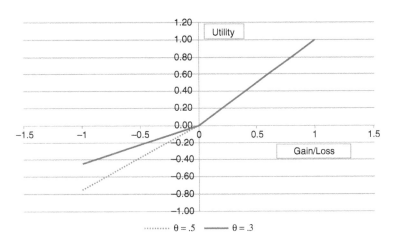

Fig. 2.12 Weak governance and risk infrastructure amplifies risk-taking behaviour. Source: Rossi (2012b:13)

In order to motivate management toward implementing effective risk management practices based on the model's structural relationships, Rossi suggests several policy solutions. *"These include financial incentives such as more rigorous assessment of risk governance and management structures at financial institutions by D&O insurers, rating agencies, and regulatory agencies, with assessments tied directly to supervisory outcomes, ratings and policy premiums."*

Rossi recommends *"the introduction of risk-based metrics into incentive compensation schemes, with particular emphasis on developing robust risk-data-warehouse capabilities that can support sophisticated risk-capital measurement".*

"Opportunities to strengthen risk governance include formalizing the reporting of the senior risk officer to the risk committee of the board, establishing a balanced scorecard taking risk heavily into account in incentive compensation structures, and raising the situational awareness of risk managers to build the stature of the risk management organization." (Rossi 2012a:38)

2.1.13 Two-Tier Board

According to the IIF Report on Governance for Strengthened Risk Management (2012), two-tier Boards usually include a Supervisory Board composed of stakeholders and independent directors and a Management Board. Members of the Supervisory Board, who represent shareholders and other stakeholders or are completely independent, are directors who would, in a single-tier Board structure, be considered non-executive and/or independent directors. The Management Board in a two-tier model is usually made up of members of the senior management team, such as the CEO, CFO, CIO, and CRO. Alternatively, this may be called the Executive Committee in a single-tier Board framework.

There should be a clear line between the executive role of management and the Board's non-executive functions, independently of the kind of Board structure adopted, as the IIF points out.

"Increasingly, dedicated Supervisory Board risk committees are being established, with terms of reference, including interactions with the Board and other Board committees, clearly spelled out." (IIF 2012:27) Risk committee members should have an understanding of risk management issues and auditing. Both the CFO and CRO usually participate in Supervisory Board risk committee meetings, and the CRO's duty when participating in those meetings is to ensure that directors on the committee are fully aware of the company's risk position. This can also be achieved by regular reports on the firm's risk appetite and risk profile. Apart from the Supervisory Board risk committee, there tends to be a risk committee of the Management Board to which the former may delegate some risk management responsibilities, including the definitions of processes, policies, and controls. The CRO typically presides and coordinates Management Board risk committee meetings (IIF 2012:27).

Regarding independent directors, who are generally thought to be better board members, *The Economist* noted that there is no evidence to this end and that eight of its ten directors were classified as independent when Lehman Brothers entered bankruptcy (*The Economist*, August 16th, 2014:52). Henderson and Bainbridge question the reason for requiring director services to be provided by natural persons, suggesting that those services could be provided in a more professional way by *"board service providers"* (BSPs), i.e. firms specializing in providing director services on company boards (Henderson and Bainbridge 2013:6 ff.). Apart from being independent from both, shareholders and senior managers, they could act more professionally, on a full time basis, thus creating *"a market for corporate governance distinct from the market for corporate control"* (Henderson and Bainbridge 2013:7). They expect such a change to increase board accountability and transparency (Henderson and Bainbridge 2013:40; 48).

Members of risk committees should bring in different risk-related experience, both nationally and internationally. They may well come from quite different industry or personal backgrounds, while it is important to include people with experiences in line with the firm's range of products and business model. Complete *"outsiders"* may bring a fresh perspective to the table and introduce new approaches regarding risk management and related practices.

"Once the Board self-evaluation is completed, the real challenge is analyzing the results and developing an action plan to strengthen Board risk management and governance. Knowing what the Board's areas of weakness might be is not very helpful without delving into where and why change is needed." (IIF 2012:28)

The IIF developed a list of warning signs in the form of responses and justifications as to why a certain business deal should be approved or carried out. They are meant to highlight specific areas of focus. The Board should, according to the IIF, react decisively when the response to a risk question is any of the following:

1. *"Every other competitor is doing this."*
2. *"There is no risk to the firm, as it has been transferred to a third party."*
3. *"The (regulator/rating agency/customer) does not mind, as they have not said anything."*
4. *"The risks are fully hedged."*
5. *"The risks are manageable without a detailed explanation and scenario examples."*
6. *"The risk metrics, which are modeled, are within the risk appetite but at the upper end of the range."*
7. *"It has not happened in (20/30/40) years, or since the 1930s."*
8. *"Closing out the position to be within the risk limit will result in an immediate loss, and it is sure to recover next (quarter)."*
9. *"We need this concentration of (risk/product/asset/liability) to be (competitive/ maintain growth/meet plan)."*
10. *"We have a higher (yield/return) with less risk."*

These responses can be grouped into the following types with relation to risk assessment:

- Justifications are not referring to the risk in question but rather compare the risk-taking to that of others (e.g. competitors as in answer 1 or 9 above) or historical *"evidence"* (answer 7).
- Answers can simply consist in the supposed mitigation of the specific risk (s) within acceptable levels, without however substantiating this in any form, as is the case with answers 2, 4 or 6, for instance.

- The response may also consist in the tertiarization of responsibility, e.g. by intrinsically or expressly transferring the obligation of assessing risk to a third party such as rating agencies, supervisory authorities etc. as happened in answer 3.
- Responses imply a positive risk/return relationship without putting this into relationship with the firm's risk policy, such as answers 5, 8, and 10.

In any case, they tend to be based on an insufficient or inexistent risk assessment against the company's risk strategy/appetite or business model. Furthermore, their use in board presentations shows the expectation of them being accepted rather than challenged rigorously. As such they do serve as warning signs regarding an insufficient risk culture and consequently may serve as a diagnostic tool to develop measures under *"an action plan to strengthen risk governance at the Board level"*. (IIF 2012:27)

2.1.14   Accounting and Controlling

When it comes to accounting with regards to corporate governance, the notion of the *"triple bottom line (3BL)"* is certainly among the first to come to mind. This concept is based on social corporate responsibility (CSR) as discussed above, and assumes that *"a corporation's ultimate success or health can and should be measured not just by the traditional financial bottom line, but also by its social/ethical and environmental performance"* (Norman and MacDonald 2004). It was coined by think tank AccountAbility in the mid-1990s and brought to a wider public by Elkington (1997), according to Wayne and MacDonald 2004, who however question that concept's promise to provide *"an agreed-upon methodology that allows us, at least in principle, to add and subtract various data until we arrive at a net sum"* (Norman and MacDonald 2004:249), i.e. to allow transforming soft factors such as ethical performance into hard numbers which may be added to or subtracted from the traditional bottom lines of financial accounting.

In reply, Pava (2007) points out that the *"aggregation claim"* implied, along with four other claims, in the criticism of 3BL by Norman and MacDonald (2004) is not generally accepted by the advocates of the triple bottom line (Pava 2007:107).

This discussion highlights one of the main challenges of issues involving corporate governance: That getting to the result that a corporation has either *"good"* or *"bad"* corporate governance is not as straightforward as finding out whether it made a profit or not. Therefore it is hard to establish a clear and direct connection between corporate governance and accounting, and while this should be further explored by practitioners of both areas, we shall take a look at the related practice of controlling.

We found the controlling topic within corporate governance already in the Cadbury Report (1992), where under sections 2.5 and 5.16 board and auditors have been given the responsibility for financial controlling of the management.

According to Berens and Schmitting (2004), controlling and internal audit are understood, from a functional perspective, as tasks delegated by the company's management. Both functions use early warning systems as a main tool of their work and jointly they play an important role for risk management which is understood as part of corporate governance.

The authors investigate the role of controlling and internal audit for corporate governance, taking into account the relationship between those two. They conclude that controlling and internal audit staff must be loyal to the company's management rather than any other organ of the entity, such as supervisory board or even external shareholders. As a consequence, they understand the controllers' and auditors' contribution to corporate governance as one limited to the support of the correctly acting management in managing the company as it should be managed. This means however, *"that in the case of wrongful or fraudulent actions committed by the company's management, controlling and internal audit won't contribute much to transparency in the sense of corporate governance"* (Berens and Schmitting, Controlling 2004).

Given that controllers and internal auditors are indeed employed by the company and therefore do not have, *per se*, any other role or duty than that of ensuring—or rather only testing—that the management's rules and policies are implemented, working, and complied with, one wonders what can or even must be expected from internal auditors and controllers in the case of illegal actions. In this case, we tend to believe that they do have a *"whistle-blowing obligation"*, not only because their professional bodies and their ethical standards—or, particularly in the case of banks: the regulators—might so stipulate, or because their inaction might later be considered as conspiratory in criminal procedures brought against the company or its management, but because this is—in the long term at least—beneficial to the company itself, which they work for and for the orderly workflows and actions of which they are ultimately co-responsible. This obviously builds on the underlying notion that corporate governance rules do not only and exclusively apply to the members of top management, but also to other professionals within an organization and especially those who do hold responsibility for the overall well-functioning of the organism which constitutes a company.

Van der Oord sees an obligation on the side of (internal) auditors to persuade managers *"to take full control of the risks that have been identified"* and to engage management *"to make sure that significant issues get holistically and sustainably resolved"* (Oord 2013).

This interrelation between corporate governance, management accounting, and risk management has been *"addressed only to a minimal extend in the academic literature"* (Bhimani 2009:3; cfr. Ballou and Heitger 2008).

2.1.15 Corporate Governance in Stock Market Organizations

Another line of investigation related to corporate governance focuses on the entities *"building"* the market for listed companies by providing the infrastructure necessary to trade their shares, such as stock exchanges, clearing houses and information providers, but also alternative competitors.

Schulte (2001:165 ff.) analyses the evolution from stock exchanges to *"stock market organizers"* analyzing the value added by corporate governance from an economic standpoint.

2.1.16 Shareholder Activism

While shareholder activism started out in the United States, it has over the course of
the past few years not only spread out to other countries such as Japan or European
countries including Germany, but it has also lost its *"distinctively negative connotation"* (Mary Jo White, Head of the Securities and Exchange Commission (SEC) as
quoted by *The Economist*, 15/02/2014:10). Confronting top managers of listed
companies has become more common—and more accepted—in line with rule
changes which made it easier. It is often seen as a means of control over the board
of directors and thus another corrective, albeit outside the classical corporate governance tool box.

On the other hand, one may argue that activist shareholders,[14] who tend to hold
their shares for relatively short periods of time, might just reap the profits of their
intervention and then leave, leading to a focus on short-term results rather than the
long-term view.

A study of around 2000 activist interventions in the U.S. between 1994 and 2007
however reveals that both the share price and the operating profits of the companies
involved increased over the 5-year period following the intervention. It also shows that
the increase is biggest towards the end of that period. (The Economist, 15/02/2014:10)

2.1.17 Social Responsibility

According to Neßler and Lis (2014:107), the increase of Socially Responsible
Investments confirms a growing appreciation by capital markets of a responsible
and thus sustainable management and company culture, serving as an *"institution-
alized risk management"* implicitly hedging their equity.

SCR is one of the few areas regulated/covered by an international standard, in this
case ISO 26000.

Figure 2.13 provides a structural overview of ISO 26000 in order to help
organizations understand how to apply this standard.

While clauses 1 to 4 deal with basic concepts of social corporate responsibility,
clause 5 deals with their recognition and shareholder engagement in order to achieve
those aims. The necessary assessment should include an analysis of the corporation's
sphere of influence and the identification of relevant action (Clause 5).

Clause 6 describes organizational governance as the structural framework which
needs to be implemented in a given organization before the implementation process
according to clause 7 can begin. The achievement of a sustainable development
depends on a successful implementation of relevant actions throughout the entity on
a regular rather than sporadic basis, supported by focused communication. This
includes integrating social responsibility into its strategy, policies, organizational
culture, and operations. Internal competency for social responsibility can be both

---

[14]E.g. Carl Icahn, Bill Ackman, David Einhorn, Nelson Peltz, to name but a few.

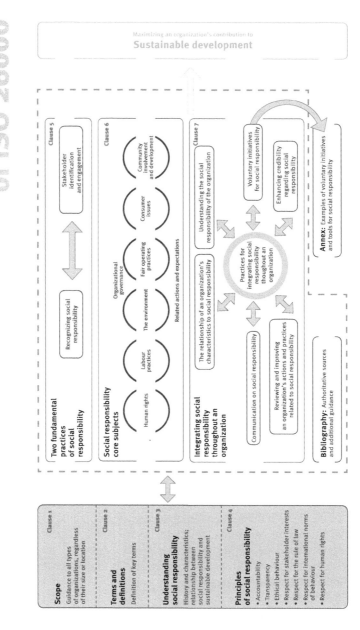

Fig. 2.13 Social Responsibility—Schematic overview of ISO 26000. Source: ISO.org (15.03.2017)

achieved and passed on by internal and external communication on this subject. As with risks, a regular review is necessary to assess and, as necessary, adjust the measures put into place with relation to social responsibility.

The overarching goal for an organization approaching and practicing social responsibility is to maximize its contribution to sustainable development.

2.1.18   Corruption

"Among crimes, corruption is a timid being. She dresses in finest fabric, does not bear arms, and rarely sheds blood. You cannot even identify the victims immediately." (Perzanowska 2006:85 as cited by Litzcke et al. 2012:1; own translation)

As a matter of fact, corruption is a crime difficult to police as both parties, the actively and the passively corrupt person, have an interest in maintaining the transaction secret. Given that the classical victim is missing, which in the case of other crimes would file a criminal complaint, it is also difficult to identify the aggrieved person, which—in the case of corruption—usually is an organization (often, the competitor's) or society as such (Litzcke et al. 2012:1).

The damage caused for the economy can only be estimated but is definitely severe, with registered damages alone accounting for EUR 4.12 bn for 2007 in Germany (Schmalhardt 2010:143).

In many cases, the participants in corruption do not think that they are actually acting illegally as they find subjective justifications for their deeds (*"neutralizing techniques"* (*Neutralisierungstechniken*)) (Litzcke et al. 2012:4).

In *TIME*'s March 3rd, 2014 issue, on page 6, Catherine Mayer and Andrew Katz refer to a WIN/Gallup International poll asking 66,806 people in 65 nations *"What's the world's top problem?"*. 21% of respondents answered *"corruption"*, roughly twice as many as those who mentioned the *"gap between rich and poor"* (12%) or *"unemployment"* (10%).

According to Fuchs and Jerabek (2009), corruption is usually understood as any kind of breach of duty up to the abuse of powers in exchange for an advantage, both in the public and private sphere. Transparency International (transparency.org) says that *"corruption is the abuse of entrusted power for private gain"*. It should always be noted that corruption exists both in its active and passive form, i.e. a crime is committed by the person who *"bribes"* another as well as by the person who accepts being *"bribed"* (Litzcke 2012:2).

According to WIN/Gallup, *"Overall, in the world, political parties are seen to be the most corrupt institution, followed by the police. Moreover, more than 1 in 4 people around the world report having paid a bribe."*[15]

Using data from Transparency International (www.transparency.org), we may establish the comparison between Brazil and Germany shown in Table 2.4 (also refer to Fig. 2.14).

---

[15]The study asked over 114,000 people in 107 countries for their views on corruption. – http://www.wingia.com/en/news/global_corruption_barometer_2013_report/61/

Table 2.4 Corruption comparison Brazil/Germany

Index	Number	Top Score	Brazil			Germany		
			Rank	Score	Value	Rank	Score	Value
Corruption Perception Index (2013)	177	100	72	42		12	78	
Bribe Payers Index (2011)	28	10	14	7.7		4	8.6	
OECD Anti-Bribery Convention (2011)				Little				Active
Control of Corruption (2010)			60%	0.056112		93%	1.700708	
Financial Secrecy Index (2011)	71		n/a	n/a	n/a	9	57	669.8
Open Budget Index (2010)			71	71	Significant	68	68	Significant
Global Competitiveness Index (2012–2013)	142	7	48	4.4		6	5.48	
Judicial Independence (2011–2012)	142	7	71	3.7		7	6.3	
Rule of Law (2010)			55%	0.00202		92%	1.627934	
Human Development Index (2011)	187		84	0.718	High	9	0.905	Very High
Press Freedom Index (2011–2012)	179		99			16	−3.00	
Voice&Accountability (2010)			64%	0.499222		93%	1.345103	

Data source: www.transparency.org; own presentation

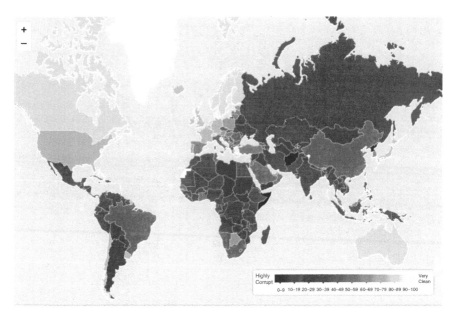

Fig. 2.14 World map—Corruption. Source: Transparency.org

This comparison shows firstly, that Germany is far more developed in terms of transparency than Brazil and that while Germany is clearly within the top ten percent, Brazil is rather in a 'midfield position'. Having said this, and on a second glance, one notices that Brazil is quite advanced in some areas. It performs well in the Open Budget Index (2010) with a score of 71, compared to Germany's 68 (both *"significantly open"*), this similarity probably being an outcome of the democratic culture in both countries.

2.1.18.1   Corruption in Brazil

According to Gallup,[16] 63% of Brazilian residents think that corruption is widespread in their government. Quite interestingly, this is only five percentage points higher than in Germany (58%), while for example Portugal stands at 88%, Tanzania at 95% and Sweden, on the other side of the spectrum, at 14%.

For a number of years now, the issue of corruption in the public sphere, especially federal and state government, has been identified as a main constraint for economic and social development in Brazil. Since it was put on the agenda by President Dilma Rousseff following the transition of power from former President Luiz Inácio Lula da Silva in 2011, a number of public officials have been charged with demanding bribes, particularly to shortcut bureaucratic processes. But also under her

---

[16]http://www.gallup.com/poll/165476/government-corruption-viewed-pervasive-worldwide.aspx

predecessors, including Lula da Silva, corruption was being fought. Between 2003 and 2012, for example, the federal auditor's office discharged nearly 4000 employees from public service, mostly based on charges of corruption or dishonesty.

The Brazilian Clean Company Act of 2013 makes also companies liable for corruption. According to the new regulations, a company can, among other restrictions, be fined up to 20% of its gross revenues or R$ 60 million, be prohibited from signing contracts with the public sector, and prevented from taking loans from state banks. This serves as an incentive for management to take issues around corruption seriously when doing business at home and abroad.

However, this law has to be actively enforced if it is to have a lasting effect. (www.transparency.org/country#BRA)

Estrin and Prevezer (2011:59) found that *"corruption is not arbitrary"* despite an inefficient judiciary system. Brazil's legal structure allows for *"many appeals so that even fairly trivial cases end up in high courts, with enormous backlogs and huge delays"*. Law-abiding and tax-paying companies, especially those which also abide by strict and complicated labor laws practically have a disadvantage with regards to those operating in the *"large black economy"*.

Thus, "[c]ompanies in the formal economy are forced to abide by expensive and enforced rules" (Estrin and Prevezer 2010:59, citing *The Economist* 2009).

Influence Peddling

Another closely related factor undermining integrity is influence peddling. Influence peddling describes *"the illegal practice of using one's influence in government to obtain favours or preferential treatment"* (Estrin and Prevezer 2011). In 2012 the former head of the presidential office was dismissed in by President Dilma Rouseff, and in 2011 two MPs were forced to resign over allegations of influence peddling. Public distrust in the public sector is also prominent.

The 'Custo Brasil' (cost of doing business in Brazil) means that companies operating in Brazil have to comply with a wide range of rules established and enforced by many regulatory agencies. This burdensome bureaucracy can increase the likelihood of corruption as it *"incentivizes"* on the one hand companies to find a shortcut to the resource-consuming and time-intensive compliance with those rules and on the other hand public officials to offer priority treatment in exchange for the payment of bribes.

Ramalho (2003) found that the values of politically connected companies in Brazil drop around the dates of anti-corruption campaigns. According to Claessens et al. (2008), companies that had contributed to campaigns of elected political candidates showed higher stock returns in the election periods of 1998 and 2002 than others and also had (improved) access to bank finance in the aftermath. (Claessens and Yurtoglu 2012:69).

As a consequence, and according to a 2009 survey (http://www.enterprisesurveys. org/Data/ExploreEconomies/2009/brazil), almost 68.8% of Brazilian business owners and top managers mention corruption as a major constraint to economic activity, whereas the figure for Latin America & Caribbean stands at 39.9% and for all countries, at 33.9%.

International Level

In addition to the national level of corruption in Brazil, there is the international sphere. The government ratified the OECD Anti-Bribery Convention in 1997, but there appears to be little enforcement. In over 10 years, only one case and two investigations have been pursued by the authorities, which shows that enforcement is almost non-existent.

As with anti-bribery laws, the existence of some of the strongest political and campaign financing regulations in Latin America does not seem to deter wrong-doing in that area, either. Brazil is being perceived as one of the countries with the highest political corruption related to the financing of political parties and individual campaigns, with important implications for the competitive situation of businesses, as donors can expect to be *"rewarded"* by the parties or politicians they sponsored. Despite of high regulation, there are no limits on donations to political parties, for example, nor are there any restrictions to party expenditure. The transparency requirements obliging parties and candidates to reveal the identity of financial backers merely establish a requirement to do so in a final consolidated report. Therefore, this disclosure only occurs well after the election, and thus remains largely without effect as it doesn't allow voters to understand before the election how politicians' public policies are influenced.

Local Governments

Another layer of complexity is added by the country's federal system which in that regard is quite comparable to the German structure, by establishing a clear separation between the local, state and federal levels, further hindering transparency as it provides politicians and bureaucrats with significant autonomy over the use of public funds on each of those political levels. According to a 2011 report, local government is particularly prone to corruption regarding business dealings with local level governments, which might show that the higher the level within the federal structure, the lower the risk of corruption (http://www.state.gov/e/eb/rls/othr/ics/2011/157245. htm). This might be explained by the fact that most businesses—which tend to be relatively small—have an easier and more direct access to local politicians than to state or federal bureaucrats, but also require favors rather on a local level, typically responsible for planning permits and business licenses, rather than on higher polit-ical levels. At the same time, the quality of corruption, understood as the degree of illegalities committed and monetary volumes involved, might well be found to be high between state and federal officials on the one side and large corporations on the other than on the local level, which should therefore probably be the focus of corporate governance and compliance concerns in big companies.

Public Procurement

This is certainly also true when it comes to public procurement in Brazil, where the legal environment is relatively mature at least on a regional level. However, also here the enforcement mechanisms do not seem to match the quality of legal statutes, making it commonplace for businesses to be faced with irregular demands in public contracting (http://www3.weforum.org/docs/WEF_GCR_Report_2011-12.pdf).

Especially in 2012, a number of corruption scandals involving public procurement put the topic as well as cabinet ministers and business leaders into the spotlight (cfr. http://www.theguardian.com/world/2012/may/15/brazil-bribery-scandal-politicians). While a number of infrastructure projects including roads, air- and seaports have been postponed, the run-up to the 2014 UEFA Cup and the 2016 Olympics left no time to review the handling of public procurement for those prestigious projects and thus ample opportunity appears to remain to improve both processes and controls on all levels of public intervention in Brazil.

(http://www.transparency.org/country#BRA)

2.1.18.2 Corruption in Germany

This follows the initiatives of many other institutions such as UNO, OECD, EU, Worldbank, and IMF regarding the information on, sensitization for and prevention of corruption, the German Grand Coalition promised in February 2014 to ratify the EU treaty on corruption and the German Parliament voted almost unanimously on the illegality of bribery of members of parliament, making it a crime to bribe parliamentarians (FAZ 21/02/2014:1/4).

Prior to this, a number of corruption scandals (Siemens, Volkswagen, Presidency of the Republic etc.) had shaken the basic idea that corruption was a rare phenomenon in Germany (Litzcke et al. 2012:7) and the geographic equation *"the further south, the more corrupt"* (Schaupensteiner 2004:117) was put into question.

With the feeling shared by a majority of Germans that corruption in Germany is growing, acceptance of stricter anti-corruption rules rises, as this appears to be correlated to the sentiment of being threatened by corruption (Litzcke et al. 2012:2). However, there seem to be no clear indications for an increase of corruption in Germany—the numbers for the period 2000–2009 indicate no increase. Still, perception is driven by the cases which become known and their exposure, and given that corruption is a *"control crime"* (*Kontrolldelikt*), i.e. the more controls take place, the more cases become known, that exposure is not necessarily an indicator for an increase in corruption itself.

The risks brought about by corruption are, above all, material damages to the economy, given that competitors, suppliers etc. of corrupt companies suffer from this phenomenon and the existence of some non-corrupt companies may be at risk. Furthermore, it undermines trust—trust in specific companies and in the economy or the State in general. Particularly companies or branches which *"sell security in a wide sense"* (Litzcke et al. 2012:3)—such as banks, insurances, and auditors depend on a 'safe' reputation, given that not only *"objective security"* but also *"subjective security"* matters, i.e. the individual perception that confidence in those companies is justified. Corruption therefore is poised to particularly afflict such companies—including banks—up to an inviabilization of their business model, and as such poses an important risk to that kind of institutions. (Litzcke et al. 2012:2f.)

2.1.18.3   Corruption in Brazil and Germany

Schlesinger (1966) opened his seminal work on political careers with the words *"Ambition lies at the heart of politics."* This somewhat provocative thesis not only reminds us of the fact that democratic politics is a very competitive game in which generally the most outgoing and ambitious people advance, but it also seems to imply that many of its problems are due to those character traits of its players. In particular professional politicians (cfr. Weber 1994) are vulnerable to monetary temptations, given that professional politics *"is about one's livelihood thrown under the imponderabilities of politics in general and the democratic election in particular"* (Borchert 2010:2).

According to Borchert, the selection of a political office is determined by three factors: (i) availability, (ii) accessibility, and (iii) attractiveness. The latter in turn is defined by the power, the status, and the material benefits of a certain position.

Brazil and Germany are two *"old federal systems"* (Borchert 2010:2), meaning that *"the distribution of competences, the status of different offices, and career patterns have had time to develop and stabilize"* (Borchert 2010:6). To that extend, both countries are comparable.

2.1.19   Corporate Governance in Emerging Markets

Shleifer and Vishny (1997) identify two main issues for corporate governance in emerging economies as (i) the nature of legal protection for investors, especially small minority shareholders, and (ii) the concentrated ownership of corporations and the presence of large shareholders in companies. They propose these are the norm for ownership structures in developing economies. (Estrin and Prevezer 2010:48)

2.1.19.1   Informal Institutions

Estrin and Prevezer (2010) argue that not only the formal institutions, but also informal institutions are central to the understanding of how corporate governance works, particularly in emerging economies: Peng and Heath (1996) found that informal institutions have a stronger impact on corporate governance in emerging countries than in OECD economies. They focus on firm ownership structures and property rights as well as the relationship between corporations and their external investors.

Table 2.5 Typology of informal institutions

Typology of informal institutions according to Helmke and Levitsky (2003)	Ineffective formal institutions	Effective formal institutions
Compatible goals between actors in formal and informal institutions	Substitutive	Complementary
Conflicting goals between actors in formal and informal institutions	Competing	Accomodating

Source: Helmke and Levitsky 2003.

With reference to Helmke and Levitsky (2003), they include in the notion of informal institutions the whole range *"from bureaucratic and legislative norms to various forms of clientelism or reliance on business or familial networks rather than formal access to banks"* and describe *"informal institutions as 'the actual rules that are being followed,' unwritten rules that often shape incentives in systematic ways"*. They continue to elaborate that *"[i]nformal institutions are usually unwritten and are created and enforced outside the official channels"* and that they include *"a variety of structures which have significance in the economy but whose power does not stem from de jure rights"* (Estrin and Prevezer 2010:43f.).

According to that research, there are two branches of literature on informal institutions, one seeing them as problem-solving, the other attributing them a problem-creating role. While the latter (e.g. Morck 2005; Steier 2009) stress the nurturing of phenomena which undermine the economic and political structures, such as clientelism, clan politics, and corruption,[17] the former (Peng 2001) focuses on the support complex formal institutions may benefit from as well as the improvement of social interaction and coordination, helping for example Chinese entrepreneurship to prosper (Estrin and Prevezer 2010:44). Understood in this way, informal institutions may be characterized as complementary to formal ones, which in effect is one of the four types of informal institutions as classified by Helmke and Levitsky (2003): in addition to complementary, there are accommodating, competing, and substitutive informal institutions with regard to formal ones, as shown in Table 2.5.

Thus, formal institutions might be supported by informal ones, however, two traits are necessary for formal institutions to be effective according to Estrin and Prevezer: (i) the existence of (market-supporting) laws and codes of governance and (ii) the enforcement of those de jure rules. The latter may be hindered by corruption and/or judicial inefficiency. *"Only when legal rights on paper are matched by* de facto *enforcement, which can come about through formal or informal institutional means, can we argue that those formal institutions are effective."* (Estrin and Prevezer 2010:45)

Regarding Brazil, they find that its corporate environment *"is characterized by 'accommodating' informal institutions which get around the effectively enforced but restrictive formal institutions and reconcile varying objectives that are held between actors in formal and informal institutions"* (Estrin and Prevezer 2010:41).

---

[17]On corruption, cfr. 2.1.18 above.

Table 2.6 Formal shareholder rights and creditor rights

	Shareholder rights index	Creditor rights index
India	5	4
Brazil	3	1
US	5	1
Average across sample	3	2.3
China	Low[a]	Low[a]
Russia	High[a]	High[a]

La Porta et al. (1998)
Source: Estrin and Prevezer (2011:50)
[a]Author estimation (Estrin and Prevezer 2010)

As major informal institutions, they single out the shadow economy which de Soto (1989, as quoted by Estrin and Prevezer 2010:48) views as the response to the *"bureaucratic and law-ridden state"* of the socio-economic system in Latin America.

Emphasizing the connection between structures of corporate governance and institutional development, Steier (2009) identifies family ownership in combination with the remnants of state ownership and financial industrial groups as the predominant mode of governance in developing market economies. Globerman and Shapiro (2003) focus on foreign direct investment (FDI) by stating that this is attracted by strong governance infrastructure such as well-working formal institutions such as property rights, regulation, legal processes, transparency and accountability. While they refer to developing and transition countries, this assessment certainly holds true for developed countries as well, and many other authors have stressed the 'importance of national governance infrastructure for growth, investment, and new firm entry' (e.g. Acemoglu et al. 2003; Djankov et al. 2002).

Estrin and Prevezer (2010) present a framework to model the interaction between formal and informal institutions, highlighting two central aspects: (i) the effectiveness of formal institutions and (ii) whether or not the aims of agents in the formal and informal institutions are *"compatible and mutually reinforcing or incompatible and in conflict with each other"* (cfr. Table 2.6).

Based on research by La Porta et al. (1998), they find informal institutions in Brazil to fall into the category *"accommodating"* for corporate governance as they have different goals from formal institutions which are regarded as *"overly restrictive"* and thus find ways to evade the formal institutions, which however are in general of a good effectiveness, based on *"a strong rule of law, strict enforcement, medium levels of corruption, and a low risk of expropriation"* (Estrin and Prevezer 2010:53). In China and India, by contrast, informal institutions for corporate governance are mainly substitutive as their aims do not contradict those by the formal institutions which are, however, ineffective. In Russia, on the other hand, the goals of informal and formal corporate governance institutions conflict with each other and the formal ones are being undermined by corruption and an absence of enforcement, thus qualifying as *"competing"* informal institutions, cfr. Table 2.7.

Table 2.7 How effective are formal corporate governance institutions?

Enforcement measures	Judiciary	Rule of Law	Corruption	Risk of expropriation
India	8	4.17	4.58	7.75
Brazil	5.75	6.32	6.32	7.62
China	Weak[a]	Weak[a]	Poor[a]	Low[a]
Russia	Weak[a]	Weak[a]	Poor[a]	High[a]
US	10	10	8.63	9.98
Average across sample	7.67	6.85	6.90	8.05

La Porta et al. (1998).
Source: Estrin and Prevezer (2011:53)
[a]Author estimation (Estrin and Prevezer 2010)

2.1.20 Corporate Governance in Brazil

"Corporate governance issues in emerging markets vary from those in advanced countries due to still-limited development of private financial markets and poor access to financing, concentrated ownership structures, and low institutional ownership" (Claessens and Yurtoglu 2012:3).

Bobirca and Miclaus (2007) identify both the ability to attract foreign investment and the privatization of formerly state-owned companies as reasons for mounting pressure on transition countries to comply with and improve their corporate governance frameworks.

Nicoletti and Scarpetta (2003) suggest that *"despite of extensive liberalisation and privatisation in the OECD area, the cross-country variation of regulatory settings has increased in recent years, lining up with the increasing dispersion in growth"*.

During most of the twentieth century, large Brazilian companies were usually financed by the State rather than financing themselves through the capital markets (Silveira 2010:176). This was mainly due to the fact that the Brazilian economy was a closed one, thus severely limiting competitiveness and innovation.

According to Black et al. (2008), the military coup of 1964 marks the beginning of a liberalisation process in Brazil through a number of legislative measures such as the approval of the Banking Reform Act (*Lei da Reforma Bancária, Lei n° 4.595/1964*) which created the Monetary Council and the Central Bank; led to the approval of the first Capital Markets Act (*Lei de Mercado de Capitais, Lei n° 4.728/1965*); the creation of the Brazilian Securities and Exchange Commission (*Comissão Brasileira de Valores Mobiliários—Lei n° 6.385/1976); and the approval of the Public Share Company Act (*Lei das Sociedades por Ações—Lei n° 6.404/1976*). This government-led trend of capital market development continued throughout the 1970s and 1980s. One example is *"Fundo 157"*, which gave taxpayers the opportunity to use part of their income taxes due to invest in equity funds (Silveira 2010:176).

As most emerging economies, BRIC countries are characterized by corporate governance structures with a *"high concentration of ownership and inside investors"* (Estrin and Prevezer 2010:49, quoting Gerlach 1992; Heugens et al. 2009).

Block holders in Brazil "*still own half of the median firm five years after IPO*", according to Claessens and Yurtoglu (2012:9). "*The consequences of the potential principal-principal-problems* [cfr. 2.1.11 above] *that follow from concentrated ownership depend largely on the way the key institutions, formal and informal, in the country work*" (Estrin and Prevezer 2010:49).

A number of studies have been carried out on specific corporate governance issues in Brazil (cfr. Claessens and Yurtoglu 2012), including Carvalhal da Silva and Leal (2006) who analyzed 236 financial and non-financial companies listed on Bovespa between 1998 and 2002, finding that government-controlled companies or those controlled by foreign and institutional investors[18] generally have significantly higher valuation and performance than family-controlled enterprises. Also, firm valuation and ROA were found to be positively related to cash flow concentration and negatively to voting concentration and the separation of voting- from cash flow rights. Silveira et al. (2007), who analyzed c. 200 companies between 1998 and 2004 found that overall corporate governance quality was still low but improving, albeit slowly. Its heterogeneity was helped by the voluntary adoption of corporate governance rules. Regarding voluntariness, Blundell-Wignall et al. (2009:26f.) state that corporate governance (reform) "*will always require companies to embrace it voluntarily, so that good principles are translated into practice. Sound governance is to a large extent cultural—within banks where shareholder rights are respected and good standards of governance are valued and reflected in long-run share price performance.*"

2.1.20.1 The Evolution of Corporate Governance in Brazil

Since the turn of the century, the Brazilian economy has undergone major changes towards a more open and modern system. After decades of political and economic instability, and following the introduction of a new and stable currency under the "*Plano Real*" in 1994, both political and macroeconomic stability have come to be part of Brazilian reality.

Following the foundation of the first Brazilian stock exchange ("*Bolsa de Valores*") in Rio de Janeiro in 1845 and that of the "*Bolsa de Fundos Públicos*"— Exchange of Public Funds—as the stock exchange in São Paulo was originally called (Silveira 2010:207), the twentieth century has seen a very limited role of capital markets in the Brazilian economy, as the State took over the "*catalyst*" function of economic activity by either providing services and products directly through State-owned firms or by granting long-term concessions over natural resources to companies which were subsidized. While the low levels of internal saving rates certainly contributed to that tamed development, the Brazilian economy has almost always been a relatively closed one, so that interventionism coupled with protectionism gave little room or impetus for a healthy competitive business environment. This led to a

---

[18]On institutional investors and corporate governance in Latin America, see Blume et al. (2007).

"tripartite corporate establishment" in Brazil (Silveira 2010:176), consisting of State-owned and controlled companies, multinationals, and Brazilian conglomerates controlled by few but very influential families, most of which were also politically well-connected.

Apart from those structures, the Brazilian economy at the beginning of the twentieth century was dependent on its exports of natural products such as coffee on the one hand and on the import of consumer and industrial goods on the other. The 1929 stock exchange crash in New York sent both demand and prices for the Brazilian commodities into a downwards spiral to which the answer was a *"policy of import substitution"* (*"política de substituição das importações"*) which not only let to the industrialization of the national economy, but also to the establishment or increase of trade tariffs and other measures which ended up closing the Brazilian market off international competition. This helped bigger family-run firms to prosper as they were almost the only ones with access to capital at a larger scale, namely by tapping State funds through their political connections. Those family businesses, many of which had grown into highly diversified groups, turned into the *"base model of Brazilian governance"* (Silveira 2010:176).

On April 30th, 2008, Standard & Poors upgraded Brazil's long-term foreign currency sovereign debt to investment-grade (*Businessweek*, May 1st, 2008). Subsequently, not only government debt has been upgraded, but also many banks and other individual companies have benefited from investment grade ratings which make them attractive—or at least eligible—for institutional international investors. Furthermore, Brazil's economy has grown steadily and did not suffer much during the Great Recession, cfr. Figs. 2.15, 2.16, and 2.17.

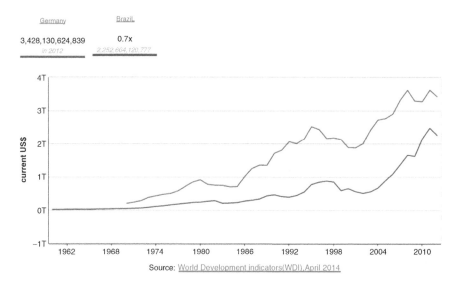

Fig. 2.15 Brazilian and German GDP, PPP (current international $). Source: knoema.com (license CC BY-ND 4.0; 03.09.2014)

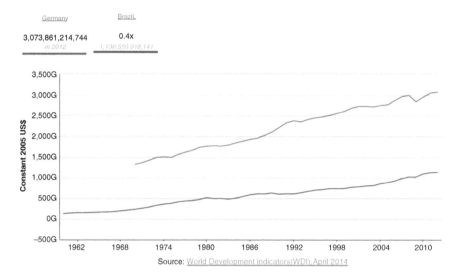

Fig. 2.16 Brazilian and German GDP, constant 2005 US$. Source: knoema.com (license CC BY-ND 4.0; 03.09.2014)

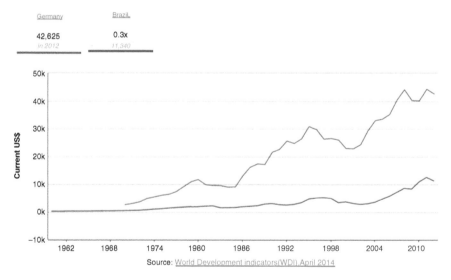

Fig. 2.17 Brazilian and German GDP per capita (current international $). Source: knoema.com (license CC BY-ND 4.0; 03.09.2014)

Another positive aspect, according to Black et al. (2012:2) was the *"development of pension funds, which became major investors in public company shares"*.

Significant changes also occurred in the stock market. Until the early 2000s, Brazil was seen as having relatively weak corporate governance, being ranked 24th for investor rights, 43rd for enforcement of corporate law, and 40th for accounting standards out of 49 countries compared by Nenova (2003). The expropriation of minority shareholders by controlling shareholders was common, helped by the existence of both voting and non-voting shares as allowed by Brazilian law. The Brazilian reality shows many companies with controlling shareholders holding a majority of voting shares, but a significantly smaller percentage of the overall issued shares. By comparing the difference between trading prices and prices paid for controlling blocks of companies in 39 countries, Dyck and Zingales (2004) found that Brazil had the greatest average benefit of corporate control, estimated at 65% of equity value.

Furthermore, there have been few independent directors on the boards of Brazilian companies (an average of 30.4% of directors were independent as of 2009 according to a study quoted by Silveira 2010:212), as well as low levels of disclosure (Cfr. Silveira 2010:184).

In 2000, in response to concern about weak protection for minority shareholders based on the realities described above, the São Paulo Stock Exchange (BM&FBovespa) created three listing levels (markets) for companies with high corporate governance standards (*Novo Mercado*, Level I and Level II). After a few years without much effect, this measure contributed to a surge in initial public offerings, which had been nearly nonexistent until 2004. Furthermore, the number of listed companies, which had been shrinking, started to stabilize and has since increased. Also, trading volumes and liquidity on the most important Brazilian and, indeed, South-American stock market rose significantly (De Carvalho and Pennacchi 2012).

Formal corporate governance structures in Brazil have clearly improved since 2000 (Lubrano 2007). Considerable legal uncertainty, prominence of non-voting shares as well as poor company performance are regarded as some of the negative consequences of poor governance. From a corporate governance perspective, the year 2000 was marked primarily by the launch of the *Novo Mercado*, but also a World Bank and IFC study, a legal reform initiative, an Investor Task Force, and an OECD Roundtable launch. In the following year further important legal reforms were passed, and in 2004, the *Novo Mercado* finally took off with 7 listings and 18 in 2005, and Banco Real created a Corporate Governance Credit Line. The year 2007 marked the 100th *Novo Mercado* listing with 92 listings in that year alone. By that time, corporate governance in Brazil had improved significantly: most new shares are now launched on the *Novo Mercado* and legal certainty has improved with regards to many relevant aspects such as changes of control, while some obstacles to takeovers (e.g. poisonous pills) remain. Examples of good corporate governance can be found in both the private and public sector nowadays and the same holds true for leadership particularly in the private sector (Estrin and Prevezer 2011:51f.).

In recent years, most new listings occurred at one of the premium listing levels and a number of already listed companies migrated their listings to a higher level, according to Black et al. (2012:7) These authors describe the evolution of corporate governance practices in Brazil.

Their data comes from three surveys about governance practices taken in 2004, 2006, and 2009. The first coincided with the beginning of the surge in IPOs in 2004;

the third was taken simultaneously with the financial-crisis-related reluctance to engage in new listings during 2008–2009. The authors covered main aspects of corporate governance by aggregating their governance information into six indices: board structure, ownership, board procedures, related party transactions, shareholder rights and disclosure. The board structure index is split into board independence on the one hand, and audit committee and fiscal board on the other. The Brazilian Corporate Governance Index (BCGI), then, reflects the average of these six indices.

Their analysis shows that *"corporate governance practices improved significantly in the 2004–2009 period"* (Black et al. 2012:4) and the authors attribute this evolution to two main factors:

- *"Growth in* Novo Mercado *and Level II listings, mainly through the entry of new firms with high corporate governance practices (IPOs); and*
- *Improvement in the governance practices of the firms that were already listed, sometimes including change in listing level."*

The corporate governance practices for firms already listed on *Novo Mercado* and Level II were found to be stable during that period.

Already listed firms showed improvements in corporate governance mainly in the fields of board independence, board procedures, shareholder rights and disclosure. Black et al. also found that many firms in *Novo Mercado* exceed the minimum *Novo Mercado* requirements and that IPO firms with private equity and venture capital (PEVC) sponsors generally provided similar results as IPO firms without these sponsors. The latter scored better on several board procedures, *"but not on the substantive aspects of governance"* (Black et al. 2012:17f.).

The legal and social frameworks now include enforcement infrastructure on the public side as well as private infrastructure in terms of education and monitoring. Important IPOs by restructured companies *"would not have been possible without these reforms"* (Estrin and Prevezer 2010:51, quoting Lubrano 2007).

In 2008, Bovespa created yet another level, called *"Bovespa Mais"*, which is similar to *Novo Mercado* but has fewer requirements.

2.1.20.2   Brazilian Corporate Governance Today

"In Brazil, formal corporate governance structures have improved markedly since 2000" (Estrin and Prevezer 2010:51, quoting Lubrano 2007). Silveira (2010:182) even sees a *"virtuous circle"*, constantly improving corporate governance in Brazil.

Estrin and Prevezer (2011:59f.) found indicators for good formal corporate governance in Brazil, including *"quite good shareholder rights, strong rule of law, and low risk of expropriation and there has been an improvement in corporate governance codes"*. On the other hand, the judiciary has been labeled as *"weak"*. Also, investor rights in Brazil were found to be weaker than the average for the sample.

Dyck and Zingales (2004:539; 550) *"estimate the value of private benefits extracted by dominant shareholders across a sample of countries. Their estimates range from close to zero for most OECD countries (but not all) to 65% of firm equity in Brazil"* (Estrin and Prevezer 2010:59). According to those findings, Brazilian

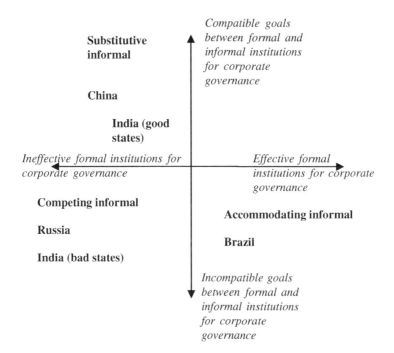

Fig. 2.18 CG institutions in BRIC countries in the Helmke-Levitsky framework. Source: Estrin and Prevezer (2011:61)

firms are very highly regulated in the formal economy, especially with regard to labor laws, by all measures of regulation of firms and its enforcement.

"This forms part of a wider corporate governance picture of tightly enforced formal laws and regulations leading to the rise of the informal economy with the aim of getting around those rules." Estrin and Prevezer (2011:59f.)

The World Bank Doing Business 2014 survey ranked Brazil 116th out of 189 countries in ease of paying taxes, hiring and firing, and on ease of starting and closing a business placed Brazil 123rd (World Bank 2013).

Estrin and Prevezer (2011:59) come to the conclusion that *"the effectiveness of formal institutions in corporate governance in Brazil is high in that the rules are good and enforced"*. In fact, they argue that the rules are too tightly enforced, pushing companies and/or dominant shareholders into the *"pervasive informal institution of the shadow economy"*.

As such, the informal institutions in Brazil are seen by the authors as a way for companies to escape the (effective) formal ones where they are being perceived as stifling in order to align the conflicting aims of both forms of institution rather than undermining the formal ones (Estrin and Prevezer 2011:59f.; cfr. Fig. 2.18). Brazilian market capitalization stands at only 54.6% of GDP as opposed to 114.9% in the United States (however higher than the 43.4% in Germany) (Worldbank.org, 2012 data).

Brazilian corporations are required to have both a Management Board (*Conselho de Administração*) and an Executive Committee (*Diretoria*), thus the differentiation between the single-board structure—typical for Anglo-Saxon and Latin corporate governance systems—and the two-tier structure of the German system does not become clear. Up to one third of Management Board members of firms in Brazil may be members of the Executive Committee, but the Board can also be composed of non-executive members only. The latter case implies an independent control function of the Board vis-à-vis the Executive Committee, thus constituting a dualist model, leading to an "*approximation between the Brazilian and the German System*" (Esperança et al. 2011:247).

Corporate governance scandals in Brazil have been relatively rare and/or less publicized, but the cases of Agrenco, Aracruz, Sadia, and Tenda (all in 2008)—which have destroyed more than half of the companies' market valuation (Silveira 2010:190) stand out as does the fall of Eike Batista's empire of energy-related companies in 2013–2014, including accusations of insider trading and market manipulation with a value estimated at R$ 1.5 billion (EUR 464 million) according to the *New York Times* (14/09/2014[19]).

2.1.20.3   The Segmentation of the Brazilian Stock Market

The Brazilian stock market has seen the introduction of several governance-related listing segments.

In addition to the traditional market, there is Level 1 and Level 2 as well as *Novo Mercado*. *Novo Mercado*, launched in 2000, requires the highest corporate governance standards. Companies which wish to list via IPO or re-list from a lower level must have only common shares, i.e. no preferred shares without voting rights; at least 25% free float; board members with non-staggered terms of max. 2 years; financial statements prepared in line with U.S. GAAP or IFRS; takeout options for minority shareholders in case of a transfer of the controlling participation; an obligation to offer the economic value of their shares to minority shareholders in case of a freeze-out or delisting; disclosure rules for trades in company stock by controlling shareholders and senior managers; an arbitrage rule to settle disputes with minority shareholders in the Brazilian arbitration panel CAM.

Level 2 does not require only common shares, but maintains the other requirements *Novo Mercado* imposes. Level 1 requires higher disclosure standards than the traditional (regular) market, particularly regarding quarterly publication of consolidated financial data, but other than that has no additional requirements beyond the legal obligations which rule the traditional market (Cfr. Black et al. 2012:5).

Novo Mercado is quite strict by Brazilian standards and excludes, for instance, companies with non-voting shares, which are quite common in Brazil, given that

---

Table 2.8 Market segmentation and investment limits for pension funds in Brazil

BM&FBovespa listing segment	Number of companies listed in segment, August 2014 (Jan.2007)	Investment limits for pension funds
Novo Mercado	132 (47)	70%
Level 2	22 (14)	60%
Bovespa Mais	9 (−)	50%
Level 1	31 (36)	45%
Traditional Market	253 (297)	35%
Total	**447 (394)**	

Source: Adaptation of Silveira 2010:181; Bovespa

corporate law allows for the issuance of up to 50% of shares as non-voting (Cfr. Black et al. 2012:5). The difference between Level I and Level II is significant and one may group *Novo Mercado* and Level II into one high-level category, while the traditional market and Level I do not require enhanced corporate governance standards.

Apart from the afore-mentioned four corporate governance practice categories, BM&FBovespa includes BovespaMais, a corporate governance differentiation for the over-the-counter (OTC) market. This is only open to companies on the stock exchange which are registered with the CVM (Aguilera et al. 2011:399).

Claessens and Yurtoglu (2012:27) describe Brazil's *Novo Mercado* as "*a notable exception where the local market has improved corporate governance standards using voluntary mechanisms, with much success in terms of new listing and increases in firm valuation*", referring to cases, as for example in the Netherlands, where self-regulation has not been successful.

Table 2.8 shows that while only 53 more companies are listed as of August 2014, compared to January 2007 (+13,5%), listings on the traditional market and Level 1 have decreased since the beginning of the financial crisis, while numbers increased in Level 2 (+64,3%) and, most notably, in *Novo Mercado*, where they almost tripled (+191,5%). According to Table 2.8 and in line with the provisions of Resolution No. 3.792/09 of the National Monetary Council (CMN), pension funds must not invest more than 35% of defined benefit or defined contribution plans into shares of the traditional listing segment. The limit rises as corporate governance levels increase, reaching 70% for *Novo Mercado*.

Another interesting rule is contained in the self-regulation standards (*Código de Autoregulação*) of ANBIMA, an association which includes Brazil's major banks, its associates shall only participate in IPOs of companies which have adhered at least to Bovespa's Level 1—or agreed to adhere to those listing standards within 6 months. Thus, the practical consequence is that any access to the capital markets in Brazil is conditional on the adherence to one of Bovespa's governance-related listing levels (Silveira 2010:181f.).

Silveira et al. (2007) found that the voluntary joining of stricter listing levels is positively associated with company-level corporate governance quality.

2.1.21   Corporate Governance in Germany

Corporate governance stepped into the spotlight of public attention in the early 2000s via a number of high-profile scandals at companies such as Deutsche Telekom (Klonoski 2012), Siemens and Volkswagen as well as the arrival of so-called *"locusts"* (*"Heuschrecken"*), an expression used by then SPD-party leader Franz Müntefering in spring 2005, comparing international, mostly Anglo-Saxon financial investors buying up traditional companies to a plague of locusts coming over the country trying to make tremendous profits at the expense of workers and society in general.

On an international level, the parallel can be found in corporate scandals which affected confidence in the (global) financial markets on a large scale, such as those of Enron, WorldCom, and Vivendi. Interestingly, the collapse of Enron also led to the disappearance of Arthur Anderson, one of the *"big five"* auditors, who, also according to Middelhoff, failed not only due to the fall of Enron, but also due to their own internal corporate governance issues (Middelhoff 2007).

Since then, public interest—as perceived and portrayed by the media—has continued to focus on scandals, also involving personalities which had so far been known in Germany for their merits with regards to corporate governance, such as Dr. Gerhard Cromme, former co-CEO of ThyssenKrupp and acting president of the Supervisory Board of Siemens AG. Given that until 2008 he acted as president of the governmental commission German Corporate Governance Code, the German Corporate Governance Code was at times referred to as the *"Cromme Code"*. Another recent example is former Arcandor AG (formerly, KarstadtQuelle AG) CEO Thomas Middelhoff, who has been under investigation since Arcandor AG entered insolvency procedures in 2009.

Apart from the scandals, however, corporate governance in Germany contrasts clearly with the Anglo-Saxon model which is the subject of the main body of literature and analysis of the topic in international terms.

One reason for this certainly is the difference in company funding. German companies rely much more heavily on bank loans to finance their growth than on accessing the stock market for capital. This turns the capital markets far less important, with market capitalization reaching only 43.4% of GDP as opposed to 122.0% in the UK (Worldbank.org, 2012 data), while this importance rests with the commercial banks.

A second difference lies in the much higher focus on stakeholders other than shareholders, particularly employees. This leads Quaresma (2011:137) to describe the German model as one of "stakeholder equilibrium as companies' main objective, to the detriment of the maximization of shareholder wealth".

One principal reason for this is regulation, as for example by the Codetermination Act (*"Mitbestimmungsgesetz"*) of 1976 (cfr. Table 2.9) which requires an equal number of representatives of shareholders and employees on the supervisory board, giving however a decisive vote to the shareholder-appointed president of the supervisory board in case of a deadlock.

Table 2.9 German Laws regarding Codetermination

Laws with Regard to the Codetermination Principle in Germany	
Law	Basic Principles Regarding the Employees' Participation in Supervisory Boards
The Montan Codetermination Act	For whom?
	Applicable to companies with more than 1000 employees in the coal and steel industry.
	How?
	It provides equal representation for employees on the company's supervisory board. In addition, a representative from the employees' side can operate as a worker on the board.
The 1976 Codetermination Act	For whom?
	It applies to companies that employ at least 2000 regular employees.
	How?
	It provides equal representation on the supervisory board. However, because of the tie-breaking vote of the chairman, who generally sides with shareholders, the law actually provides 'quasi-parity'.
The 2004 Third Part Act	For whom?
	It applies to firms that usually employ 500–2000 workers, whether the firms are corporations, partnerships limited by share, limited liability companies, mutual insurance associations, or cooperative, industrial and provident societies.
	How?
	It assigns a third of the seats on the company's board to the employees, although it does not dictate the exact number of board members.

Source: Bordean and Pop (2012:23f)

Thirdly, and most prominently, Germany has a two-tier board system, consisting of above-mentioned supervisory board (*"Aufsichtsrat"*) and the management board (*"Vorstand"*) which is responsible for the day-to-day management of the company and no person shall simultaneously participate in both boards. This two-tier structure is not only applicable to public companies (*Aktiengesellschaften*/AGs) but also to limited liability companies (*Gesellschaften mit beschränkter Haftung*/GmbHs) with more than 500 employees.

In GmbHs with more than 500 employees as well as AGs with less than 2000 employees, shareholders chose two thirds of the members of the supervisory board (*"Vorstand"*), while the other third gets elected by employees. In AGs with more than 2000 employees, half of the supervisory board members are chosen by shareholders and the other half by employees. The usual setup of the supervisory board consists of twenty members who are elected for 4 year terms, meeting at least quarterly.

The supervisory board has two main responsibilities. One is to ensure the accuracy of the company's financial reporting, the other regards the advisory, nomination, remuneration and dismissal of the members of the managing board.

The members of the board of directors (*"Vorstand"*) are nominated for maximum terms of 5 years each. The managing board consists usually of five to ten members which meet regularly, usually weekly, and report to the supervisory board. The board represents the company collectively and each director has only one vote, all being jointly and severally responsible for the board's acts. This is another difference with regards to the Anglo-Saxon system with an extremely powerful CEO. This responsibility of each director for the board's acts—regardless of an organizational separation of tasks—ensures that German management boards usually strive for unanimous decisions, resulting in long decision-making processes.

The Anglo-Saxon Board of Directors, which is made up of both *"inside"* and *"outside"* directors, thus *"unites"* *"Vorstand"* and *"Aufsichtsrat"* in one body. Whereas the CEO and other core functions such as CFO, COO, etc. are taken by inside members, the current tendency apparently is for their relative number to decrease, while outside directors' relative representation increases.

The codetermination system in particular necessarily leads to a much wider stakeholder approach than most other systems. Apart from employees' interest, also those of other stakeholders and society in general are normally respected. This is also supported by strict legislation on environmental protection and other areas of the social environment. Although all these factors have contributed to a sustainable growth of the German economy and social peace over the past 60 years or so, especially international investors are reluctant to invest in companies the fate of which is codetermined by the employees and not primarily driven by share-holders' interest in profits.

Yet again, shareholder activism is rarely seen in Germany in the intensity and effectiveness witnessed in the US, for instance. One of the rare cases was the success of activist shareholders in TUI, a German travel and container operator, to force the separation of the container business, Hapag-Lloyd, from the tourism section.

On the other hand, returns in the stock market appear to be less volatile in Germany than in the Anglo-Saxon area and might as such serve as a natural hedge (cfr. Silveira, 2010:151 ff.).

Still, criticism of the German corporate governance model is regularly back on the agenda.

Then president of the governmental commission on corporate governance in Germany, Gerhard Cromme, already in 2002 demanded that the codetermination rules be reviewed.

However, a commission set up to review codetermination by then chancellor Gerhard Schröder ultimately yielded no results as positions of those who wanted to curtail employees' participation and those who wanted to extend it couldn't be reconciled.

Also above-mentioned scandals at Volkswagen and Siemens, mainly related to bribery, and which left Siemens with less than half of its share value in 2008/2009, lead politicians, managers and the public alike to demand for changes in the German system.

Furthermore, the German capital markets are characterized by a high level of concentration of shareholders. Goergen et al. (2008:16) analyzed 402 large German

Table 2.10 Empirical Studies—Compliance within German CG

Selected empirical studies attempting to assess the issue of compliance within the german corporate governance model	
Authors/Year of study	Aims and results
Werder and Talaulicar (2006)	Study aimed at assessing the compliance of the DAX firms with the recommendations and suggestions of the GCGC.
	Results:
	1. The firms surveyed comply on an average with 95.3% of the mandatory recommendations.
	2. On an average, 85.2% of DAX companies comply with these suggestions (comply or explain).
Goncharov et al. (2006)	What value relevance does the extent of compliance have?
	Result:
	The study reveals that there is a significant value relevance to compliance.
Werder and Talaulicar (2009)	Is the GCGC followed by the German companies?
	Result:
	The Code is being followed to a great extent.

Source: Bordean and Pop (2012:22f)

companies and found that the main shareholder on average holds 59.7% of overall voting rights, while the respective figure for NYSE-listed firms stands at only 8.5%. In a separate study of 416 listed German companies, only 12% were found not to have at least one shareholder owning over 20% of the shares (Gadhoum et al. 2005). At the same time, however, one should note that the types of the largest shareholder are quite diversified, being the largest group that of other firms with 21.0% (37.5% in Belgium), followed by families with 7.4% (68.6% in Italy) and banks with only 1.2% (16.0% in France) (Goergen et al. 2008:17).

Table 2.10 summarizes a few studies on the compliance with Corporate Governance in Germany.

Rott (2009) criticizes the German corporate governance system as too much in line with the Anglo-Saxon system and as such not easily applicable to the German business reality, particularly regarding the high share of *insider* shareholders.

2.1.21.1 The Segmentation of the German Stock Market

Market capitalization in Germany stood at only 24% of GDP in 1993, i.e. lower than in other *"bank dominated countries"* such as France with 36% of GDP or Japan which at the time was still very prosperous with 71% market capitalization. The gap was far wider when compared to market oriented financial systems such as the United States (82%) or Great Britain (140%) (Burghof and Hunger 2003).

Between 1997 and 2002, there were four segments within the German equity market: the Official Trading (*Amtlicher Handel*), the Regulated Market (*Geregelter Markt*), the Unofficial Regulated Market (*Freiverkehr*), and the New Market (*Neuer Markt*).

The *Neuer Markt* had been introduced in 1997 in order to accommodate small and medium sized companies of innovative, growing sectors, thus comparable in its aim and purpose to the successful NASDAQ. The *Neuer Markt* was not the first attempt at allowing a wider range of companies access to equity capital, but none of those earlier attempts had been very successful (Burghof and Hunger 2003:2).

Consequently, the *Neuer Markt* was rather aimed at new technology SMEs than at raising corporate governance standards. Nevertheless, publication requirements were somewhat stricter at the New Market than for the *Geregelter Markt*, to which companies had to be admitted in order to achieve a listing at the *Neuer Markt* through a simultaneous waiver. Apart from minimum requirements regarding equity and number of shares, the issuer needed to prove at least 3 years' track record and free-float had to be at least 25% of the aggregated nominal volume. Beyond the requirements of the *Official Trading*, companies had to include information about risk factors in their securities prospectus. Such risk factors are *"information regarding any factors which could have a substantial negative influence on the financial condition of the issuer or which could endanger the issuer's business success"* (Deutsche Börse AG, 2001, No. 4.1.16).

By trying to gain investors' trust, the rules for the *Neuer Markt* were designed in such a manner that they actually helped raise corporate governance standards by introducing higher levels of transparency.

The success story of the *Neuer Markt* is best evidenced by its strong performance relative to the other German markets, mainly the Official Trading as shown in Table 2.11.

However, this *Neuer Markt* was discontinued at the end of 2003 after what Burghof and Hunger (2003:1) describe as *"its stunning temporary success and its ultimate failure"*.

After having grown from two companies at the start on March 10th, 1997, to 339 listed firms with a market capitalization of c. €234 billionat the peak in 2000, the burst of the bubble along with insolvencies, cases of alleged fraud and insider-trading, ended its good reputation and brought down the market capitalization of entities listed on the *Neuer Markt* by 87.5% to 29 billion € only (Burghof and Hunger 2003).

2.1.21.2 The *"Hausbank nature"* of the German Economy

The German financial system has been described by Burghof and Hunger (2003) as *"bank based and relationship oriented"* in which a company's longstanding relationship with its main bank, the so-called *"Hausbank" (home bank)*, compensates disadvantages such as an apparent lack of flexibility or the absence of disciplining effects an active stock market may have, through shareholder control or aggressive take-over strategies. The main advantages of such a system seem to be *"a higher degree of long term thinking, better conditions for long term and specific investments and better support of firms in financial distress through their relationship lender, the so called* 'Hausbank'*"* (Burghof and Hunger 2003).

Table 2.11 German stock market comparison

	Official Trading	Regulated Market	Unofficial Regulated Market	Neuer Markt	Total
Number of IPOs[a]	70	45	22	298	435
Number of IPOs (in percent of total)	16.09	10.34	5.06	68.51	100.00
IPO-Underpricing (Mean)[b]	**11.16**	**17.30**	**39.65**	**53.64**	42.34
Gross Proceeds (in Mio. EUR)	25,648.64	784.10	145.19	20,415.55	46,993.48
Gross Proceeds (in percent of total)	54.58	1.67	0.31	43.44	100.00
Gross Proceeds on average (in Mio. EUR)	366.41	17.42	6.60	68.51	108.03
Initial Capital (in Mio. EUR)	5754.28	272.97	66.49	4183.16	10,276.90
Nominal Capital (in percent of total)	55.99	2.66	0.65	40.70	100.00
Initial Capital on average (in Mio. EUR)	82.20	6.06	3.02	14.04	23.62

Source: Hunger (2002)

[a] The total number of IPOs was about 457. For 22 IPOs no sufficient data was available; thus, the data refr to the remaining 435 IPOs only

[b] Initial Return, market-adjusted with the DAX-100 index refering to the preriod of the end of the offer period and the first trading price

Germany was, however, not the only European country to create a New Market: Similar initiatives led to formations of New Markets in Europe between 1995 and 1999, namely the *Nouveau Marché* in Paris, the SWX New Market in Zürich, Euro. NM in Belgium, Amsterdam's *Nieuwe Markt*, and Milan's *Nuovo Mercato*, Brussels' now defunct Easdaq and London's Alternative Investment Market (Burghof and Hunger 2003, footnote 23).

2.1.22   *Corporate Governance and Financial Institutions*

Regalli and Soana (2012:4f.) affirm that the *"decision to focus on the financial sector is dictated by the awareness that financial intermediaries are "special", that is, different from corporations"*, because of the following factors:

- There is a higher number of capital providers—generally depositors but also a more diverse shareholder structure;
- Historically, corporate governance faults have led to significant losses and scandals on a scale not usually found at non-financial organizations;

- Financial institutions are systemically important as they are most relevant to the seamless functioning of the economic and monetary system, and therefore *"heavily regulated"*.

According to Claessens and Yurtoglu (2012:30f.), the financial crisis *"has shown that the corporate governance of financial institutions has been an underhighlighted area, as there were massive failures at major institutions in advanced countries. Corporate governance at financial institutions has been identified to differ from that of corporations, but in which ways is not yet clear—besides the important role of prudential regulations, given the special nature of banks. In this area, more work is needed for emerging markets as well, in part related to the role of banks in business groups. While there is some research on state ownership, corporate governance of banks in emerging markets is little analyzed. Clarifying this will be key, as banks are important providers of external financing, especially for SMEs".*

The present analysis and comparison between Brazilian and German banks should also be helpful to determine reasons for differences in corporate governance systems of both countries, given that *"[i]t is clear that one of the major determinants of corporate governance patterns is the structure of domestic finance"*, as for example, *"[d]ebt finance is notably much more important in Japan, Italy and Germany than in France or the United States and the United Kingdom"* (FMT 1995:14). Or Brazil, we may add. While ownership concentration in listed companies is rare in English-speaking countries, it tends to be high in continental European countries, including Germany. The involvement of major German banks, is *"rather unidirectional"* when compared to Japan, for instance, where multi-directional cross-holdings (*"vertical and horizontal integration"*) are commonplace (*"keiretsu"*) (FMT 1995:18).

Regarding the role of banks in the governance of large corporations, and according to FMT (1995:19), major OECD countries can be divided into three groups:

- Market-based countries, such as the United States or the United Kingdom;
- Bank-based countries, like Japan and Germany; and thirdly,
- Other countries, including France and Italy.

In so-called market-based countries, long-term finance is provided by the capital markets (equities), while banks—in the form of commercial banks as opposed to investment *"banks"*—mainly provide short-term finance. Rather than relationship banking, based on reciprocal confidence, the arm's-length approach still prevails in those Anglo-Saxon countries. The banking markets of the Netherlands and Switzerland had moved somewhat into that direction (FMT 1995:19f.) well before the financial crisis, but we may assume that they are nowadays (again) closer to the German model.

Bank-based economies like Germany and Japan therefore rely on relationship banking even in their relationships with large corporations, providing both short- and long-term finance, thus triggering much higher leverage ratios. Banks in these countries offer a wide variety of financial solutions and as a consequence, they continue to have a dominant influence on businesses, especially SMEs, in those bank-based countries, leading to the association of two concepts with these countries, *"universal banking"* and *"house bank"* (cfr. 2.1.21.2 above).

At the same time, they are serving as "active monitors of corporations on behalf of other stakeholders", being represented on many supervisory boards, while their influence seems to have diminished since the onset of international competition in banking. *"On balance, the degree of monitoring and control by the supervisory board in the German two-tier board system seems to be very limited in good times, while it may play a more important role when the corporation comes under stress."* (FMT 1995:20f.)

Aguilera et al. (2011:382) even suggest that *"in German [. . .] corporate governance, monitoring by relationship-oriented banks may effectively substitute for an active market for corporate control"*. (Cfr. also Byers et al. 2008) More generally, i.e. independently from the jurisdiction, Aguilera et al. (2011:388) argue that *"it can be argued that banks are able to reduce the monitoring efforts needed, which may have an influence on other elements of the corporate governance bundle"*. While there is still much to improve in German banks' corporate governance systems, one may doubt if it makes sense to let banks take that role.

France, where *"house bank"* relations with large companies are not the rule, serves as an example for an economy within the group of *"other countries"*. Due to their rather 'independent' position, banks in those countries *"may be able to play a more active role in governance"* and provide *"long-term corporate finance"*. (FMT 1995:21)

2.1.23   Comparative Corporate Governance

Aguilera et al. (2011:390) describe the *"quintessential question"* in corporate governance as: *"What describes and explains variation in corporate governance systems across countries?"*

Although corporate governance is a global topic, and the corporate world continues its tendency to be ever more independent of national boundaries, significant differences can be observed in both the corporate governance frameworks (rules, institutions) and the underlying economic fabric. This section therefore provides an overview on a few recent studies investigating to what extend countries differ regarding corporate governance aspects, paying special attention to differences between emerging markets (including Brazil) on the one hand, and advanced economies (such as Germany) on the other.

In their 2012 survey, Claessens and Yurtoglu (2012:5) find that *"emerging markets differ in some key aspects from advanced countries, but they also show that there is much variation in some of these features across emerging markets"*.

They stipulate that two factors are shaping the challenges around national corporate governance systems: the *"country's overall economic development"* on the one hand, and its *"institutional environment"* on the other.

Main determinants to establish these for an individual country would therefore be:

- Economic environment;
- Financial environment;
- Institutional environment.

Economic and financial conditions differ significantly between advanced and developing economies (Claessens and Yurtoglu 2012:5), and this is not different between Brazil and Germany.

The institutional environment would include not only the existence and organization of certain institutions, but above all their efficiency. Here, the concept of the Rule of Law comes to mind, which appears to be more often used than clearly defined.

"For the United Nations, the rule of law refers to a principle of governance in which all persons, institutions and entities, public and private, including the State itself, are accountable to laws that are publicly promulgated, equally enforced and independently adjudicated, and which are consistent with international human rights norms and standards. It requires, as well, measures to ensure adherence to the principles of supremacy of law, equality before the law, accountability to the law, fairness in the application of the law, separation of powers, participation in decision-making, legal certainty, avoidance of arbitrariness and procedural and legal transparency." (Report of the Secretary-General on the Rule of Law and Transitional Justice in Conflict and Post-Conflict Societies (http://www.un.org/en/ruleoflaw/))

From a more economic point of view, Kleinfeld Belton (2005:13) suggests that a *"predictable, efficient legal system allows businesses to plan, enables law-abiding citizens and businesses to stay on the correct side of the law, and provides some level of deterrence against criminal acts. It enables a free market by providing for efficient adjudication of contract disputes"* and thus implies the ease of contracting.

While Claessens and Yurtoglu (2012:5) claim that *"[s]pecific corporate governance issues and the role of corporate governance for economic development and well-being are best understood from the perspective of ownership structures and the related structures of business groups"*, this appears to concentrate too heavily on classic concepts of corporate governance, namely the agency theory and the protection of minority shareholders, i.e. a merely shareholder-based view of corporate governance rather than the wider stakeholder approach.

Under the latter, the wider socio-economic fabric of a country would have to be taken into account and serve as a basis for comparison.[20]

The ratio of credit to GDP as a share of GDP show, according to Claessens and Yurtoglu (2012:6), that *"there remain relatively large differences between advanced countries and emerging markets and transition economies"* and that the financial systems of advanced economies are *"much deeper"*.

---

[20]For indicators, please refer to section 2.1.20.1 above.

According to the same authors, market capitalization as a share of GDP amounts to around 90% in advanced economies, but only 23% in transition countries and 67% in emerging markets.

The idea of comparing a *"basket"* of emerging markets to another one of advanced economies—as appealing as it appears—bears risks of comparing groups with each other the members of which are not quite as homogeneous as they probably should be in order to be compared. Likely the most prominent example is the much-referred to acronym of BRICs we mentioned under Literature Review above, which—maybe excessively—underlines the positive similarities of four quite different nations (Brazil, Russia, India, and China) and has been replaced on Wall Street by the rather pessimistic acronym BIITS (Brazil, India, Indonesia, Turkey, and South Africa) which has been come up with due to their high current-account deficits. The only two countries those two acronyms have in common are Brazil and India, and both have significantly improved their current-account deficit in comparison to the three other *"BIITS"* (Sharma 2014).[21] So while at least those two countries appear to have a lot in common in terms of economic development and prospect, probably at least as many significant differences can be observed. Therefore, even comparing only those two jointly with any set of advanced economies would certainly be a tricky exercise.

Likewise, it will be hard to find a bundle of economically advanced countries which are sufficiently similar to one another to allow for a joint comparison with others. What does come immediately to mind are the United States and similar, *"Anglo-Saxon"* economies such as Canada or the United Kingdom. But even those differ—particularly when it comes to corporate governance issues and risk management—and especially the US and the UK have served as the main points of reference in these fields for an almost infinite number of studies and comparisons. Not least due to different legal systems, other large advanced economies such as Japan, Germany, France, and others are hardly homogeneous enough to form part of a wider basket consisting of them in order to be compared to others.

Klonoski, for instance, found that *"German corporations have been much more willing than American firms to adopt a universal set of ethical guidelines for business"* as he analyzed the adoption of the U.N. Global Compact (Klonoski 2012). While he identified similarities which may not exist between Germany and Brazil, such as *"Protestant Work Ethic"*, he found for example that union strength is *"still more widely accepted and favourably viewed in Germany than it is in the U.S."* (Klonoski 2012)

The remainder of this study shall therefore be dedicated to the comparison of two big economies which do bear some similarity in that they are predominant powers in their respective regions, relatively big in terms of macro-economic criteria such as population, GDP and economic diversity, but at the same time are distinctively

---

[21]Ruchir Sharma is the head of emerging markets and global macro at Morgan Stanley Investment Management. (http://www.morganstanley.com/views/perspectives/thought-leadership-07072012.html)

different in terms of socio-cultural and economic history and present development: Brazil and Germany.

2.1.24   Corporate Governance During and After the 2007–2009 Financial Crisis

Depending on which country and financial system we look at, the perception of start and end of the latest financial crisis may differ significantly. For many, the crisis started with the sale of Merrill Lynch to Bank of America for $ 50.1 billion (cfr. Friedland 2009:51) and the insolvency of Lehman Brothers in September 2008, for instance, and ending after the global economic downturn during 2009, while in many countries and (financial) entities, especially in Southern Europe, the repercussions are still being felt and their economic and financial situation even appears to deteriorate further in some instances.

A 'consensus timing' in the literature however appears to be the 2007–2009 period (cfr. Dallas 2012:267; Lister 2010:295; Kindleberger and Aliber 2011:9), which may generically be described as the build-up and aftermath of the Lehman Brother *'debacle'*.

Chuck Prince, CEO of Citibank at the time, is quoted as commenting on *"concerns about "froth" in the leveraged loan market in mid 2007 that "while the music is playing, you have to dance" (i.e. maintain short term market share)"* (Kirkpatrick 2009:65)

"By mid 2008, it was clear that the crisis in the subprime market in the US, and the associated liquidity squeeze, was having a major impact on financial institutions and banks in many countries. Bear Stearns had been taken over by JPMorgan with the support of the Federal Reserve Bank of New York, and financial institutions in both the US (e.g. Citibank, Merrill Lynch) and in Europe (UBS, Credit Suisse, RBS, HBOS, Barclays, Fortis, Société Générale) were continuing to raise a significant volume of additional capital to finance, inter alia, major realised losses on assets, diluting in a number of cases existing shareholders. [. . .] In Germany, two state owned banks (IKB and Sachsenbank) had been rescued, following crises in two other state banks several years previously (Berlinerbank and WestLB). The crisis intensified in the third quarter of 2008 with a number of collapses (especially Lehman Brothers) and a generalised loss of confidence that hit all financial institutions. As a result, several banks failed in Europe and the US while others received government recapitalisation towards the end of 2008." (Kirkpatrick 2009:64)

The beginning of the build-up to that financial crisis was chosen as the beginning of our period of analysis, also taking into account that *"organization's capabilities are tested in times of crisis"* (Jacob 2012:259; Sharma and Narwal 2006).

According to Jacob (2012:259f.), *"the financial crisis of 2008 can be seen as a result of the lack of self regulation and irresponsibility of financial institutions even in areas that are crucial for their own survival"* and made it *"clear that this global*

*crisis revealed an urgent need to call for "binding global minimum standards"
when it comes to corporate responsibilities"* (Emeseh et al. 2009).

As one of the main contributors to the financial crisis of 2007–2009, Dallas
identifies *"short-termism or myopia, which is defined as the excessive focus of
corporate managers, asset managers, investors, and analysts on short-term results,
whether quarterly earnings or short-term portfolio returns, and a repudiation of
concern for long-term value creation and the fundamental value of firms"* (Dallas
2012:268), with a lot of market participants engaging in *"myopic behavior, including mortgage originators, securitizers, credit default-swap sellers, rating agencies,
and investors. Contrary to the efficient market hypothesis, market prices of subprime
mortgage-related securities failed to reflect underlying risk in the wake of a massive
decline in lending, underwriting, and rating standards and over reliance on the risk
reduction capacities of derivative transactions and on models that failed to account,
among other things, for low-frequency economic shocks"*, leading to excessive risk
taking (Dallas 2012:267; 274). Dallas explores therefore why firms engage in short-
termism and looks for ways to mitigate this risk. Behavioral concepts help to explain
this tendency of individuals to discount or disregard low-frequency events in the
future (over-optimism), including the availability hypothesis and threshold heuristics
(*"disaster myopia"*) (Dallas 2012:270). Culture, especially firm culture, has also
been identified by Dallas as a contributor to such managerial myopia (Dallas
2012:272). Thus, the phenomenon of managers *"caring too much"* under managerial myopia theories contrasts with the agency cost theory which argues that managers are disciplined by market pressures such as (the risk of) hostile takeovers
(Dallas 2012:273). This view supports the empowerment of long-term shareholders
and the imposition of a fiduciary duty of directors and officers to focus on long-term
interests of their firms, including deferred compensation arrangements. Likewise,
group polarization phenomena should be avoided, particularly in boards, as they
result *"in more extreme positions such as excessive risk-taking"*. (Dallas 2012:276f.)

2.2 Risk Management

*"Perhaps one of the greatest shocks from the financial crisis has been the widespread failure
of risk management. In many cases risk was not managed on an enterprise basis and not
adjusted to corporate strategy. Risk managers were often kept separate from management
and not regarded as an essential part of implementing the company's strategy. Most
important of all, boards were in a number of cases ignorant of the risk facing the company."*
(OECD 2009:8)

According to Kaplan and Garrick (1981), *"we are not able in life to avoid risk,
but only to choose between risks"*. In order to make that choice, to take that decision,
on a rational basis, one needs to identify, assess, and weigh the concurrent risks.
Therefore a framework is needed to quantify risk and to put it into relation to the
expected returns to see if it is indeed worthwhile taking.

This section intends to give a short overview over the risk-return relationship as
far as it concerns the decision-taking processes of investors and companies by briefly

reviewing the relevant literature. This is followed by the attempt at the presentation and a systematisation of risk management, with a particular focus on credit risk management.

2.2.1   Risk

"Nichts geschieht ohne Risiko. Aber ohne Risiko geschieht auch nichts."—*"Nothing happens without risk. But without risk, nothing happens at all."* (Walter Scheel, former President of the Federal Republic of Germany)

"A risk analysis is essentially a listing of scenarios. In reality, the list is infinite. Your analysis, and any analysis, is perforce finite, hence incomplete. Therefore no matter how thoroughly and carefully you have done your work, I am not going to trust your results. I'm not worried about the scenarios you have identified, but about those you haven't thought of. Thus I am never going to be satisfied." (Kaplan and Garrick 1981:15 f., paraphrasing one of the criticisms regarding the Reactor Safety Study).

In the so-called *"Western World"*, *"risk"* has a clearly negative connotation and the usual reaction to any mentioning of risk would be that risk is to be avoided. Quite to the contrary, the Chinese expression for *"risk"* or a *"risky situation"* is *"Wei-ji"*, combining two symbols which individually stand for *"threat"* and *"opportunity"*, thus reflecting the general concept that every risk-taking implies opportunities but also that each opportunity comes with its share of general and specific threats. On a higher level, the Chinese philosophy calls two of its central elements *"Yin and Yang"*, alluding to an equilibrium which as we shall see is also desirable in the domain of risk management, i.e. to understand risk and opportunity as two sides of the same coin, appreciating that with opportunity comes risk and very high opportunities come with a very high risk, and that in any case, both opportunities and risks have to be managed (Cfr. Maier 2007:1).

2.2.1.1   Definition of Risk

"Risk is the probability that an [undesired] event will occur." (Burt 2001:3)

Many different kinds of risk are discussed: financial risk, operational risk, business risk, social risk, economic risk, safety risk, investment risk, military risk, political risk, etc.

While the literature mainly focuses on quantifiable aspects of the notion of risk (cfr. portfolio models etc.), there is obviously, and in addition to the quantitative aspect of risk, a qualitative side to it. In what follows, and based on Kaplan and Garrik (1981), the qualitative and quantitative aspects of risk shall be summarized.

2.2.1.2 Qualitative Aspects of Risk

The Distinction Between Risk and Uncertainty

Kaplan and Garrik (1981) give the example of a rich relative who had just died and named someone as their sole heir. Until the assets are inventorized, the heir is not sure how much he or she will get after estate taxes. While this would clearly be a state of uncertainty, one could hardly say that this means facing a risk. The notion of risk, therefore, involves both uncertainty and some kind of loss or damage that might be received. Symbolically, Kaplan and Garrik (1981) write this as:

Risk = uncertainty + damage.

The Distinction Between Risk and Hazard

It is necessary to draw a distinction between the ideas of risk and hazard.

Kaplan and Garrik (1981) find hazard defined as *"a source of danger."* Risk is the *"possibility of loss or injury"* and the *"degree of probability of such loss."*

Hazard, therefore, simply exists as a source. *"Risk includes the likelihood of conversion of that source into actual delivery of loss, injury, or some form of damage. This is the sense in which we use the words."* (Kaplan and Garrik 1981:12)

As an example, an ocean can be said to be a hazard. Trying to cross it in a rowboat constitutes a great risk. If we use a cruise ship, the risk is small. The *cruise ship* thus is a device that we use to safeguard us against the hazard, resulting in small risk. Kaplan and Garrik (1981:12) express this idea symbolically in the form of an equation:

$$\text{risk} = \frac{\text{hazard}}{\text{safeguards}}$$

This equation also brings out the notion that risks can be reduced by increasing the safeguards—or mitigants—but it may never, as a matter of principle, come down to zero. *"Risk is never zero, but it can be small."* (Kaplan and Garrik 1981:12)

2.2.1.3 Awareness of Risk

Included under the heading *"safeguards"* is the idea of simple awareness. That is, awareness of risk is both a precondition to risk-mitigation and a mitigating factor in itself. I.e. if one does not know that there is a risk, one cannot try to avoid it. If however one is aware that there is a risk—and is maybe even able to define it—the risk can be mitigated. Yet, the more precisely a risk is known and understood, the better it can be mitigated. This is not only so because more specific safeguards can be applied which better confine the respective risk, but any mitigation should also be reasonable in relation to the risk itself, given that any safeguard has its *"costs"* which may at some point outweigh the desire for risk mitigation.

2.2.1.4   Relativity of Risk

There does not appear to be an *"absolute risk"*, and insofar the term *"perceived risk"*—while making clear that risk is the risk perceived by a given individual—is somewhat misleading insofar as it implicitly suggests that there is something other than a perceived risk, i.e. an objective or absolute risk. However, according to Kaplan and Garrik (1981:12), *"the notion of absolute risk always ends up being somebody else's perceived risk"*.

2.2.2   Quantitative Aspects of Risk

2.2.2.1   Set of Triplets

According to Kaplan and Garrick (1981:13), *"risk analysis consists of an answer to the following three questions:*
  (i) What can happen? (i.e., What can go wrong?)
  (ii) How likely is it that that will happen?
  (iii) If it does happen, what are the consequences?"
   To answer these questions the first step is to make a list of outcomes or *"scenarios"* as suggested in Table 2.12.
   The *i*th line in Table 2.12 *"can be thought of as a triplet:*
   (s_i, p_i, x_i)
   where s_i is a scenario identification or description;
   p_i is the probability of that scenario; and
   x_i is the consequence or evaluation measure of that scenario, i.e., the measure of damage."
   If this table contains all the scenarios one can think of, then that is to say that the table is the answer to the question and therefore is the risk.
   "More formally, using braces, { }, to denote "set of" we can say that the risk, R, "is" the set of triplets:

$$R = \{< s_i, p_i, x_i >\}, i = 1, 2, \ldots, N."$$

(Kaplan and Garrik 1981:13)

2.2.2.2   Unknown Factors

The above assumption would however require that all the risks *"one cant think of"* really cover all possible scenarios. As discussed above, risks are perceived risks and furthermore, it is hard to take into account all and every possible course of future

Table 2.12 Scenario list

Scenario	Likelihood	Consequence
s_1	p_1	x_1
s_2	p_2	x_2
$\vdots$	$\vdots$	$\vdots$
s_N	p_N	x_N

Source: Kaplan and Garrick (1981:13)

Table 2.13 Scenario List with Cumulative Probability

Scenario	Likelihood	Consequence	Cumulative probability
s_1	p_1	x_1	$P_1 = P_2 + p_1$
s_2	p_2	x_2	$P_2 = P_3 + p_2$
$\vdots$	$\vdots$	$\vdots$	
s_i	p_i	x_i	$P_i = P_{i+1} + p_i$
$\vdots$	$\vdots$	$\vdots$	
s_{N-1}	p_{N-1}	x_{N-1}	$P_{N-1} = P_N + p_{N-1}$
s_N	p_N	x_N	$P_N = p_N$

Source: Kaplan and Garrick (1981:13)

development and respective consequences, particularly as some may not yet have occurred in the past. Moreover, arguably the worst risk is the one which has not been identified and therefore cannot be taken into consideration for mitigation.

Kaplan and Garrik (1981:15) therefore suggest to add a scenario category s_{N+1} and applying a probability to it. This brings the *"unknown factor"* into the consideration but it still does not make a realistic consideration of possible consequences (*"losses"*) and relevant probabilities possible.

2.2.2.3 Risk Curves

Adding a fourth column, *"cumulative probability"* to Table 2.12 and arranging the scenarios by increasing severity of damage results in Table 2.13.

Plotting the points $<x_i, P_i>$ results in the staircase function shown as dashed line in Fig. 2.19. Given that the scenarios are in reality categories of scenarios as they bundle different kinds and sizes of each *"scenario"*, the staircase function can be regarded as an approximation to a continuous reality. Graphically, this can be expressed in a smoothed curve, R (x), through the staircase which should represent the actual risk and is therefore called the *"risk curve"* as illustrated in Fig. 2.19.

A practical illustration is Fig. 2.20 which depicts the frequency of man-caused events in relation to fatalities.

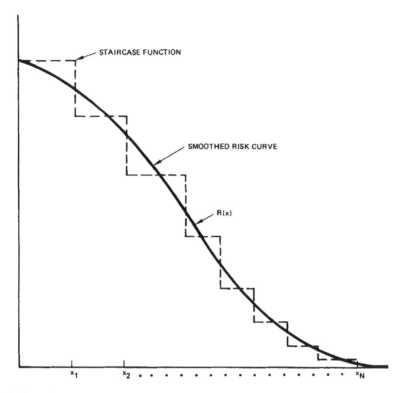

Fig. 2.19 Risk curve. Source: Kaplan and Garrick (1981:14)

2.2.2.4   Multidimensional Damage

Often, there is not only one possible damage, as the loss of life, but a combination of several types of losses, such as the loss of life and the loss of property etc.

This can be taken into account by regarding the damage "*as a multidimensional or vector quantity rather than a single scalar*", thus turning the risk curve into "*a risk surface over the multidimensional space*", cfr. Fig. 2.21 (Kaplan and Garrik 1981:14):

2.2.3   Probability

Probability, i.e. the likelihood of an event taking place, has been discussed by various schools and different approaches have been made to establish what exactly probability means and how to quantify it. Among those, "at least three seem to be widely accepted" (Gilboa et al. 2008:3): the "Classical" approach, the "Frequentist" approach, and the "Subjective" approach which shall briefly be presented as follows.

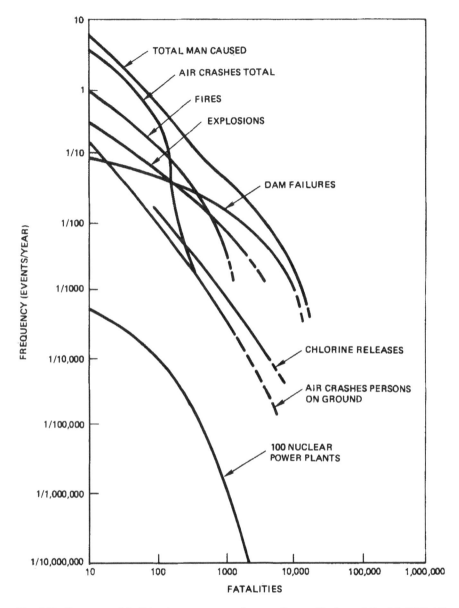

Fig. 2.20 Frequency of fatalities due to man-caused events. Source: Kaplan and Garrick (1981:15)

2.2.3.1 The "Classical" Approach

Under the "Classical" approach, also referred to as the "Principle of Insufficient Reason" or the "Principle of Indifference", all possible outcomes will have the same probability. A real-life example for a case in which this assumption would be correct,

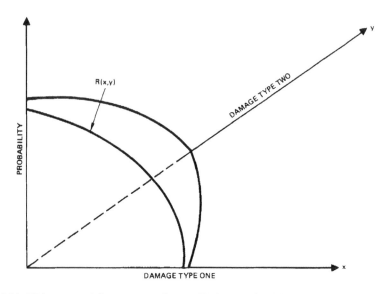

Fig. 2.21 Risk curve and damage types. Source: Kaplan and Garrick (1981:16)

is the tossing of a coin, where the probability that it lands heads up is just as high (50%) as the probability of it showing the other side. Most situations requiring a calculation of probability are however more complex as for example the decision whether or not to take out a specific insurance against a specific risk. It would *"hardly be rational"* to assume that the probability for the insured event to occur during the term of the policy is as high as it not occurring. (Gilboa et al. 2008:3 f.)

2.2.3.2 The "Frequentist" Approach

This view advocates a probability derived from the *"empirical frequency of an event in past observations"*, assuming that *"independent and identical repetitions of an experiment will result, with probability 1, in a relative frequency of occurrence of an event that converges to the event's probability"* (Gilboa et al. 2008:3).

As such, this approach works for tossing a coin and may provide for the same result as the "Classical" approach if the coin is fair. But it would also work if the coin was not fair and landed more often on one side due to its specific characteristics, something unaccounted for by the "Classical" approach.

The "Frequentist" approach also would be able to give a meaningful answer to the question regarding an insurance policy. If there were enough data for risk occurrences under the same circumstances (e.g. for car theft insurance: theft of the same type of car in the same neighbourhood etc.), these could be used to calculate the probability of the insured event occurring over a certain period of time.

It would not, however, be very helpful for situations which are basically unique and as such not comparable to other cases which might serve as sample. Gilboa et al. (2008) give the example of a patient considering whether or not to undergo an elective operation with a number of (high) risks. Given that similar cases may not be comparable, because patients had different individual characteristics, underwent surgery carried out by different surgeons in different hospitals etc., no single case may be exactly equal to the one at hand.

2.2.3.3 The "Subjective" Approach

*"The "*Subjective*" approach views probability as a numerical measure of degree of belief that is constrained to satisfy certain conditions (or "axioms")."* (Gilboa et al. 2008:3)

These subjective probabilities change from person to person and therefore contain a high degree of personal bias, as they are intuitive. An example of subjective probability could be asking German soccer fans, before the world championship starts, about the chances of Germany winning the world cup. Although there is no absolute mathematical proof behind the answer to the example, fans might still give specific replies, for instance that the German team has a 30% chance of winning the world cup.

"Interpreting the function as "utility" and the measure as "subjective probability", his theorem provides a behavioral definition of subjective probability, coupled with the principle of expected utility maximization." (Gilboa et al. 2008:3)

Thus, the patient in above-mentioned case could select a group of cases deemed comparable (e.g. all similar surgeries carried out by the same surgeon), in order to derive the individual probability of realization of a specific risk from that group.

This may indeed be applicable even to cases as straight-forward as tossing a coin, given that each experiment is still unique, if only by the exact time and place of its realization.Thus, similarity (an individual perception) could be used to solve this dilemma. The so-called *"similarity-weighted frequency approach"* could therefore eliminate some of the shortcomings of the frequentist approach (Gilboa et al. 2008:7).

The specific *"Default Probability"* or *"Probability of Default"* shall be discussed later.

2.2.3.4 Distinction Between Probability and Frequency

Kaplan and Garrik (1981) try to resolve the apparent antagonism between the *"objectivist"* or *"frequentist"* school on the one hand, and the *"subjectivist"* viewpoint on the other by declaring that those are both correct and call the objectivist approach *"frequency"* and the subjectivist viewpoint *"probability"*, thus leading to a distinction between probability and frequency. For those authors, the mathematical framework of *"frequency"* establishes the ground on which to apply and introduce subjective data (*"probability"*).

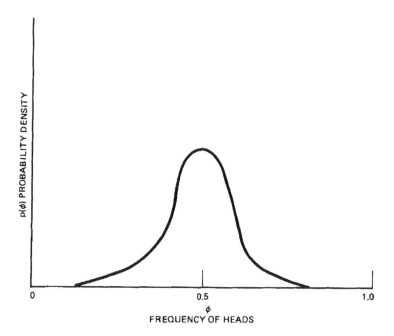

Fig. 2.22 Probability curve. Source: Kaplan and Garrick (1981:19)

2.2.3.5   Probability Curve

Using the example of tossing a coin, the probability of heads in the next toss would correspond to the formula

$$p(\text{heads}) = \int_0^{10} \phi p(\phi) d\phi$$

where ϕ stands for outcome and the respective curve would look as shown in Fig. 2.22.

This reflects the Gaussian concept of normal distribution.

2.2.3.6   Inclusion of Uncertainty

By including uncertainty as a factor, the result is an area, rather than a curve, defined by several curves which are sensible to a specific P value (i.e. 0.90 for 90% certainty) as shown in Fig. 2.23, according to Kaplan and Garrik (1981).

2.2.4   *Risk Management in Financial Institutions*

> "*[S]ound corporate governance and strong riskmanagement culture should enable banks to avoid excessive leverage and risk taking. But human nature being what it is, there are likely always to be some players eager to push complex products and trading beyond the sensible*

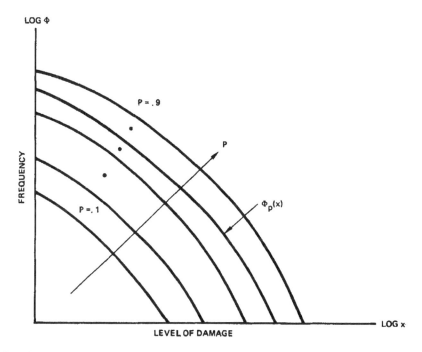

Fig. 2.23 Risk curve in probability of frequency format. Source: Kaplan and Garrick (1981:21)

needs of industry and long-term investors in order to drive profits." (Blundell-Wignall et al. 2009:12)

In the financial area, the term risk stands for the possibility that an investment's actual return will be different from what was expected. This includes the chance of having a lower or no return at all, as well as the possibility of losing a part or all of the original investment. One way of measuring risk is to calculate the standard deviation of the historical returns of a specific investment. Whenever this value is elevated, a high degree of risk has to be assumed.

Both, financial and non-financial firms invest heavily in developing risk management systems and strategies to manage risks associated with their business and investment dealings in a professional way. However, the results can only be as good as the (human) input, and a number of tasks still have to be performed by human beings, such as risk assessment, which involves the identification and description of the firm's or project's risks.

Indeed, as Jorion highlights as the first lesson learned from the financial crisis, experienced risk managers should be in charge of risk management. It *"should be driven by people, not machines."* (Jorion 2009:930)

2.2.5 Beta

An important measure of risk for investments is beta, which indicates the volatility of an investment in relation to the overall market. Beta is used in the capital asset pricing model (CAPM), a model which computes the expected return of an investment taking into account its beta and expected market returns. As such, Beta—also known as *"beta coefficient"*—is a risk index (Levy 2010:43).

Beta is being calculated using regression analysis, thus analyzing an investment's sensitivity to market fluctuations. A beta of 1 indicates that the investment will move in line with the market. A beta of below 1 indicates that the equity, for instance, will be less volatile than the market, while a value above 1 means that the investment's price will be more volatile than the market. A beta of 1.2 consequently implies an expected volatility of that stock or bond of 20% more than the respective market. This means, as a result, that returns may be higher, but also significantly lower, i.e. granting higher opportunities as well as riks.

2.2.6 Risk-Return Relationship

Simply speaking, there is no risk-free return, and the higher the potential return, the higher the associated risk. Or, in other words, the greater the amount of risk that an investor is willing to take on, the greater the potential return. The reason for this is that investors need to be compensated for taking on additional risk (Cfr. Fama 1973).

Markowitz (1952, 1959) pioneered in what has become known as portfolio theory, explaining the traditional objectives of either minimizing risks for given levels of return or maximising returns for given levels of risk.[22]

This is not to say that riskless assets cannot or should not be assumed for study purposes—in fact, they are (Levy 2010, 48)—, nor that no assets are described as risk-free (as, for instance, happens with US Treasury bonds (Altman et al. 1998:1730)). As recent developments not only in Europe have shown however, no investment is absolutely free of risk, but treasury bonds typically provide a lower rate of return than e.g. US corporate bonds. This is easily explained given that a corporation is much more likely to go bankrupt than the U.S. government. Consequently, as the risk of investing in a corporate bond is higher, investors are offered a higher rate of return.

This so-called risk-return trade-off implies that low levels of uncertainty—i.e. low risk—correspond to low potential returns, and vice versa, high levels of uncertainty (high risk) are associated with high potential returns.

---

[22]Regarding portfolio performance, see Blume (1968).

2.2.7 Risk Management

"People who don't take risks generally make about two big mistakes a year. People who do take risks generally make about two big mistakes a year." (Peter F. Drucker)

Risk Management is one of the central aspects of corporate governance (Buhleier and Splinter 2013) and thus one of the topics the supervisory board has to oversee. This obligation is derived from article 4.1.4 of the German Corporate Governance Code (GCGC) which refers to section 91 II AktG (German Public Company Law). The latter stipulates that the managing board has to take adequate measures— especially by establishing systems of supervision—in order to ensure that developments which might put the continuity of the corporation at risk be identified at an early stage.[23]

"Risk management is largely an exercise in quantifying uncertainty and then working to find ways to mitigate risks outside the company's risk appetite" (Rossi 2012a:33).

Risk management covers the assessment, the mitigation, and the monitoring of risks, based on a risk strategy (cfr. Froot et al. 1993). Optimally, it should cover all risks an organization is exposed to, such as:

- Financial Risk;
- Credit Risk;
- Operational Risk;
- Organizational Risk.

This list could be extended almost infinitely (insurance risk, etc.), or shortened to just Financial and Operational Risk as it appears to us that the former includes Credit Risk and the latter incorporates Organizational Risk. Some risks, such as reputational risk[24], may even transcend the most general categorization, as this risk in particular, for instance, may result from both internal errors (e.g. hiring of a (convicted) fraudster) and external factors attributable to market disruptions.

More important than these categorizations, however, appears to be the need for inclusion of each and every risk which might affect the organization, including risks as diverse as internal and external fraud, re-financing risks, natural hazards, and changes in (tax) legislation to name just a few.

---

[23]*"Der Vorstand hat geeignete Maßnahmen zu treffen, insbesondere ein Überwachungssystem einzurichten, damit den Fortbestand der Gesellschaft gefährdende Entwicklungen früh erkannt werden."* – *"The management board has to take adequate measures, particularly to establish a surveillance system, so that developments which might put the continuation of the company at risk be recognized at an early stage."* (Section 91 II AktG)

[24]Reputational risk can be defined as *"the range of possible gains and losses in reputational capital for a given firm"* or as *"a stakeholder's overall evaluation of a company over time"*, being this evaluation *"made up from the stakeholder's experience of the visible behavior of the company, as well as the images based on the company's communication and in addition its symbolism in comparison with its major competitors"* (Jacob 2012:263, quoting Fombrun et al. 2000 and Gyomlay and Moser 2005).

Also extremely important is the pro-active management of those risks, rather than a reactive management (*"fire-fighting"*) of risks which have already materialized. In truth, the latter should not even be considered *"risk management"* but rather called *"workout"*, given that risk, as seen above, implies the possibility of an event, not the dealing with an event which has already materialized. Although this is all quite obvious and self-explanatory—as it is clear that a fire department's main task should be to avoid fires rather than to actually fight them—, reality shows that many organizations either have no structured risk management in place at all, or regard it as an obligation or *"nice-to-have"* option which above all is seen as a cost factor.

So, in order to achieve this organization-wide, pro-active management, a number of steps, which shall be presented in the following section, need to be taken—and regularly reviewed—to ensure that the likelihood of their occurrence is limited and that for the case of a hazardous event the relevant policies are in place and ready to be executed. The latter includes the proper distribution and training of those policies.

"Enterprise Risk Management (ERM) has traditionally been a qualitative and subjective discipline with a focus on annual risk assessments, risk registers and board reports." (Shinkman and Herd 2014) Recently, however, ERM and risk management in general have come to rely more heavily on quantitative approaches to identify emerging risks and reflect risk exposure, risk apetite and risk tolerance, due to the increased volatility and velocity of change in the business environment. In order to achieve this aim, a certain standardization of risk management parameters was necessary and found in what are called the key risk indicators (KRIs) in an analogy to the key performance indicators[25] (KPIs) best known from production, accounting and controlling, but also commonly used in general management and finance (Cfr. Shinkman and Herd 2014; Sobel and Reding 2004).

According to Shinkman and Herd (2014), their employer CEB found that *"78% of companies would like to improve their process of developing more mature key risk indicators"* but find it difficult to find the right set of metrics.

They suggest the so-called S.M.A.R.T.-approach to key risk metrics, where S.M. A.R.T. stands for:

- **S**calability, allowing a consistent application throughout the organization;
- **M**easurability, requiring that KRIs ideally be quantified but in any case reasonably measurable;
- **A**ctionability, to support management's decision-taking process and the taking of action;
- **R**eliability, allowing for their recurring monitoring and measurement;
- **T**imeliness, providing early warning signals of emerging risks or gaps in preparedness

(Shinkman and Herd 2014, quoting CEB, Develop SMART KRIs, Arlington, VA 2013:6)

---

[25]For a good overview on KPIs in German, cfr. http://www.controllingportal.de/Fachinfo/Kennzahlen/Key-Performance-Indicators-KPI.html

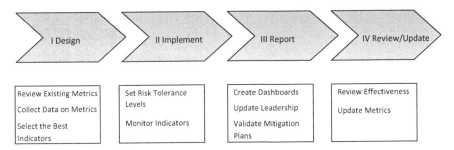

Fig. 2.24 The *"KRI Process Road Map"*. Source: Shinkman and Herd (2014)

As part of an early warning system, KRIs may be used to identify and monitor changes in risk exposure, as well as compare them to the risk strategy defined, thus alerting to a deviation of exposure from the entity's thresholds.

KRIs may be used to define an organization's risk appetite as well as risks and opportunities. The mapping of KRIs to risk tolerance levels helps senior management to define and implement their organization's risk appetite, while by specifically designing and analyzing KRIs to that end, one may discover trends which could adversely affect their aims or unveil the presence of opportunities.

By monitoring KRIs in that way, they can kick off a process of risk mitigation before those risks materialize, and may be used as controls by establishing limits for certain actions (*"risk treatment"*).

In terms of risk reporting, data obtained by KRIs can be summarized and thus provide for reports with different levels of detail to different levels of management.

Finally, and crucially for financial institutions within their regulatory environment, KRIs may be used to track compliance efforts and their effectiveness in risk-related areas such as capital adequacy and risk reserves (Shinkman and Herd 2014) (Fig. 2.24).

According to Kirkpatrick (2009:70), it is not sufficient for risk management systems in the technical sense to work properly, but it is of the utmost importance that the transmission of risk information occurs through *"effective channels, a clear corporate governance issue"*. *"[R]obust risk management"* is—together with qualified board oversight—important not only to financial institutions, but also for *"large, complex nonfinancial companies"* (Kirkpatrick 2009:62). The author also found that readability of risk disclosures is difficult and that there is a lack of generally accepted risk management accounting principles, underlining that *"[l]eading disclosure practices were first enunciated by the Senior Supervisors Group in early 2008"* (Kirkpatrick 2009:84) (Fig. 2.25).

Friedland (2009:50 f.) cites the FSF, an organization of regulators affiliated with the Bank for International Settlements as stating that *"[w]hile it is the responsibility of firms' board and senior managers to manage the risk they bear, supervisors and regulators can give incentives to management so that risk control frameworks keep pace with innovation and changes in the business model"*.

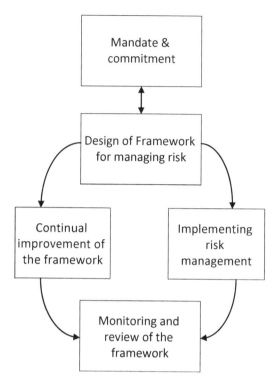

Fig. 2.25 Risk
Management Framework.
Source: Safetyrisk.net

2.2.8   Risk Assessment

As a first step in the risk management process, all relevant risks have to be identified. One of the difficulties this implies is that some risks may yet have to materialize for the first time, so that a mere dependence on past experience may be insufficient. Secondly, a clear measurement (assessment in the stricter sense) of the risks identified needs to take place, in order to be able to, thirdly, classify those risks in *"Risk Classes"*.

2.2.8.1   Risk Identification

In order to identify (almost) all risks which may potentially affect an organization during the course of its existence, all areas of actuation need to be identified. This must not be limited to the the core- and non-core-activities of the entity, but also to all internal and external activities, for example those related to human resources management as an internal activity, or the external relationship with public entities etc.

Once these areas of actuation have been defined, all intrinsic risks need to be identified. This may well lead to the finding that some risks are cross-sectional, i.e. appear in various divisions, that risks in once section may mitigate or increase the risk in others—which leads us to the next section on the measurement of risk.

2.2.8.2 Risk Measurement

Risk measurement (cfr. Altmann et al. 1998) is probably the most complex and difficult of the tasks covered in this part of our monograph, given that it relates directly to the quantification of risk which has been discussed above and cannot be realistically separated from its qualification.

As such, serious, realistically applicable risk measurement will hardly ever be the result of an exact mathematical process, but rather involve the combination of various means, such as the mathematical models (Monte Carlo simulations etc.), personal experience and sector-specific knowledge.

To illustrate the measurement of risk a relatively simple, yet very important area of risk management shall be chosen: credit risk management, arguably the most important risk for financial institutions. This excludes a priori many of the factors which make other areas, such as operational risk management, particularly complex as they may have multiple and/or cross-sectorial effects, which may increase or decrease each other. Also, by having a very measurable basis, namely credit as expressed in currency amounts (money), it has per se a more *"measurable nature"*.

At the same time, it is not limited to banks, as sometimes assumed, but actually applies to almost all organizations and even private persons: By granting payment terms or delivering goods or services without immediate payment, firms contract a credit risk. The same is true for private individuals who for instance make purchases for others, trusting that they will be reimbursed for the purchase price etc.

Neither is credit risk management incomparable to other areas of risk management. Actually, risk management is in essence quite comparable across the board, and findings from one area are easily applicable to another.

Having said this, the very basics of credit risk management can be summarized as follows.

2.2.8.3 Default

The main (again, not the only) risk with regards to credits is that the terms of the same will not be complied with, be it in terms of repayment of the loan amount, payment of interest, compliance with (re-)payment dates, etc. Cumulatively, these *"breaches of contract"* are known as *"default"*.

2.2.8.4 Loss

While in operating a production plant, for example, one of the risks involved is the loss of property or the loss of lives, in credit operations the main risk is in fact the loss of money. This may be because the loan amount is not (fully) repaid or because it is repaid late, thus precluding other opportunities of earning money during that time.

2.2.8.5 Probability of Default (PD)

Probability of Default (PD) is consequently understood as the degree of likelihood that the borrower of a loan or debt will not be able to comply with its obligations, mainly regarding repayments. Whenever certain covenants are not met, the borrower may be declared to be in default and different (legal) measures can be taken by the bank to recover at least part of the owed amount, for instance by enforcing collateral.

The spread, i.e. the margin over and above the refinancing rate is usually calculated on the basis of the borrower's or project's probability of default. Consequently, a high PD will lead to a higher interest rate (or a refusal of the loan application) and vice versa.

Probability of Default is usually expressed in a percentage value, where:

$PD = 100\%$—certainty of default, i.e. borrower has defaulted on a loan;
$PD = 0\%$—certainty of full compliance, i.e. borrower has already complied with all terms (i.e. fully repaid).

As an example, then, a PD of 10% implies that the specific borrower has a one in ten probability to default on his loan.

2.2.8.6 Loss Given Default (LGD)

Loss given Default is the amount of funds that is estimated to be lost by an entity when a borrower defaults on a loan. Also here, the quantification, usually expressed in percentage, is a difficult task, for it depends on the point in time at which the borrower may default under any given loan, as parts of the loan may have been repaid (or not yet drawn) by that time. It further depends on the quality and liquidity of granted collateral etc.

In brief, LGD may be summarized as follows:

$LGD = 100\%$—all of the original amount will be lost, i.e. the lender will not recover anything (highest (total) risk of loss);
$LGD = 0\%$—all of the original amount will be recovered, i.e. the lender will not lose anything even in a default situation, normally due to very valuable and liquid collaterals (lowest (no) risk of loss).

As an example, then, an LGD of 50% implies that under a specific loan, the default of a borrower would result in the loss of half of the original amount (for example, the execution of a mortgage takes time, costs money, and in a forced sale process only part of the original loan amount can be recovered).

2.2.8.7   Expected Loss (EL)

Finally, the Expected Loss simply reflects the result of multiplying the LGD with the PD in order to obtain a final risk measure for a loan:

$$EL = PD \times LGD$$

To apply above example, and given a Probability of Default of 10% and a Loss Given Default value of 50%, Expected Loss would in this case amount to 5%:

$$EL = 10\% \times 50\% = 5\%$$

Therefore, had a EUR 1 million loan be given, the Expected Loss in this example would amount to EUR 50,000.

EL Values for individual loans may vary sharply, and usually a more important figure taken into account is the EL value of a whole portfolio of loans. This is then compared to the internal rate of return (IRR) of the relevant loan or portfolio.

Historical data over past losses in comparable portfolios provides for a comparable, but does not necessarily serve to change that value as (i) historical figures will usually have entered into the risk measurement process, thus leading to a double-accounting should they be taken into account, and (ii) changing (economic) environments may disturb the comparability of historical EL figures even in very comparable portfolios.

In this context it is important to note that such an approach may underestimate actual losses, i.e. the (additional) risk is that of *unexpected* losses (Altman and Saunders 1998:1736).

2.2.8.8   Risk Classification

As a final step of the risk assessment process, risks may be classified in order to simplify the subsequent risk mitigation process (thus however to some extend jeopardizing it) or rather to give a high-level risk overview.

Risk classes may be different from entity to entity as they should reflect all the risk groups and only those groups of risk the specific entity faces (or, at least, has identified).

Coning back on our above example, one way of classifying credit risk would be to establish EL-classes, e.g.:

$$EL = 0 - 0.5\% - ELC\,1;$$
$$EL => 0.5\% - 1.0\% - ELC\,2;$$

. . ..

In practice, this may be used to create sub-portfolios to subject them to different *"intensities"* of risk management, i.e. loans in higher (riskier) EL classes will be reviewed more frequently, handled by more experienced staff, moved into special (sub-)entities or sold off to venture funds etc.

2.2.9   Risk Mitigation

The aim of risk mitigation is to minimize risk by taking measures intended to reduce the probability of occurrence of the risks assessed as per above.

Again, there are innumerous forms and means of risk management, including:

- Hedging[26] (interest rate, foreign exchange, etc.);
- Insurance (either directly or by taking a pledge over the same);
- Payment controls;
- Etc.

These measures will typically address both the probability of loss generation and the amount of the expected loss.

2.2.10   Risk Monitoring

In addition to the above, ongoing risk monitoring and re-assessment is essential in order to ensure the relevance of all measures within the risk management framework at all times. This includes legal and tax reviews as well as regular review of (risk-prone) processes.

In the cases where the realization of one or several risks is imminent or already partly materialized, special treatment such as intensive care or separation (e.g. into off-balance vehicles) to avoid contamination may be applied (*"Workout"*).

2.2.11   Risk Strategy

Risk Strategies are important management tools as they not only define the risk management process but also the *"risk appetite"* of the relevant organization. They should also depend on factors such as shocks to investment and financing opportunities (Froot et al. 1993).[27]

2.2.12   Risk Management Under ISO 31000

"Risk management must be transformed into a cornerstone of corporate governance and business strategy and fully integrated into executive decisions, organizational structures and corporate cultures." (Martin, II May 2013:16)

ISO 31000—Risk Management—, a norm approved in late 2008 and published in 2009, established risk management as an international standard and is characterized by three main traits, according to Brühwiler (2009a:24).

---

[26]For details on hedging, please refer to Froot et al. (1993:1629 ff.).

[27]Please refer to Sect. 2.2.7 for more detail.

Firstly, risk management is based on a top-down-approach dealing on a broad basis with the positive and negative effects uncertainties may have on the performance and achievements of organizations. This includes strategic risks (economic environment, products, technologies, markets, clients etc.) as well as operational and process-related risks on a management level. The top-down-approach reflects the corporate governance belief—also stated in the OECD and German corporate governance codes—that risk management is *"one of the main tasks of the upper management"* (Brühwiler 2009a). Consequently, Supervisory Board, Management Board and top managers need to constantly assess the risks of their organization, in constant exchange with the other stakeholders.

Secondly, risk management is now seen as a management function rather than looking mainly at the mere risk assessment or risk quantification role. As such, risk management includes the management functions of the so-called Deming cycle (PDCA cycle—Plan-Do-Control/Check-Act or, Plan-Do-Study-Act (PDSA)). The risk management process as such feeds into the *"Do"*-function and includes the necessary steps to identify, analyze, evaluate/quantify and mitigate/deal with risks, as shown in Fig. 2.26.

This process has to be accompanied by constant communication and information exchange as well as monitoring and verification of risks.

Thirdly, ISO 31000 is a generic norm—or base norm—and is meant to significantly extend the American COSO-rules. It gives a general guidance on risk management, rather than the many area-specific risk management norms for several sectors and industries such as building, IT, machinery, financial reporting, safety at work etc. As such, ISO 31000 deals with all potential risks of an organization on a

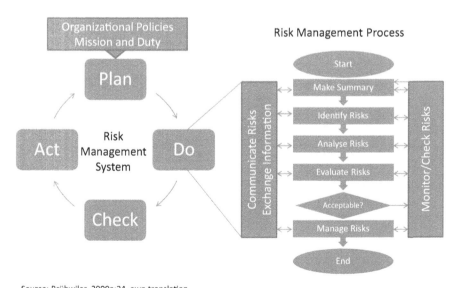

Source: Brühwiler, 2009a:24, own translation

Fig. 2.26 Risk Management System

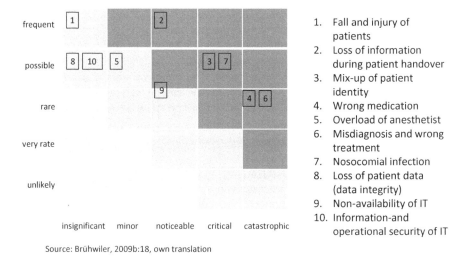

Source: Brühwiler, 2009b:18, own translation

1. Fall and injury of patients
2. Loss of information during patient handover
3. Mix-up of patient identity
4. Wrong medication
5. Overload of anesthetist
6. Misdiagnosis and wrong treatment
7. Nosocomial infection
8. Loss of patient data (data integrity)
9. Non-availability of IT
10. Information-and operational security of IT

Fig. 2.27 Risk profile (patient security)

global scale and serves as blueprint for technically or locally specific editions, such as British Standard's BS 31100 or the ONR 49000 series.

ONR 49002-2 groups the many methods of risk assessment into five groups as follows:

1. Creativity techniques such as brainstorming, the Delphi method, and morphological matrix;
2. Scenario analyses as for example the root cause analysis, fault tree and event tree analysis or worst-case-scenario analysis;
3. Indicator analysis such as critical incidents reporting system (CIRS) or change-based risk management (CBRM);
4. Functional analyses, like, for example, failure mode and effects analysis (FMEA), general hazard analyses, a hazard and operability study (HAZOP) or hazard analysis and critical control points (HACCP); and
5. Statistical analyses, including standard deviation, confidence interval (value at risk), and Monte Carlo simulations.

An important task of risk management is not only the identification of the most appropriate methods for solving a given issue, but rather to combine several methods in order to achieve that aim. Brühwiler (2009a) gives the example of combining the classic risk profile (see Fig. 2.27) with a quantitative evaluation by means of a value at risk (confidence interval) calculation using a Monte Carlo simulation.

Brühwiler (2009b:17 f.) stresses that each method has its own advantages and disadvantages which need to be known in order to perform above-mentioned selection of applicable methods.

A way of getting an overall view of risks and priorities is the worst-case-scenario-analysis, for example, which is characterized by a top-down-approach and includes a list of threats; risk owners are the managers. Its disadvantage lies primarily in the subjectivity of the risk assessment.

The critical incidents reporting system (CIRS) provides for one of the most valuable results, based on the generation of risk information stemming from numerous inputs about errors. A basic requirement however is a so-called *"error culture"*, i.e. a working environment in which all professional groups acknowledge errors and are willing to record and share information on those mistakes with their colleagues and managers. Pre-conditions therefore are anonymity, lack of fear of repression or sanctions, voluntary participation, good examples set by management (*"management by example"*), and—generally—a corporate culture based on mutual trust.

Hazard analyses on the other hand are based on a bottom-up approach including process analysis which is comparable to process failure mode and effects analysis. This too provides for a high level of detail and can be very effective if paired with a well-working quality management system.

The issue with statistical analyses is that most organizations simply cannot provide the amount of data which is required to obtain relevant output from a statistical analysis of internal data. Therefore, external data—including academic research—has to be used, but the latter can only serve as an indication and consequently, specific conditions of each organization need to be taken into account.

The root-cause-analysis only makes sense in order to analyze an incident which already occurred with a significant impact. This method is case-specific, therefore without general validity, and relatively expensive.

Among its eleven key principles, ISO 31000 states that *"risk management is an integral part of organizational processes"* and that it is *"part of decision-making"* (Brühwiler 2009a:25). The processes of an organization are split by ISO 9001 into management processes, resource processes, processes of products and services, and ancillary processes. As with other management processes, risk management cannot exist on its own, isolated from the other parts of the process environment, but rather embedded into it as shown in Fig. 2.28.

ISO 31000 however omits areas as important as emergency-, crisis-, or continuity management (recovery), although those are crucial and, according to Brühwiler (2009a:26), risk management would be *"unthinkable"* without them. ONR 49002-3, by contrast, integrates crisis management into risk management. Emergencies are defined as unexpected, sudden events with severe consequences for an entity of an organization, such as explosions, natural catastrophes, legal attacks, etc. Crises—which may result from emergencies—however are situations which do affect the whole organization and require extraordinary measures. Both require immediate action (*"response"*), followed by an effort to re-establish the productivity of the organization (*"recovery"*). Continuity management shall be part of Enterprise Resource Planning (ERP) which should not only plan and prepare for normality, but also for exceptional situations, i.e. emergencies and crises.

Another important, practical aspect of risk management is the allocation of tasks towards each responsible. While this is and should be basically a question of internal organization of each entity, norms such as ISO 31000 and ONR 49001 mention the

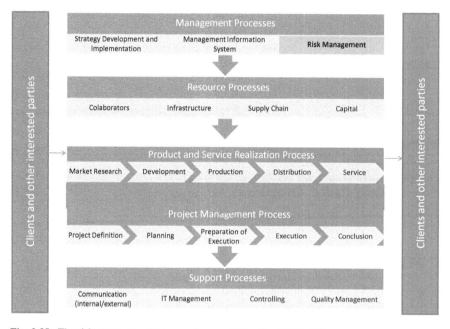

Fig. 2.28 The risk management process. Source: Brühwiler (2009a:25)

risk owner, ONR 49001 further refers to the person appointed by top management (further on, the *"appointee"*) and to the risk manager.[28]

The risk owner shall ensure that the principles of risk management be respected in all decision-making, that uncertainties relating to opportunities and threats be minimized, and that risks be evaluated according to recognized standards and methods. Furthermore, the risk owner shall make sure that the results from risk assessments be implemented and enable communication about risk topics with all relevant parties.

The appointee for his part shall have responsibility for the risk management system in general, the nomination of risk owners and risk managers, he or she shall provide the necessary resources and ensure risk communication in the whole organization. Apart from this, the appointee shall ensure the operational implementation of the organization's risk policy and the evaluation of the risk management system with all

---

[28]Brühwiler (2009e) describes the function of a risk manager in quite some detail and based on ONR 49001/49003, highlighting that this is not an officially recognized profession and comparing the risk manager with his inter-disciplinary and multi-task activity, a specific toolset, and the necessity to communicate and analyze across an organization's functions and areas to a "Superman". An important part is his cooperation with risk owners by whom he has to be respected and accepted despite of not necessarily mastering their business. The risk manager should also be well integrated into the organization and its decision processes and therefore needs not be as independent as, for instance, an auditor. However, the effective application of the "four-eyes-principle" should be ensured. Another important trait is the direct link (reporting line) to the top management via an "appointee" or directly to the Chief Risk Officer/Head of Corporate Risk Management (or, in absence of such a position, often the Chief Financial Officer).

its elements as well as reporting on performance and effectiveness of risk management and the necessity of improvements.

Lastly, the risk manager has to make sure that spirit and purpose of risk management is being understood by top management and managers as risk owners, that the risk management process is duly being implemented in the organization, and that the methods used are appropriate for the risk assessment which itself shall fulfill at least a minimal, generally accepted standard. Furthermore he or she shall report on the effectiveness of risk management to the appointee who has to ensure that measures from risk assessments as well as adequate interfaces to other management tools and processes be implemented in a relevant fashion and lastly, that the elements of the risk management system be designed, implemented and maintained in a practical manner on behalf of top management.

An internal control system (ICS) is always dependent on several factors such as effectivity, traceability and efficiency. In a first phase of introduction, effectivity will be ensured by the selection and implementation of adequate aims and activities of control, while traceability is granted by sufficient documentation. Efficiency—or even increased performance—however is not immediately associated with an internal control system which is rather seen as an administrative burden. In order to use an ICS efficiently, two actions are helpful, according to Scheffner (2012), reporting on relevant experience at major German utility EnBW: Firstly the separation of ICS into financial reporting and business steering; secondly, the segmentation of ICS's 'secondary effects' into risk diversification, transparency, and increase of effectivity and efficiency.

ICS—financial reporting reflects the common or classical understanding of ICS and aims at ensuring reliable and correctness of control mechanisms regarding the external financial reporting.

ICS—business steering, by contrast, aims at identifying and avoiding—at an early stage—any mistakes, risks and resulting damage for the company. In addition to legal requirements, it can be used to controlling the achievement of internal guidance. This can happen by segmentation of the corporate processes into their individual steps and analyzing each regarding their financial, reputational, and fraud-related risks.

This separation could in our opinion and in ultimate consequence lead to a separation of the overall responsibility for risk management in two different *"appointees"*, one in the finance area and another in the operative realm of an organization. It still appears to be common to locate the main risk responsible in the finance section (cfr. Brühwiler 2009c:22 (A3)). This might lead to an excessive focus on financial risks (such as credit risk, liquidity risk etc.[29]) to the detriment of other (rather operational, strategic, and policy[30]) risks, while both are crucially

---

[29]For an overview on risks in the finance area, cfr. Keitsch, Risikomanagement (2007).

[30]Golub and Crum (2010:38) identify policy risk as a major contributor to market volatility and see it as a primary source of risk in many markets.

important to an organization, and may even result in the realization of the same risks (e.g. reputational risk).

With its authors, ISO 31000:2009 can thus be described as *"a generic risk management approach that can be applied to all organizations to help achieve their objectives"*.

2.2.12.1 Risk Diversification

Regarding the second set of segmentation, Scheffner (2012) explains that ICS leads to an increased sensitivity of all participants in the processes regarding the avoidance of risks and thereby has a pre-emptive effect on them and the organization as a whole. Apart from the risks covered by KonTraG, this includes particularly process risks which are not part of the official reporting system but which nonetheless contribute to a minimization of risks.

2.2.12.2 Transparency

The intense analysis of business processes leads not only to the identification of lacks of control, but—beyond that—shows required action, including the attribution of missing responsibilities or a clear definition of governance functions, once more stressing the point that transparency is a major element of good corporate governance.

2.2.12.3 Increased Effectiveness and Efficiency

The implementation of an ICS exposes existing control mechanisms and tests them with relation to their relevance and extent. This allows the exclusion of both excessive and insufficiently controlled processes which can be remedied while streamlining may occur by dropping unnecessary and repetitive controls.

In summary, ICS—just as labor law induced risk management or other legally prescribed measures to deal with risks—can be used beyond the mere compliance with obligations to improve the overall performance and risk profile of an organization.

Apart from those areas, there are many which are unregulated and require each firm to establish their own risk management standards and processes. This is not altogether bad as it provides for company- and sector-specific design of risk management rather than a *"one size fits all"* approach. Brühwiler (2009c:21) makes that point for financial institutions when he writes that *"almost all financial institutions which succumbed to the present financial crisis had many risk management activities in place, as for example the management of credit risk according to Basel II or the control of financial risks under the Sarbanes-Oxley-Act. Risk management was doubtlessly very intense, but unfortunately with the wrong focus, in the wrong place"*.

2.2.12.4 Risk Management Policy

This leads to the requirement for each organization of firstly identifying its relevant risks and decide which direction its risk management shall take (cfr. ISO 31000, Principles and Guidelines, chapter 6.3—*"establishing the context"*) in order to deal with the right risks in the right way, thus defining its risk management policy. This is defined by ISO 31000 as *"[t]he statement of the overall intentions and direction of an organization related to risk management"*. It describes how risk management shall be performed by the organization and includes, according to Brühwiler (2009c:21) the motivation of the organization as well as roles and responsibilities, the management of conflicts of interest, the attitude towards approach, resources, measurement of effectiveness and the function and responsibility of top management. Whether an organization really needs its own risk management policy depends primarily on its size, given that SMEs usually work quite well with an informal process supported by direct communication between employees and management.[31] Other factors however are the density of the relevant regulatory environment and risk exposure of each entity. For those reasons, above all the regulatory element, it appears necessary for all financial institutions to have a formal risk management policy and the respective processes in place, even for small institutions, where however the volume and depth of such policy and procedures may be adapted relative to the size of the organization and above all the business areas it is active in.

Risk management policy is also based on the Deming cycle described above and can be amended and illustrated by translating "Do" into "Implement", "Check" into "Appraise", and "Act" into "Improve", as suggested by Brühwiler in Figs. 2.29, 2.30, 2.31, 2.32.

Planning therefore includes the general direction of risk management set by top management, defining what risks have to be dealt with in which manner, attribution of necessary resources and capacities, as well as the definition of individual roles, competences and responsibilities. Another important factor at this stage is the integration of risk management into the overall organization and an open communication.

The Do or Implement phase covers the several applications of the risk management process, as well as the decision whether risk management shall be fully integrated into the management system or rather run independently. The risk assessment and crisis-management have to be dealt with, as well as the documentation of the risk management process. This also exemplifies the common structure of a central management of the risk function but a de-centralized implementation and realization.

The Check or Appraisal phase verifies the effectiveness of the risk management system and checks whether the expected improvements of efficiency, corporate strategy and operative tasks really took place. This may happen by means of an *"audit"* process and may comprise qualitative and quantitative assessments.

---

[31]On risk management in small and medium sized enterprises (SME), cfr. Brühwiler (2009d).

Source: Brühwiler, 2009c:22 f., own translation

Fig. 2.29 Plan

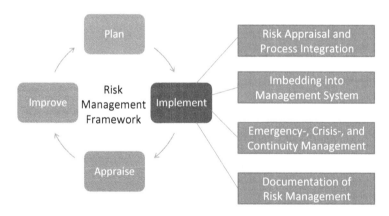

Source: Brühwiler, 2009c:22 f., own translation

Fig. 2.30 Implement

In summary, the risk management policy is necessary to ensure a continuous surveillance and improvement of the risk management process. Initially, this process can consist of three phases. First comes the definition of principles, followed by an implementation phase which is then, on an ongoing and even permanent basis, succeeded by integration into the corporate management, processes and its culture (*"risk culture"*), thus spreading its roots in the organization's corporate governance. (Cfr. Brühwiler 2009c:22 f.) The integration might happen by various means and

Source: Brühwiler, 2009c:22 f., own translation

Fig. 2.31 Appraise

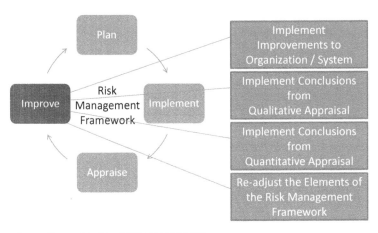

Source: Own continuation of Brühwiler, 2009c:22 f.

Fig. 2.32 Improve

through different processes, but one way might be to integrate risk management into the quality management process or the business development function as suggested by Brühwiler (2009c:23 (example C1); 2009e:24). In any case, employees have to be trained accordingly—constantly followed up by relevant continuous professional development measures—and minimal risk management tools such as lists of risks, support material and process descriptions showing how risk management is being introduced and integrated have to be always available.

2.2.12.5   Risk Assessment and Mitigation

The assessment of risk management measures (phase C in the Deming (PDCA) cycle) will happen both by qualitative and quantitative measurement (cfr. Fig. 2.31).

The **qualitative assessment** will, according to Brühwiler (2009e:21), analyse the following aspects:

- Were the measures suited to influence the risks;
- Were the measures effectively implemented;
- Have the measures had a diminishing impact on the probability of occurrence and/or the effects of risks;
- Can the effect of the measures be proven by early warning signs?
- What is the risk experience (occurrence of risk, positive and negative) and which consequences were drawn from that?

The **quantitative verification** will focus on a mathematical analysis of the risk profile, comparing an earlier to the latest version of the organization's risk profile. There is a simple and a more sophisticated approach to this (Brühwiler 2009e:21 f.).

Finally, within the Check or Improve phase of the circle the conclusions from the Appraisal shall be implemented and the risk management framework re-adjusted on the basis of the newly implemented improvements, as shown in Fig. 2.32.

By the simple multiplication of probability (P) with effect (E) of each risk (R) will provide a number to the risk (usually expressed in the organization's main currency): $P*E = R$. Each of those results may be added and/or compared individually to the relevant figures of the earlier risk profile, showing changes in the overall and/or individual risk weight. This quantitative approach bears two main weaknesses however: (i) it focuses on the worst case scenarios which reflect extremes and thus lead to a negative risk burden; and (ii) extreme but rare risk potentials tend to be *"watered down"* by the multiplication with (low) probabilities of occurrence.

The more sophisticated method for quantifying risk is based on the Gaussian distribution of each risk's probability of occurrence based on a high number of relevant data. Given that those data are not usually available, the common approach is to simulate it in form of many *"runs"* (several thousands, usually) in a Monte Carlo simulation. To this end, a number of questions have to be answered (Brühwiler 2009e:22):

- Does the risk bear only loss potential or also upside chances?
- Which is the maximum loss potential (credible worst case)?
- Is there a mean and optimal value for the risk?
- Is the risk normally distributed or differently (equal, one-sided. . .)?
- How does the risk behave in extreme effects (both positive and negative)—do they increase strongly or slightly, decrease strongly or slightly etc.?

By means of *"risk aggregation"* via the Monte Carlos simulation, the distribution of individual risks will be united. One of the main results is the so-called Value at Risk (VaR) which expresses the amount at stake which will not be exceeded with a given certainty (typically, 90%, 95%, 99% or 99.9%). The equity of a company should be significantly higher than (or at least as high as) the Value at Risk (at a significant threshold, say 99.8%) in order to ensure the long-term survival of the organization. Consequently, a Value at Risk perspective also helps to establish the creditworthiness of a borrower or issuer, given that the probability of default can be measured by relating equity to loss potential which can be derived from the risk assessment. In addition to this, other factors either of a quantitative nature (annual results) or qualitative (management, technologies, markets) are being taken into account by credit bureaus and rating agencies (Brühwiler 2009e:22 f.; Jorion 2009:926 ff.).

Under the sub-title *"Risk management is already a profession; now it needs to be professionalized"*, Martin (2013:16) demands that *"risk managers should be trained, licensed and regulated, just like accountants, lawyers and actuaries"*. He goes on to argue that as with other responsible jobs, risk managers should acquire the knowledge and experience necessary to be a professional risk manager, prove this in exams, and adhere to professional standards. He further raises the topic of independence which the US Federal Reserve Board required by establishing new rules by which large financial institutions must have a risk committee chaired by an independent director and integrating at least one member in that committee who has real risk management experience (Cfr. Federal Reserve, 2014 (http://www.federalreserve.gov/aboutthefed/boardmeetings/memo_20140218.pdf)).

Martin argues that *"one of the reasons Canadian banks fared better in the past financial crisis is that they followed written risk standards promulgated by the government. These regulations require companies to use* "a knowledgeable person with familiarity with risk management" *" (Martin 2013:16)*.

"Though the boards of most mutual funds are in the habit of hiring outside counsel when needed or contracting the services of accounting firms, they are unaccustomed to engaging experts to oversee risk on an ongoing basis." (Martin 2013:16).

Martin suggests to first define what risk management expertise and experience really are, *"and then require boards to include someone with these qualities or to seek qualified advice as they make their decisions"* (Martin 2013:16).

"Risk managers cannot rely on the past to predict the future. Most risk models are based on historical performance and work well—up to a point" (Martin, II May 2013:16). This implies that humans may be better at evaluation risk than statistical models. However, and at least for the medical field, psychoanalyst Paul Meehl gave evidence that statistical models almost always yield better predictions and diagnoses than the judgment of trained professionals (Meehl 2003).

"Professionalizing risk management also means creating standards, including benchmarks that provide some basis for the comparison of risk. For example, most regulators require stress tests to determine the adequacy of capital reserves. The general approach is to stress a company's portfolio based on predetermined scenarios. It would be far more interesting to know instead what would happen if regulators decided on a single benchmark portfolio and then had all financial institutions run it through their risk systems. Using this model, each company would produce hypothetical loan-loss reserve measures, value-at-risk and stress

Fig. 2.33 The Crisis in
Crisis Management. Source:
Plamper (2010:124); own
translation

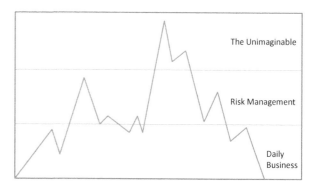

test results. The different systems would almost certainly produce different results. The benchmark portfolio would help regulators determine how institutions think about risk." (Martin 2013:16)

"I look forward to the day when firms will have chief fiduciary officers with independent reporting responsibilities for audit, compliance and risk." (Martin 2013:16)

"Risk management minimizes the possibly occurring disadvantages as a result of expectations which did not materialize or unexpected events." (Plamper 2010:123)

Plamper states that risk management may either:

- Prevent the occurrence of a (specific) risk or the consequent damages;
- Distribute the disadvantages onto several individuals or entities (as in the case of insurances) or even transfer them altogether;
- Prepare for the occurrence of a consequent damage.

He goes on to describe risk management as the attempt at *"optimizing"* the probability of the occurrence of a damage as well as its extent or to more accurately define them (Plamper 2010:124). Discussing crisis management, Plamper identifies three levels of crises: Daily Business (*"Tagesgeschäft"*), Risk Management (*"Risikomanagement"*), and The Unimaginable *("Das Unvorstellbare")*, according to Fig. 2.33.

This identification of three levels of escalation appears to make a lot of sense, however, one might be tempted to think of risk management as a set of tools to identify, quantify, assess, and mitigate risks, taking into account all risks within those three levels. Accordingly we believe that the second level should, following Plamper's rationale, rather be labelled as *"the imaginable"* or *"the thinkable"* and risk management be the generic term. Consequently, risk management should perform its above-mentioned role on those three levels (cfr. Fig. 2.34):

- Daily Business (normal situations);
- Imaginable deviations (special situations);
- Unimaginable deviations (very special situations).

Fig. 2.34 Crisis in Risk Management. Source: own presentation based on Plamper (2010:124)

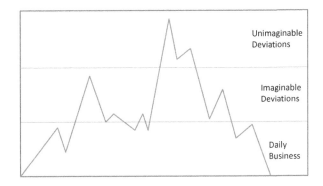

As an example for *"the unthinkable"*, Plamper refers to natural catastrophes such as the flooding of Hamburg in 1962 or that of New Orleans in 2005, arguing that with those *"very special situations"* come very special, *"unthinkable"* solutions such as the participation of the public in helping victims and re-building the damaged cities, or the intervention of the military which was in itself unthinkable at the time of the Hamburg flooding (but pushed through by then Hamburg's Secretary of the Interior and later Chancellor of the Federal Republic of Germany, Helmut Schmidt) (Plamper 2010:124).

Jorion (2009:926) also classifies risks into three categories: *"'known knowns', 'known unknowns', and 'unknown unknowns', corresponding to different levels of uncertainty"*.

Regarding risk management, KPMG demand and suggest the following (http://www.kpmg.com/Global/en/industry/Financial-Services/Pages/Risk-management.aspx):

- *"Risks are often managed in departmental silos;*
- *Risk management needs to be integrated across the entire business;*
- *Firms need to monitor key indicators which show early warning signs of potential problems, and have pre-planned strategies to address potential risks."*

2.2.13 Risk Management in Brazil

A 2011 study carried out by KPMG among 67 companies from different industries in Brazil revealed that at the time only 44% of those had a risk management system implemented in their organizations.

The consultancy explained that cultural aspects were partly responsible for delays in the implementation of such systems as they were seen as a *"control mechanism"* which turns the entity more bureaucratic. Furthermore, insufficiencies in the definition and allocation of roles and tasks pertaining to the risk management system were identified as roadblocks in the implementation of adequate structures.

The existence and nurturing of a strong risk culture within the company was seen as the most important factor for successful risk management, as indicated by 20% of the respondents. 17% of the managers interviewed considered support by senior management as the second most important factor, without which many related projects would simply not be put into practice.

34% of the managers at the time mentioned that their risk indicators were not very effective, pointing towards a strong lack of risk measurement instruments, according to the consultancy (KPMG Risk & Compliance 2011).[32]

The Brazilian risk management rules for financial institutions are mostly published by the Brazilian Central Bank on behalf of the National Monetary Council, however focusing on individual aspects such as market risk.

In June 2007, the Brazilian Central Bank published Resolution 3.464 (dd. 26/06/ 2007), establishing rules for the implementation of risk management structures in Brazilian financial institutions regarding market risk. Those structures have to be in line with the institutions' operational nature, include clearly documented risk management strategies and policies as well as systems to identify, measure, monitor, and control market risks for each individual institution as well as for the group.

In a similar fashion, Resolution 3.721 covers the implementation and structure of a credit risk management framework for Brazilian banks which should also adequate to the nature of their business and the complexity of products and services.

Resolution 4.090 dd. 24/05/2012 covers those aspects for liquidity risk, dedicating individual sections to transparency (sec. 6) and governance (sec. 7 ff.)

Furthermore, Resolution 3.380 of 29/06/2006 provides for the implementation of an operational risk management framework, while Resolution 3.988 of 30/06/2011 covers the capital management framework required to be implemented by financial institutions active in Brazil.

2.2.14   Risk Management in Germany

Plamper (2010:126f.) refers to a *"Zero-Risk-Mentality"* in Germany and draws particular attention to the question whether and how risk management on the level of a parent company covers the risks within participated companies and whether those subsidiaries have their own risk management systems. Especially in the case of mergers and acquisitions (M&A), by which organizations end up controlling a number of culturally and sectoral diverse subsidiaries, and which at times create situations, in which a number of controlled entities depend even on more than one parent company, individual companies or groups thereof may try and succeed in pitting one parent against another (just as in real family life). In other words, risk management and control may not only fail to work in a top-down direction, but may

---

[32]http://www.kpmg.com/br/pt/estudos_analises/artigosepublicacoes/paginas /release_pesquisa_ger enciamento_de_risco.aspx

be further compromised by interference from one or several subsidiaries in an upwards direction (*"bottom up"*) leading to what Plamper describes as *"a tail wagging the dog"* or even *"a tail wagging several dogs"* (Plamper 2010:127).

Also, following a merger or an acquisition, companies may succumb to the temptation of thinking that risk is now being shared or diversified rather than acknowledging that several layers may add to the overall organizational risk which has to be managed in a structured way (cfr. Plamper 2010:127; Weisman 2013). Another incentive beyond the size increase of the acquisitive company might be managers' remuneraton. As Abell et al. (1994) found, remuneration of the top directors increases *"over and above what one would expect because of the growth in 'size'"*.

Ladipo et al. (2008:45) found that risk management is not deeply embedded in the organization, which has been labeled as *"a clear corporate governance weakness"* by Kirkpatrick (2009:78).

Ladipo and Nestor (2009:12) summarized their findings by stating that *"most of the banks in our peer group were models of "best practice" in so far as they had established a central risk management function—responsible for all the bank's principal risks—headed by a chief risk officer whose direct reports were "embedded" within, but independent of, individual lines of business. Many of these banks subsequently discovered that the independence of the risk management function was not the critical issue. What ultimately proved more important was the degree of authority and cultural standing possessed by the risk functions within their organizations and the extent to which information on risks was shared across different business areas"*.

2.2.15 Conclusions

Finance theory has contributed a great deal to the advancement of risk management by developing ever more testable and practically relevant theories and tools, as well as portfolio theory in general. Particularly for hedging mechanisms and insurance applications, these are extremely helpful as they allow to quantify a risk-return relationship which is essential to decision-making as to whether or not entering a market or transactions as well as for adequately pricing the calculated risk. Nonetheless, a main element of risk assessment depends on the *"correct"* estimation of probabilities which these tools can support, but they do not seem to be able to replace human experience and judgement (yet).

"Both financial and non-financial companies face a similar range of risks that need to be managed including operational, strategic and market risks. However, for financial companies the volatility of risk tends to be greater requiring even more efforts by them to manage risks." This assessment by the OECD (2009:8f.) underlines the particular importance of risk management within financial institutions but at the same time implies that the common focus on credit risk management may be

dangerous as *all* material risk factors[33]—including, for instance, reputational risks—need to be taken care of and managed in line with the firm's risk appetite and the resulting risk strategy.

2.3 Governance, Risk Management, and Compliance

2.3.1 Corporate Governance and Risk Management

As we have seen above, *"Corporate governance is the system by which companies are directed and controlled."* (Cadbury 1992:chapter 2.5)

We have also learned that risk management consists, in essence, of the identification and mitigation of risks.

Still we struggle to find a clear and universal link and hierarchy between those two concepts. Van der Oort shows that link when he states that *"[i]n business, corporate governance is often equated with proxy voting, shareholder rights, and board directors' oversight duties. But its fundamental purpose is to ensure that an organization is effectively directed and controlled, which is a significant undertaking (to put it mildly). Being 'in control' means that all risks to the success of the business have been properly identified and mitigated by management."* (Van der Oort 2013)

Adiloglu and Vuran (2012:554) demand, as item 14 of their 27-item Financial Information Transparency Check-List, *"Detailed explanation about the foreseeable **risk factors** regarding future operations"* (our emphasis).

In summary, risk management is about the risk/return balance, while corporate governance is to establish a system of checks and balances. As such, we may say that the common denominator is *"balance"* (cfr. GARP[34]).

As we have seen before, risk management is mostly being regarded as a less important part of corporate governance or it is being neglected altogether when discussing corporate governance. Mostly it is even interpreted as credit risk management and thus immediately and exclusively associated with financial institutions.

We have demonstrated however, that risk management is not only an important part of corporate governance, but also that it goes far beyond the specific area of credit risk management, including effectively all areas of economic activity as they are all exposed to both general and specific risks.

Following the financial crisis and the apparent shortcomings in risk management practices, the Institute of International Finance (IIF), which was founded in 1982, established a Task Force on Risk Governance in order to continue the Institute's work in this area.

---

[33]Risk factors differ by work area, geography, and over time. An extensive list of risk factors regarding mergers and acquisitions was presented by Nwogugu (2005:23 ff.).

[34]http://www.garp.org/media/991488/theroleofriskgovernanceineffectiveriskmanagement_tunji_ad esida_071312.pdf

2.3.2 Risk Governance

"The concept of risk governance comprises a broad picture of risk: not only does it include what has been termed 'risk management' or 'risk analysis', it also looks at how risk-related decision-making unfolds when a range of actors is involved, requiring co-ordination and possibly reconciliation between a profusion of roles, perspectives, goals and activities."
(Renn 2005:11)

The 2012 IIF Report (p. 1 ff.) on Governance for Strengthened Risk Management identifies the following structure for what is known as *"Risk Governance":*

1. Risk Culture,

   a. Embedding Risk Culture
   b. Conducting Risk Assessments
   c. Implementing a Risk Education Program
   d. Aligning Compensation

2. Risk Appetite,

   a. Linking Risk Appetite to the Planning Process
   b. Cascading Risk Appetite
   c. Developing Risk Metrics

3. Role of the Board and Board Risk Committees,

   a. Strengthening Risk Governance Committees
   b. Interaction of Board Risk Committees
   c. Board Risk Reporting
   d. Stress Test Results
   e. Conducting Board Self-Evaluations

4. Role of the Chief Risk Officer (CRO)

   a. Ownership of Risk

Another important aspect of risk governance is accountability. *"Ownership of risk by the business and ensuring its accountability for risk are among the greatest challenges in risk governance. The risk function has an important orchestration role, which includes playing a leading role in establishing the risk appetite and the risk management frameworks, as well as monitoring and aggregating risk. However, neither the risk function nor the CRO "owns" risk, nor can either be involved in policing every risk decision made throughout the organization. Ownership and accountability for risk ultimately lies with the front-line business."* (IIF 2012:37)

According to the IIF (2012:37) report, there are three "lines of defense":

- Line management
- Risk management
- Internal audit

"Ultimately, aligning the firm's risk governance structure with its broader corporate governance framework and strategy will make for a more robust and lasting improvement in risk management." (IIF 2012:42)

"In many cases, quantitative limits will not be sufficient if the metrics used do not cover all risks, especially such non-financial risks as reputational or legal risk." (IIF 2012:2)

Such *"non-financial risks"* may however have severe financial consequences up to the ultimate failure of a company due to its harmed reputation, for instance.

The reputational risk in particular showcases the relevance of an adequate *"risk culture"* to be implemented in each organization in order to instill in each employee a sense for its meaning and a framework in which they ultimately can answer the question *"what is the right behavior/measure/decision to be adapted now in such a case?"* Once this question can be answered by the employees, the firm's risk culture has properly been integrated into—rather than imposed onto—the structure. This, however, must not be seen as a completed task, but rather the beginning of a new period during which this successfully implemented risk culture must be nurtured and grown because else it might very quickly *"fade away"* due to changes in leadership, the economic situation, etc. (IIF 2012:1)

"Regardless of the committee structure chosen, as noted in the Walker report (Walker, David, A Review of Corporate Governance in UK Banks and other Financial Industry Entities—Final Recommendations, November 2009), it is important that the whole Board is ultimately responsible and accountable for risk governance.

It is worth noting that governance committee structure, both at the Board level and at the executive management level, is an area that shows the widest variation across different financial institutions. In many cases, this is due to varying regulatory requirements in different jurisdictions, which in some cases mandate specific committees and membership structures and obligations. It is also due, appropriately, to significant differences in the size, complexity, and cultures of firms— smaller, less-complex financial institutions do not need the same governance processes that a very large international organization requires. Another key factor is differences in legal regimes, in which directors of subsidiary Boards in some countries face varying degrees of personal liability, and therefore have a much stronger interest in risk governance at the local level." (IIF 2012:26)

2.3.3 Compliance

Having discussed Governance and Risk Management, a few words should be spent on the topic of Compliance, the third area in the often-used acronym GRC (Governance, Risk (Management) and Compliance). (Cfr. Standke 2010) Compliance means the following of external or self-set rules; many of them are the output of risk management initiatives. One example would be the four-eyes-principle which requires two or more persons or entities who are not directly dependent one from another, to take or formalize a decision, or execute a transaction. (Plamper 2010:125)

Plamper notes that excessive compliance, i.e. too many and too strict/limiting rules, can be detrimental and 'suffocate' the entity they are aimed to control. A particularly important factor for that risk is the fact that creating compliance-rules is 'cheap'. It is neither difficult nor expensive to create rules and the costs of their implementation and compliance usually materialize much later and on a different level, usually within the entity they are aimed at. According to Plamper, it was only those 'compliance costs' which brought compliance into the spotlight of economic discussion. (Plamper 2010:125)

According to data from the German Government (Normenkontrollrat 2007), compliance costs amounted to 16.4 billion Euros in companies in the Netherlands alone as of 31st December 2002, representing 3.7% of Dutch GDP. This further justifies the application of the *"Standard Cost Model"* which has been implemented in the Netherlands based on the *"Mistral"* measurement model introduced in 1993 by André Nijssen (Normenkontrollrat 2007:4), before being adopted by other countries like Denmark (bureaucracy costs as of 31st December 2001: 4.4 billion Euros p.a. or 2.2% of Danish GDP), Great Britain (60 billion Euros—3.6% of GDP) and Germany (39 billion Euros—c. 1% of GDP on the Federal level only) in the following years. In order to assess the impact of its regulation on a European basis, the European Commission (EC) created the Impact Assessment Board as an internal organ of the EC (Normenkontrollrat 2007).

Despite the fact that Compliance does not constitute one of the main aspects to be covered in this thesis, there is no denying the fact that there are close ties between Corporate Governance, Risk Management and Compliance, as shown above. Therefore, it would be short-sighted not to mention further negative or collateral effects which may be caused by compliance with external or internal rules with regards to other controls. One of those aspects has been identified by Plamper (2010:128) who fears that the nomination of Supervisory Board members by a public entity may—in the case of companies subject to codetermination—cut down the power of the people in favor of the power of employees. *"This does not lead to more democracy, as postulated by the equilibration of market and capital, but the power of the people is being (partly) substituted by the power of the employees"* (Plamper 2010:128; cfr. Plamper 2005:67 ff.). Within our scope of work, this might be particularly relevant for public banks, both in Brazil and Germany.

2.4 Financial Institutions and Banking

2.4.1 Financial Markets Today

The use of global data and communication networks enables financial markets and intermediaries to provide for basic financial services, such as transfers of payments—including foreign exchange—and equity trading non-stop, virtually without limitations by national borders, time zones, and different jurisdictions. Those financial markets include equity markets, foreign exchange, fixed-income as well as the markets for 'derivative' securities such as futures, options, and swaps or, somewhat exotic sounding combinations of those such as swaptions[35]. While those *"plain vanilla products"* are also offered and executed through financial intermediaries such as banks and insurance companies, along with stock exchanges, broker houses etc., financial intermediaries *"provide customized products and services—the kind that do not lend themselves to the standardization necessary to support a liquid market"* (Bodie and Merton 1995:3).

The complexity of those products along with the necessity to protect the final client—i.e., generally, the consumer but also public entities such as municipalities— from severe financial losses potentially caused by a lack of understanding of those products or the financial markets in general, exposes banks and insurers in a particular way to regulatory oversight.

Despite of the standardized and globalized flow of funds, trading of equities etc., the regulation of financial institutions still differs immensely across national borders. The reasons for this are manifold and include differences in the size, economic power, complexity and available—or allowed—technologies of the national econo- mies, as well as diverse socio-cultural, historical, and political backgrounds.

2.4.2 Financial Institutions

By definition of the European Central Bank (ECB), there are three groups of financial institutions:

- Monetary financial institutions—MFI
- Investment funds—IF
- Financial vehicle corporations—FVC

""Monetary financial institutions" (MFIs) are resident credit institutions as defined in European Union (EU) law, and other resident financial institutions whose business is to receive deposits and/or close substitutes for deposits from entities other than MFIs and, for their own account (at least in economic terms), to grant credits and/or make investments in securities. More precisely, Regulation ECB/2013/33 concerning the balance sheet of the monetary financial institutions sector (recast) defines MFIs as resident undertakings that belong to any of the following sectors:

Central banks, i.e. national central banks of the EU Member States and the European Central Bank;

Credit institutions as defined in Article 4(1)(1) of Regulation (EU) No 575/2013 of the European Parliament and of the Council of 26 June 2013 on prudential requirements for credit institutions and investment firms;

Other deposit-taking corporations which are

---

[35]*"An option to enter into an interest rate swap where a specified fixed rate is exchanged for floating."* (Hull, 2010:529)

1. *principally engaged in financial intermediation and whose business is to receive deposits and/or close substitutes for deposits from institutional units, not only from MFIs and for their own account, at least in economic terms, to grant loans and/or make investments in securities, or*
2. *electronic money institutions, as defined in Article 2(1) and (2) of Directive 2009/110/EC, that are principally engaged in financial intermediation in the form of issuing electronic money;*

Money market funds *(MMFs), i.e. collective investment undertakings as defined in Article 2 of Regulation ECB/2013/33."* (http://www.ecb.europa.eu/stats/money/mfi/html/index.en.html)

Brazil's Central Bank (Banco Central do Brasil—BCB) distinguishes five types or groups of financial institutions:

- Conglomerates;
- Commercial and diverse banks as well as Caixa Econômica;
- Credit Cooperatives;
- Investment banks, development banks, stock traders and money exchange insititutions, stock dealers, credit, financing and investment companies, real estate finance companies and savings and loan associations (associações de poupança e empréstimo—APEs), leasing companies, investment companies, credit companies for micro-entrepreneurs, and development agencies;
- Consortium manager/lead arrangers. (http://www.bcb.gov.br/?RELINST)

According to David F. Hastings, a financial institution is an organization with the aim of optimizing the allocation of own or third-party financial capital, obtaining a co-relation of risk, cost, and term. This organization should act in the interest of its stakeholders. The financial institution thus works by managing a difficult balance between currencies, terms and taxes for the funds received and invested, within the limits given by regulators (Hastings 2006).

While the names and definitions of several types of financial institutions vary (monetary financial institutions, credit institutions, commercial banks etc.) as per above, we shall—for the purpose of this monograph—use this term in the sense of *"credit institutions"* as defined by the European Union or as described by BCB as *"Commercial and diverse banks as well as Caixa Econômica"*, i.e. banks in the common sense of the word, including development and state banks but excluding mere investment banks, stock brokers or even central banks and insurers.

2.4.3 Banking

What is called *"bank"* in one country is not necessarily the same as a *"bank"* in another one, as differences between U.S. banks and their European 'namesakes' show. *"They also change over time."* (Bodie and Merton 1995:3)

Bodie and Merton (1995:4) describe the evolution of the financial system as an *"innovation spiral, in which organized markets and intermediaries compete with each other in a static sense and complement each other in a dynamic sense. The functional perspective views financial innovation as driving the financial system toward the goal of greater economic efficiency".* They distinguish four levels of analysis regarding financial institutions:

- System-level;
- Institution-level;
- Activity-level; and
- Product-level.

According to Bodie and Merton 1995:5), the *"single primary function"* of the financial system, as is alas that of an economic system, is the allocation of resources. They identify six *"core functions"*:

Function 1—Clearing and Settling Payments

Firstly, the provision of an infrastructure to enable settlement of payments and clearing in order to facilitate the trade in goods, services, and assets.

Function 2—Pooling Resources and Subdividing Shares

Secondly, the financial system is expected to provide ways of pooling resources and of subdividing shares in different companies, thus leading to more diversification.

Funtion 3—Transferring Resources Across Time and Space

A third function is the transfer of economic resources between industries and countries as well as through time.

Function 4—Managing Risk

The fourth function is to provide ways *"to managing uncertainty and control risk".*

Function 5—Providing Information

Furthermore, the financial system shall provide price information, thus helping to manage *"decentralized decision-making in various sectors of the economy".*

Function 6—Dealing with Incentive Problems

This sixth function is *"[t]o provide ways of dealing with the incentive problems created when one party to a transaction has information that the other party does not or when one party acts as agent for another"* (Bodie and Merton 1995:5).

While the first three functions may be described as *"providing infrastructure"*, and the fifth deals with (price) information, the other two focus on the management of two areas which are both far less easily definable: risk management and aspects of corporate governance, namely asymmetric information and agency theory.

Of particular interest for our study are those two functions.

As mentioned before, Regalli and Soana (2012:4 f.) point out that an awareness exists that financial institutions are different from other corporations and as such *"special"* for a number of reasons (cfr. 2.1.22 above).

Another, not altogether new, aspect of banking is the so called *"shadow banking"*, a practice of providing financial services without holding a banking license, and as such usually not being subject to (strict) supervision (Cfr. Cheng 2014:40 ff.).

2.5   The 2007–2009 Financial Crisis

According to Lister (2010:295 f.), the latest financial crisis was triggered by two courses of action.

Firstly, originators used low interest levels to extend loans also to lower-income families for real estate finance, thus increasing demand for housing, particularly in the lower-priced section of the market. Due to the increased demand, real estate prices increased, leading to higher bank valuations of the main collateral. The combination of higher valuations—including re-valuations increasing debt-levels of already highly indebted households—and low interest led to an ever-increasing sale of real estate finance to low-income borrowers. When the Federal Reserve increased interest rates in order to reign in on inflation, many were unable to service their debt and had to (fire-)sell their property, leading to falling prices.

Secondly, and in parallel to the developments in loan origination, credit risks became tradable by means of credit derivatives. Thus, the originators of the loans—mostly commercial banks—gained the opportunity to pass on part or all of their underwritten risk to other market participants—usually, investment banks[36] seeking high returns—thus also making room for more lending within their respective exposure limits. When interest rates rose, property prices tumbled, and borrowers became unable to service their debt, the derivatives lost most or all of their value.

As a result of this development which can be blamed on the failure of banks' pricing and risk models, financial institutions suffered significant losses and lost liquidity. A lack of liquidity and mutual trust triggered the break-down of the interbank market, leading to the insolvency of many banks (Lister 2010:295).

While the underlying reasons as described above can mainly be found in the U.S., the break-down of the interbank markets in particular affected the financial systems in almost all countries. The effects of the financial crisis between 2007 and 2009 are shown by Fig. 2.35 which illustrates the GDP growth rate for Brazil, Germany, Portugal, and the United States.

It becomes obvious that Brazil almost avoided a negative growth rate altogether, while the other countries shown suffered from a pronounced GDP reduction in 2009. Portugal, then, was the only country to fall back into negative growth rates, but also the other countries have approached the nil-line again, with only the U.S. showing a positive trend in 2012.

"The financial crisis provides an opportunity to study the dynamics of risk governance at financial institutions." (Rossi 2012a:37)

According to Rossi (2012a:37 f.), most failures of financial institutions during the latest financial crisis *"could be traced back to deficiencies in risk governance and risk management."*

---

[36]*"Banks that were driven by investment banking were much more problematic in terms of contagion and counterparty risk regardless of their balance sheet size."* (Blundell-Wignall et al. 2009:22)

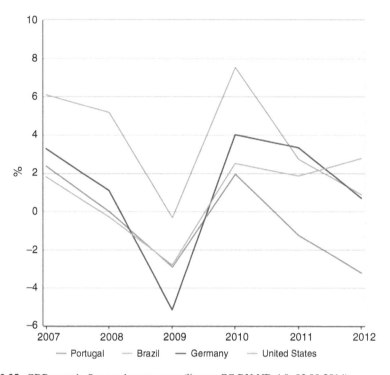

Fig. 2.35 GDP growth. Source: knoema.com (license CC BY-ND 4.0; 03.09.2014)

"There have been big shifts in corporate behavior since the '08 crisis. Companies across the U.S. are stockpiling cash and avoiding big new investments that could help rev up the economy. Both trends [...] are fueling the new proliferation of shareholder activism." (*TIME*, December 16, 2013:35)

Shareholder activism has been gaining importance in the corporate governance sphere, with interventions in the USA going up 21% from 2010 to 204 in 2011 and 2012. As per the end of August 2013, there were already 138 actions in that year. (TIME, December 16, 2013, p. 35)

Also the targets of the *"corporate raiders"*, as they were formerly called, have changed. While in the 80s and the following decade or so, poor performers were in the crosshairs of activists, the Citi report found that 57% of the campaigns waged in 2013 against S&P 1500 firms involved companies whose share prices outperformed the index. (TIME, December 16, 2013, p. 35)

Furthermore, the sheer volume of 'activist money' increased drastically. Between 2008 and 2013, the amount managed specifically by activist funds went up from $32 billion to $84 billion. During the period 2009-30/06/2013, the return of activist hedge funds averaged nearly 20% (annualized), while the S&P 500 returned 12%. (TIME, December 16, 2013:35)

Differences about the perception of the crises also become apparent in the annual reports of banks. Itaú, for instance, refers to *"Subprime"* for 2007, *"Lehman Brothers"* regarding 2008, and the *"European crisis"* for 2010/2011 (Itaú AR 2012:75), while Bradesco simply refers to *"the 2008 crisis"* (Bradesco AR 2011:12).

2.5.1 Lessons Learned from the Crisis

Overall, as Jorion (2009:923) puts it, *"this crisis has reinforced the importance of risk management"* and this *"should be driven by people, not machines."*

As another lesson learned from the financial crisis, Jorion (2009:932) mentions the use of reverse stress tests as recommended by the BCBS, which *"start from a known stress test outcome (such as breaching regulatory capital ratios, illiquidity or insolvency) and then asking what events could lead to such an outcome for the bank".*

To this, Golub and Crum (2010:22 ff.) add *"the paramount importance of liquidity"*, differentiating in line with the BCBS between *funding liquidity risk* and *market liquidity risk*.

They also find that *"market risk can change dramatically"* in a very short time and refer to a *"changing nature of market risk"* towards policy risk, requiring *"politically oriented analysts"* (Golub and Crum 2010:35 ff.).

Those authors also advocate the need for investors in securitized products to *"look past the data to the underlying behavior of the asset"* (Golub and Crum 2010:30 ff.).

Golub and Crum (2010:34 f.) also think that *"certification is useless during systemic events"*, referring to *"'certifiers' of financial products"*, such as bond insurers, auction managers and rating agencies.

The final lesson learned is that *"by the time a crisis strikes, it is too late to start preparing"* (Golub and Crum 2010:39).

2.6 Summary

As we have seen, both corporate governance and risk management are difficult to define and to break down into all their elements, which appear infinite. However, this does not have to be a bad thing. Bhimani (2009:3) states that *"[t]he lack of precise definitional characteristics endows concepts such as risk and governance with possibilities of effecting organisational changes".*

Corporate governance seems to work well on a voluntary basis, even when linked to compulsory rules for specific areas. The establishment of a remuneration and risk management committee should be contemplated where it is not yet an obligation. Proper person tests help to improve the quality of management in general so that board members serve as a good example.

Domestic finance seems to have an important impact on structures and the effectiveness of corporate governance structures. In any case, corporate governance seems to be moving more towards an integrative approach, including SCR, away from the mere Principal-Agent-Conflict.

Uncertainty is not only the main feature of risk, but it also characterizes risk: *"Perhaps it is the uncertainty around what constitutes risk which lends it the capacity to alter, define, and reshape management activities in particular ways"* (Bhimani 2009:3).

Chapter 3
Institutional Background

Changing the law on the books does not guarantee corporate governance improvement (Licht et al. 2005:230)

This chapter puts the various aspects of corporate governance, risk management, and compliance identified before in context with the reality of banking regulation and reporting, particularly in Brazil and Germany.

Properly working legal and judicial systems (for a schematic overview, refer to Fig. 3.1) are, according to Claessens and Yurtoglu (2012:6), crucial for both, corporate governance and financial markets development. Generally, the ease of contracting has been referred to above with relation to the Rule of Law, equally property rights—including shareholder rights—, the enforceability of legal rights within an acceptable timeframe, and the absence of corruption. With regards to corporate governance, specific rules aiming at increasing transparency, such as disclosure obligations, are important. Those are difficult to quantify and cannot be compared easily, as they are of a rather qualitative character. Nonetheless, even a more abstract comparison can yield significant differences between countries (Claessens and Yurtoglu 2012:6).

Generally speaking, Common Law is said to offer better protection of property and creditor rights and a swifter enforcement of claims.

Based on this categorization and the work performed by LaPorta (1996), Licht et al. (2005:250) present the *"value dimensions approach"*, studying relations between culture (Williamson's Level I) and law (Williamson's Level II) and the causal relations among institutions and economic performance. Licht et al. affirm that *"the present evidence that culture matters does not imply that law does not matter"* and likewise state that proponents of the notion *"law matters"* do not imply that there was a direct causal link between legal rules and economic performance. (Licht et al. 2005:250)

Aguilera et al. (2011:379) question a common conceptualization of governance models in a *"dichotomous world of common-law/outsider/shareholder-oriented system vs civil law/insider/stakeholder-oriented system"* and propose that many companies do not fit into one of those two models because they either belong to

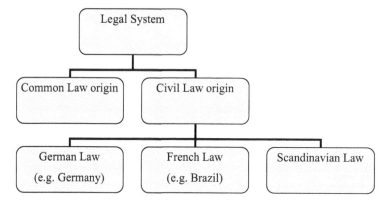

Fig. 3.1 Legal Systems

the opposite model despite of their legal environment or *"nationality"*, combine aspects of both categories, or constitute a category of their own, as firms in emerging markets (Cfr. also Bordean and Pop 2012:20; FMT 1995:13).

They further state that the three governance characteristics legal system, ownership, and board of directors are interdependent (Aguilera et al. 2011:380).

Licht et al. (2005:253) demonstrate that *"corporate governance laws relate systematically to the prevailing culture. Consistent relations between cultural emphases and the degree of formalism in civil procedure laws also emerge."*

Access to equity markets is quite low in Brazil where only 3–4% of firms participate in those markets, compared with 12–16% in China and India or c. 8% in Germany. Access to international capital markets for long-term finance is restricted to larger companies, according to Estrin and Prevezer (2010:52) who blame *"the underdeveloped nature of capital markets as much as poor governance structures"*.

But even on a national level, larger corporations in older industries have much better access to bank finance as local banks in Brazil tend to provide small and medium-sized companies or those in new markets with far lower volumes of credit granted, higher interest rates, and stricter requests for guarantees (Cfr. Campos and Iootty 2007). According to a World Bank report (2003), over 50% of Brazilian companies do not even apply for bank loans due to complex requirements and procedures, compared with 32% in China and 16% in India (Estrin and Prevezer 2010:52).

Before taking a closer look at both Brazilian and German banking regulation, one should bear in mind that on 1st April 2014, the Dodd-Frank-Act came into full effect with a transition period until 21st June 2015 for a number of rules.

The Federal Reserve promulgated so-called *"Regulation VV"* under Section 13 of the Bank Holding Company Act of 1956, which implements what is popularly known as the *"Volcker Rule"* (section 619 of the Dodd–Frank Wall Street Reform and Consumer Protection Act of 2010). Regulation VV generally prohibits *"banking entities"* from sponsoring and/or acquiring (as principal) or retaining an *"ownership interest"* in, *"covered funds."* (12 CFR § 248.10 (a) (1)). Affected institutions have until July 21, 2015 to conform their activities and investments to the rule.

The prohibition generally applies to *"banking entities."* This term includes any company treated as a bank holding company under the International Banking Act of 1978, along with any affiliates of such a company (12 CFR § 248.2 (c) (1)).

The term *"covered fund"* is defined to include, among other things, an issuer that would be an investment company, as defined in the Investment Company Act of 1940.

This rule aims at limiting banks' participation in such "covered funds", thus limiting their ability to invest in what are regarded as risky investments.

3.1 Banking Regulation

The present chapter aims at identifying and understanding the differences between banking regulation in Brazil on the one hand and in Germany on the other.

3.1.1 Basel Committee on Banking Supervision

The Basel Committee on Banking Supervision, part of the Bank for International Settlements (BIS)—a *"bank for central banks"* (http://www.bis.org/about/index.htm)—*"provides a forum for regular cooperation on banking supervisory matters. Its objective is to enhance understanding of key supervisory issues and improve the quality of banking supervision worldwide."* (www.bis.org./bcbs/)

The Committee's members come from many countries, including Brazil and Germany.

The original Basel III rules date back to 2010 but have been subject to several reviews ever since. While this set of rules establishes capital requirements as its predecessors, Basel I (1988) and II (2008), Basel III introduced a minimum leverage ratio as well as two liquidity-related ratios, the Liquidity Coverage Ratio and the Net Stable Funding Ratio. As such, Basel III goes beyond the stipulations of Basel I and II[1], as it has a different focus: While the early versions dealt primarily with loan loss reserves, Basel III is concerned mainly with the avoidance of and preparation for a "run on the bank". The rules introduced by Basel III will become effective in a staggered form and the implementation phases shall end by 2019.

---

[1] *"[T]he failure of Basel II to address the issue of systemic risk and the role of particular classes of asset price inflation associated with such risk means that the opportunity to push these benefits further has been missed."* (Docherty 2008:104)

According to Docherty (2008:84), the "*logic of bank regulation is to impose restrictions on banks designed to limit this risk-taking behavior in the presence of safety net availability and to reduce the general likelihood that losses will emerge in the first place*".

Bengtsson (2012) found that the Basel III accord is "*relatively less beneficial for large international banks and the traditional BCBS member countries. This suggests that a tilting of power in favor of emerging markets and publicly accountable authorities has occurred in the political economy of banking regulation and the international financial architecture*". In his 2013 version of that article, however, Bengtsson (2013) states that "*while BCBS still seem[s] to develop **standards that favor their traditional member countries, large international banks no longer seem as clearly favored** by its latest capital accord. And while private actors still seem to dominate the exertion of influence over the committee, the governance structure of BCBS has changed towards a more transparent and politically account-able set-up*" (own emphasis).

The Basel Committee on Banking Supervision (BCBS) also published guidelines to enhance corporate governance for banking organizations, with the following principles:

- Principle 1: Board qualifications, capabilities and responsibilities
- Principle 2: Board's role regarding the bank's strategic objectives and corporate values
- Principle 3: Lines of responsibility and accountability
- Principle 4: Ensuring oversight by senior management
- Principle 5: Auditors and internal control functions
- Principle 6: Board and key executive compensation
- Principle 7: Transparent governance
- Principle 8: *"Know your operational structure"*

(BCBS 2006:6 ff.)

As the international regulatory framework for banks, Basel III establishes capital requirements for banks (June 2011) as well as for liquidity (January 2013), cfr. Table 3.1.

"*"Basel III" is a comprehensive set of reform measures, developed by the Basel Committee on Banking Supervision, to strengthen the regulation, supervision and risk management of the banking sector. These measures aim to:*

- *improve the banking sector's ability to absorb shocks arising from financial and economic stress, whatever the source*
- *improve risk management and governance*
- *strengthen banks' transparency and disclosures.*

The reforms target:

- *bank-level, or microprudential, regulation, which will help raise the resilience of individual banking institutions to periods of stress.*

Table 3.1 Basel III phase-in arrangements

(All dates are as of 1 January)

Phases		2013	2014	2015	2016	2017	2018	**2019**
Capital	Leverage Ratio		Parallel run 1 Jan 2013 – 1 Jan 2017 Disclosure starts 1 Jan 2015				Migration to Pillar 1	
	Minimum Common Equity Capital Ratio	3.5%	4.0%		4.5%			4.5%
	Capital Conservation Buffer				0.625%	1.25%	1.875%	2.5%
	Minimum common equity plus capital conservation buffer	3.5%	4.0%	4.5%	5.125%	5.75%	6.375%	7.0%
	Phase-in of deductions from CET1*		20%	40%	60%	80%	100%	100%
	Minimum Tier 1 Capital	4.5%	5.5%		6.0%			6.0%
	Minimum Total Capital			8.0%				8.0%
	Minimum Total Capital plus conservation buffer		8.0%		8.625%	9.25%	9.875%	10.5%
	Capital instruments that no longer qualify as non-core Tier 1 capital or Tier 2 capital		Phased out over 10 year horizon beginning 2013					
Liquidity	Liquidity coverage ratio – minimum requirement			60%	70%	80%	90%	100%
	Net stable funding ratio							Introduce minimum standard

* Including amounts exceeding the limit for deferred tax assets (DTAs), mortgage servicing rights (MSRs) and financials
– – transition periods

Source: BIS.org (a)

- *macroprudential, system wide risks that can build up across the banking sector as well as the procyclical amplification of these risks over time.*

  These two approaches to supervision are complementary as greater resilience at the individual bank level reduces the risk of system wide shocks." (http://www.bis.org/bcbs/basel3.htm)

3.1.2 Banking Regulation in Brazil

According to World Bank data, countries such as Brazil, Ecuador, Uruguay and Venezuela have very weak disclosure requirements, while other emerging market countries such as Malaysia, Thailand and South Africa which compare very well with those of advanced economies (Claessens and Yurtoglu 2012:7).

The main sources of banking regulation in Brazil are Acts from the 1960's, including *Lei* 4.595 (*Lei do Sistema Financeiro Nacional*—National Financial System Act) of 31/12/1964 with its subsequent changes and accompanying legislation.

That code covers the main legal topics of banking activity in Brazil and establishes that the Brazilian financial system is mainly made up of the following entities:

1. Conselho Monetário Nacional (National Monetary Council);
2. Banco Central do Brasil (Brazilian Central Bank);
3. Banco do Brasil S.A.;
4. Banco Nacinoal de Desenvolvimento Econômico e Social (BNDES), the National Bank for Economic and Social Development;
5. Other financial institutions, both private and public.

According to section 3 of *Lei* 4.595, the National Monetary Council is the main regulatory body for banking activities in Brazil. Its regulations, which have a generic nature, are called *Resoluções* (Resolutions), more specific rules are issued by the BCB as *Circulares* (Circulars).

In addition, specific legislation has been enacted in order to fight financial crimes, such as *Lei* 7.492 dd. 16/06/1986 (*Lei do Colarinho Branco/Crimes Financeiros*— White Collar/Financial Crimes Act) and *Lei* 9.613 (*Lei da "Lavagem" de Dinheiro*—Money "Laundry" Act) of 03/03/1998.

In order to be allowed to operate in Brazil, financial institutions have to receive approval from the Cental Bank of Brazil and mostly need to be incorporated as *Sociedades Anônimas*. They may not lend more than 25% of their adjusted shareholders' equity to any one person or group of companies (Resolution 2.844 dd. 29/06/2001), provide loans to shareholders who hold more than 10% of their equity, nor to their directors and officers or their family, or companies held by those persons ($> 10\%$). Banks in Brazil are subject to further restrictions, such as on real estate investments (*Lei* 4.595, section 35 II), own investments ($> 50\%$ of equity according to Resolution 2.283 dd. 05/06/1996, as amended in 2002) and repotransactions. They must maintain transactions confidential, comply with at least bi-annual reporting requirements and reserve requirements.

Regarding capital adequacy requirements, Resolution 2.099 dd. 17/08/1994 requires financial institutions in Brazil to abide by the rules on capital adequacy set by the Basel Committee for Banking Supervision (cfr. 3.1.1 above). (*Global Legal Insights*[2])

Regarding the remuneration of board members of financial institutions, rules were introduced by Resolution n° 3,921, which establishes the requirement to establish and maintain a remuneration committee from 2012 onwards (sec. 11 ff.) and lays out principles of a remuneration policies with the following limits:

1. At least 50% of variable remuneration is to be paid out in stock or equivalent, which have to be accounted for at fair value (sec. 6);

---

[2]http://www.globallegalinsights.com/practice-areas/banking-and-finance/banking-regulation-1st-ed/brazil

2. Payment of at least 40% of variable remuneration has to be deferred in time by at least 3 years, and subject to adjustment of unpaid tranches if the entity's earnings decrease significantly over that period (sec. 7);
3. Contracts with clauses exceeding those rules have to be compatible with "value creation and risk management over the long-term" (sec. 8);
4. No minimum bonus guarantees shall be given except for special circumstances like the transfer of a board member to another business unit or city, and in any case should be limited to 1 year after the occurrence of the relevant fact (sec. 9).

3.1.3 Banking Regulation in Germany/Europe

In preparation of its taking on the role of a supervisory body for major European banks, the European Central Bank has been carrying out, during 2014, an evaluation of important banks. The assessment consists of three elements: (i) a supervisory risk assessment to review, quantitatively and qualitatively, key risks, including liquidity, leverage and funding; (ii) an asset quality review (AQR) to enhance the transparency of bank exposures by reviewing the quality of banks' assets, including the adequacy of asset and collateral valuation and related provisions; and (iii) a stress test to examine the resilience of banks' balance sheet to stress scenarios. (ECB press release of 23 October 2013: *"ECB starts comprehensive assessment in advance of supervisory role"*, http://www.ecb.europa.eu/press/pr/date/2013/html/pr131023.en.html)

The German Financial Reporting Reform Act (*"Bilanzreformgesetz"*) of 2006 lead to detailed sustainability reporting in annual reports (cfr. Gebauer et al. 2008:15) which now address a wide range of different stakeholders such as clients, investors, employees, analysts and also neighbors of their production plants etc. (Goldmann et al. 2010:189).

On October 28, 2013, senior board member of the European Central Bank, Benoit Coeure, said the Euro Area was now out of the immediate *"danger zone"* but added that it risked a Japanese-style stagnation unless its banking sector was cleaned up.

"In one direction lies the Japanese experience, and in the other direction that of emerging East Asia," the Frenchman said. *"Europe has emerged from the danger zone. It's time for us to get our act together, to reform and to grow."* (As reported by GARP in: Put the banks in order, ECB board member tells euro zone http://www.garp.org/risk-news-and-resources/risk-headlines/story.aspx?newsid=67894&utm_source=informz&utm_medium=email&utm_campaign=newsletter)

As is the case with Japan, financial institutions in Germany control important parts of the corporate sector (La Porta et al. 1998; Claessens et al. 2000; Faccio and Lang 2002; Claessens and Yurtoglu 2012).

3.2   Corporate Governance Frameworks

While in most countries, corporate governance rules seem to have been improved and underlying regulations tightened, there also are exceptions to that rule. For instance, it became known in 2013 that Honk Kong authorities plan to ease identification rules for Directors by removing the necessity to register their home address and by allowing to hide several digits of the Honk Kong identity-card (HKID), which *"since many local names are similar, [. . .] serves as the only practical unique identifier available"* (*The Economist*, March 2nd 2013, p. 63). While real concerns regarding privacy may be one (legitimate) reason (cfr. a document issued on December 5th, 2013 by the Hong Kong Office of the Privacy Commissioner of Personal Data, http://www.pcpd.org.hk/english/infocentre/files/annex20131205_e. pdf), many fear that this measure would primarily help to disguise illegitimate business, given that the cross-referencing of HKID numbers has helped to build trust and enforce legitimate claims (*The Economist*, March 2nd 2013:63 f.).

3.2.1   Global Reporting Initiative (GRI)

The Global Reporting Initiative (GRI)[3], founded in Boston in 1997 as a union of experts, institutions, and rating agencies developed a standard for sustainability reporting which states that transparency in companies shall be increased by better communication in order to improve management, governance, and communication with their stakeholders. Sustainability reporting shall provide for an adequate and balanced presentation of sustainable action by a company, cover all aspects which are relevant for the stakeholders, and increase comparability (Goldmann et al. 2010:189).

A majority of the banks under analysis in this thesis use the GRI Reporting Principles and Standard Disclosures for their reporting system (Banco do Brasil, BNDES, Bradesco, Commerzbank, Itaú, DZ Bank).

The process for defining reporting content under GRI is illustrated by Fig. 3.2.

As always with reporting, the quality of the report itself may not always fully reflect the quality of the underlying reality. However, researchers assume that there is a positive link between a good report and a strong performance, while a weak report is not necessarily a sign of weak performance (Goldmann et al. 2010:189).

For the eighth time, business association *future e.V.* and the Institute for Ecologic Business Research (IÖW) have analyzed the sustainability reports of the 150 top German companies in 2011 (http://www.ranking-nachhaltigkeitsberichte.de/). Among the top 10, there is only one (public) bank, Landesbank Baden-Württemberg

---

[3]https://www.globalreporting.org/Pages/default.aspx

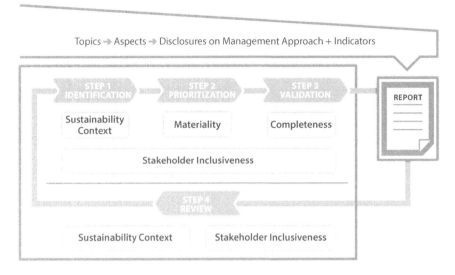

Fig. 3.2 Defining material aspects and boundaries—process overview. Source: GRI (2013:90)

(LBBW), private banks follow on rank 20 (HypoVereinsbank), and 22 (Commerzbank); and DZ Bank occupies rank 30. Kirchhoff's "Good Company Raking 2013" of the 70 largest European corporations ranks Deutsche Bank at 34 and Commerzbank at 41 out of the top 70, while the financial industry as one of 11 sectors ranks 9th, only followed by commodities and energy. That study takes into account several criteria related to stakeholders, clients, supply-chain, and society. (Kirchhoff 2013:11 ff.)

3.2.2 Corporate Governance Rules in Brazil

3.2.2.1 Brazilian Corporate Governance Code

For 15 years now, the *Instituto Brasileiro de Governança Corporativa* (IBGC) has been *"disseminating the best practices"*, currently with an *"initial public audience"* by means of an online survey to prepare the fifth edition of its *"Code of Best Practice of Corporate Governance"* (*"Código das Melhores Práticas de Governança Corporativa"*—BCGC) going on until 31st August, 2014 (https://pt.surveymonkey.com/s/23R5XR5).

The current, 4th version of the BCGC was published in 2009, following editions since 1999. It is divided into six chapters, excluding a preface consisting of foreword, introductions, and concept and principles of corporate governance.

Part 1 covers *"Ownership"*, i.e. shareholder-related issues, such as *"one share = one vote"*, shareholders' meetings, transfer of control, anti-takeover mechanisms (*"poison pills"*[4], for instance), but also a *"Family Council"* for family organizations, *"a group formed to discuss family issues and the alignment of its members' expectations with regard to the organization"*. The main tasks of such a Family Council would be:

- *"Setting boundaries between family interests and business interests;*
- *Preserving family values (history, culture and shared vision);*
- *Defining and agreeing on standards for asset protection, growth, diversification and management of securities and real property;*
- *Creating mechanisms (e.g.: an equity fund) for the purchase of other partners' holdings in case they leave the organization;*
- *Succession planning, transfer of property and inheritance;*
- *Viewing the organization as a uniting and family continuity factor;*
- *Preparing family members to succeed in the organization, considering their willingness and aptness, their professional future, and continuing education; and*
- *Defining rules for the appointment of members who will make up the Board of Directors"*. (BCGC 2009:27 f.)

Part 2, then, deals with the Board of Directors, its composition and mission, details such as directors' qualifications, age, term of office (max. 2 year terms) and time avilability, limiting the service on other boards and committees to one for senior executives, two for the CEO and internal Directors, up to three board memberships for the Chairman and a maximum of five for external and/or independent Directors in total, and a CEO or Chairman should not chair the board of another (unrelated) organization. The BCGC is based on a one-tier board structure, requesting that *"the positions of Chairman and CEO should not be held by the same person"* (BCGC 2009:34 f.), and adding that a *"clear separation of roles between the two positions and clear power and action limits are of fundamental importance"*. (BCGC 2009:49)

Whereas the BCGC only mentions a Supervisory Board once (regarding other functions of Board members), it describes an Advisory Board, *"preferably made up of independent members"*, as *"good practice, particularly for organizations taking the first steps in the adoption of good practices of corporate governance. It allows independent members to contribute to the organization and gradually improve its corporate governance."* (BCGC 2009:43).

The Brazilian Code clarifies that board members *"have their duties to the organization, and therefore to all shareholders. The Board is, therefore, bound to none"*. (BCGC 2009:32)

---

[4]For details on poison pills, please refer to Monks (2004:200 ff.).

The recommended number of board members is between five and eleven, whereas the *"existence of alternate Directors is not a good corporate governance practice, and should be avoided"*, arguing that *"[t]he alternates for occasional absences are not sufficiently familiar with the organization's issues"*. (BCGC 2009:36)

The Board's role is being described by the BCGC *"to be the link between shareholders and Management, to guide and oversee Management and its relationship with other stakeholders"* (BCGC 2009:29) and its responsibilities under section 2.3, including three sub-sections:

- 2.3.1 Corporate risk management;
- 2.3.2 Sustainability;
- 2.3.3 Spokesperson policy.

The responsibilities include the *"discussion, approval, and monitoring of decisions involving [. . .] [r]isk appetite and tolerance (risk profile)"*.

The BCGC understands risk profile as the *"conjunction"* of risk appetite and risk tolerance regarding the *"exposure to risk the organization is willing to accept"* and defines risk appetite as *"the level of risk the organization can accept while seeking and attaining its mission/vision (an activity which is more associated to a prior analysis of risks)"*. Risk tolerance is being described as *"the acceptable level of variability in attaining defined targets and objectives (more associated to the monitoring of risks)"*. (BCGC 2009:30)

The BCGC does not set a fixed minimum for the number of independent directors, stating solely that this depends *"on the level of maturity of the organization, its life cycle, and its characteristics"*. The code recommends however *"that the majority of members be independent, hired through formal processes, and with a well-defined scope of work and qualifications"*. (BCGC 2009:37)

Section 2.28 describes committees of the board of directors, naming a few as example, such as Audit, Human Resources/Compensation, Governance, Finance, and Sustainability Committees.

Part 3 of the BCGC deals with Management, particularly the CEO's role of *"managing the organization and coordinating Management"* (BCGC 2009:54). It establishes rules for Officers' nomination and their personal responsibility as well as the organization's relationship with stakeholders, defined by the Brazilian Code as *"individuals or entities that assume some kind of direct or indirect risk related to the organization's activities"* and the obedience of international standards in section 3.5.1. (BCGC 2009:54 f.)

Regarding management compensation (section 3.9), the BCGC establishes that this *"should be linked to results, with short and longterm goals, clearly and objectively associated to the creation of economic value for the organization"*, whereas the incentive structure should include a system of *"checks and balances"* (cfr. above 2.1.3) and requires the disclosure of *"all kinds of compensation payments made to officers"*, for variable compensation namely:

- *"Variable compensation mechanisms (% profit, bonuses, stock, stock options, etc.);*
- *The performance indicators/metrics used in the variable compensation program;*
- *Target award levels (paid for attaining 100% of the targets);*
- *The main features of any stock option plan (eligibility, strike price, vesting period and exercise period, standards to define the number of options, granting frequency, maximum dilution, annual dilution, etc.);*
- *The description of the benefits offered;*
- *The potential and actually paid mix (percentage) of total compensation, i.e., how much each part (fixed, variable, benefits, and share plans) represents of the total"* (BCGC 2009:56 f.)

Having already described the audit committee in quite some detail under its section 2.30, the Brazilian Code dedicates its Part 4 to *"Independent Auditing"* and Part 5 to the *"Fiscal Council"*. (BCGC 2009:62 ff.)

Part 6, finally, addresses a corporation's *"Conduct and Conflict of Interest"*, establishing that *"every organization should have a Code of Conduct binding administrators and employees. [...] The Code [of Conduct] should accurately reflect the company's culture and state, as clearly as possible, the principles on which it is based. It should also implement ways to complain or report problems of an ethical nature (complaints channel, ombudsman)"*. (BCGC 2009:66) Such a code of conduct should deal with a list of issues, including *"questionable payments made or received"*, *"nepotism"*, *"exploitation of adult or child labor"* or *"use of alcohol and drugs"*, to name but a few. (BCGC 2009:66 f.)

The chapter about conflicts of interest (section 6.2 of the BCGC) includes related party transactions and establishes the temporary removal of the conflicted person, to be noted in the meeting minutes. (BCGC 2009:68 f.) Part 6 also covers capital markets related issues such as the use of insider information and a stock trading policy, made mandatory by the Brazilian Code, as well as information disclosure (*"transparency"*), contributions and donations, concluded by the requirement to establish a policy *"to prevent and fight illicit acts"*. (BCGC 2009:70 f.)

3.2.2.2   Brazilian Rules on Corporate Governance

Corporate governance legislation in Brazil is based on Acts dating back to the 1960s and 1970s, as for example *Lei* 4.728 (*Lei do Mercado de Capitais*—Capital Market Act) dated 14/07/1965, and *Lei* 6.385 of 07/12/1976 (*Lei do Mercado de Valores Mobiliários*—Stock Market Act) with their respective amendments over time and ancilliary legislation.

In 2007, an interministerial commission on corporate governance was established by Decree 6.021 (22/01/2007), in order to adopt and promote corporate governance best practices in State holdings and companies, thus also applying to State banks such as Caixa Econômica Federal. For further examples of Brazilian regulation, cfr. 3.1.2 above.

3.2.3 Corporate Governance Rules in Germany

3.2.3.1 German Stock Companies Act (*Aktiengesetz*—AktG)

The German Stock Companies Act (AktG) codifies the rules for German corporations in as far as they are not subject to other legislation, such as the Limited Liability Company Act (GmbHG).

Section 161 AktG is entitled *"Declaration on the Corporate Governance Code"* and requires, in its first paragraph, Management Board and Supervisory Board to declare complinace with the provisions of the GCGC or name and explain any deviation.

Paragraph 2 requires the declaration's permanent publication on the company's internet site.

Section 120 par. 4 AktG allows for board managers' compensation system to be approved by the general assembly, but this does not constitute rights or obligations, nor does it interfere with the Supervisory Board's authority and its responsibilities.

The Management Board's right to exercise their discretion in managing the company (*"on their own authority"*) according to section 76 par. 1 AktG is limited, in accordance with case law, to the interest of the company.

Section 91 II AktG stipulates that the managing board has to take adequate measures—especially by establishing systems of supervision—in order to ensure that developments which might put the continuity of the corporation at risk be identified at an early stage (Cfr. 2.2.7 above).

Drennan and Beck (2001:1) note (primarily for the UK) that the "gradual expansion of the duties of managers and boards [...] has not been accompanied by the provision of detailed guidelines, leaving it up to individual companies to decide how to manage strategic, operational and reputational risks".

3.2.3.2 German Commercial Act (*Handelsgesetzbuch*—HGB)

Section 289a HGB (*Handelsgesetzbuch*/German Commercial Act) requires listed companies in Germany to make declarations on their corporate governance (*"Unternehmensführung"*), naming those practices which exceed the legal minimum requirements as well as indications as to where they are publicly available. Furthermore, they have to describe the working practices of management board and supervisory board as well as the composition of their committees. A remittance to the internet publication of such data is also accepted. Another obligation of section 289a HGB is the declaration in accordance to section 161 AktG.

Since 2006, there is a specific CSR reporting obligation for the largest companies in Germany (sections 289 (par. 3), 315 HGB).

3.2.3.3   KAGB and AIFM

On 22nd July 2013, the new German Investment Law (*Kapitalanlagegesetzbuch—* KAGB) came into force, regulating the closed-end fund industry in unprecedented depth and breadth. This law implements fund manager regulations (*"Erlaubnispflicht für Manager"*) in sections 17 ff., specific product regulations as well as detailed rules for sales, prospectus (*"Prospektpflichten"*) and valuations.

Apart from those product-related rules, the KAGB closes in on the very organization of the issuing entities which will now have to maintain their own equity base and comply with strict rules on issues as sensitive as the top management and risk management.

But not only the fund managers will have to adopt new organizational structures: the same will be true for the regulating entity, the German banking supervisory board (*"Bundesanstalt für Finanzdienstleistungsaufsicht"*—BaFin). BaFin will have to review their own structures as well as the communication with the supervised entities, in accordance with the specific rules of the law, given that a number of topics have been regulated in detail already. For those cases in which the law is not that specific, BaFin has already been issuing decrees (*"Verordnungen"*) in order to limit the scope for interpretation and help define processes which still need to be tested. (Mario Caroli, *"Den Dialog mit der Bafin suchen"*, in: FAZ:41, 11/10/2013)

Both, AIFM and KAGB, aim at avoiding conflicts of interest by implementing organizational and administrative processes. Furthermore, a special focus rests on risk management and liquidity management, implying *"that the risk management function be separated from the operative areas of the portfolio in functional and hierarchical terms"*.

Apart from this, remuneration not only of the top management, but also of employees who do have a significant influence on the risk profile of the portfolio, shall be in line with a *"solid risk management"*, thus avoiding the underwriting of excessive risk.

The banking sector has created working panels and groups coordinating the work of the banking sector in agreeing on processes and measures with BaFin. (Mario Caroli, *"Den Dialog mit der Bafin suchen"*, in: FAZ:41, 11/10/2013)

3.2.3.4   KonTraG and Other Relevant Legislation

The *Gesetz zur Kontrolle und Transparenz im Unternehmensbereich* (KonTraG 1998), an Act regarding control and transparency in the corporate sphere, establishes a personal liability for board members regarding their decisions and actions in as far as they lead to (significant) losses for the company. This appears to be a sensible way to mitigate the principal-agent-conflict as directors who are usually not significant shareholders in the corporation they preside are thus potentially feeling a direct link between their mismanagement and their personal financial situation. Reportedly, around 5000 cases against former managers were pending in Germany in the first semester of 2014.

The flip-side of this approach however is the consequence that managers demand D&O insurances and/or higher remuneration for taking such risks and exposing their personal wealth to potential claims by shareholders in an unforeseeable future, thus increasing the costs for the corporation they are supposed to manage in a cost-conscious way.

Other relevant norms can be found in the TransPuG (*Gesetz zur weiteren Reform des Aktien- und Bilanzrechts, zur Transparenz und Publizität*—Act for further reform of the stock- and accounting rules, for transparency and publicity) of 2002, the BilReG (*Bilanzrechtsreformgesetz*—Act for the reform of accounting laws, 2004) and the VorstOG (*Vorstandsvergütungs-Offenlegungsgesetz*—Act regarding the disclosure of management board's compensation, 2005) as well as the BilMoG (*Bilanzmodernisierungsgesetz*—Act regarding the modernization of accounting rules) of 2009, also regarding internal control systems (ICS).

3.2.3.5 German Corporate Governance Code

The German Corporate Governance Code (GCGC) was last amended on May 13, 2013 and is subject to an annual review and shall be amended, if necessary, to reflect national and international developments in the area of corporate governance. (GCGC 2013:2)

"The German Corporate Governance Code (the "Code") presents essential statutory regulations for the management and supervision (governance) of German listed companies and contains internationally and nationally recognized standards for good and responsible governance. The Code aims to make the German Corporate Governance system transparent and understandable. Its purpose is to promote the trust of international and national investors, customers, employees and the general public in the management and supervision of listed German stock corporations." (GCGC 2013:1)

The GCGC has been issued by the Government Commission German Corporate Governance Code and is organized as follows:

Part 1 (Foreword) explains its purpose and aims, giving also an overview of the German corporate system, especially regarding the dual board system with its compulsory division into Management Board and Supervisory Board (with the exception of a European Company (SE)) as well as the participation of employee representatives on supervisory boards (codetermination, cfr. 2.1.21 above).

It is noteworthy that the passage *"In practice the dual-board system, also established in other continental European countries, and the single-board system are converging because of the intensive interaction of the Management Board and the Supervisory Board in the dual-board system. Both systems are equally success-ful."* has been eliminated by the May 2013 revision of the GCGC.

It further establishes the *"comply or explain"* rule for its recommendations (identifiable by the expression *"shall"*) and distinguishes them from mere suggestions (preceded by the word *"should"*).

Finally, its primary focus on *"listed corporations and corporations with capital market access"* is stressed, while its application is recommended also for other companies (GCGC 2013:2).

The second part deals with *"Shareholders and the General Meeting"* including details on the submission of the annual reports, invitation and proxies for the General Meeting etc.

Part 3 addresses the *"Cooperation between Management Board and Supervisory Board"* focusing on the enterprise's strategy and, interestingly, declaring the provision of sufficient information to the Supervisory Board as *"the joint responsibility of the Management Board and Supervisory Board"* (section 3.4 GCGC). The third part also establishes provisions for the Boards' actions in case of a takeover offer (*"appropriate cases"* in the previous version) and, independently from this, defines individual board members' liability and requires a min. 10% deductible for any D&O policy. Furthermore, rules on loans to managers and their relatives as well as the obligation to publish a Corporate Governance Report annually can be found in this section.

Part 4 then deals with the duties, dealing with conflicts of interest, composition and compensation of the Management Board and its members. Regarding the latter, the following passage was introduced by the 2013 review, i.a.: *"The Supervisory Board shall consider the relationship between the compensation of the Management Board and that of senior management and the staff overall, particularly in terms of its development over time. The Supervisory Board shall determine how senior managers and the relevant staff are to be differentiated. [...] The amount of compensation shall be capped, both overall and for individual compensation components. [...] For pension schemes, the Supervisory Board shall establish the level of provision aimed for in each case—also considering the length of time for which the individual has been a Management Board member—and take into account the resulting annual and long-term expense for the company."* (section 4.2.2 f. GCGC). Section 4.2.5 GCGC also sets out the details to be included in the annual compensation report (see Table 3.2), with a specific introduction by the 2013 review: *"In addition, for financial years starting after 31 December 2013, and for each Management Board member, the compensation report shall present:*

- *the benefits granted for the year under review including the fringe benefits, and including the maximum and minimum achievable compensation for variable compensation components;*
- *the allocation of fixed compensation, short-term variable compensation and long-term variable compensation in/for the year under review, broken down into the relevant reference years;*
- *for pension provisions and other benefits, the service cost in/for the year under review.*

Table 3.2   GCGC Appendix Table rel. 4.2.5, 1. bullet point

		I	II	III	IV				
a		Name				Name			
b		Function				Function			
c		Date joined/left				Date joined/left			
d	Benefits granted	$n-1$	n	n (min)	n (max)	$n-1$	n	n (min)	n (max)
1	Fixed compensation								
2	Fringe benefits								
3	**Total**								
4	One-year variable compensation								
5	Multi-year variable compensation								
5a	Plan description (plan term)								
…	Plan description (plan term)								
6	**Total**								
7	Service cost								
8	**Total**								

Notes:

a—Name of the Management Board member

b—Function of the Management Board member, e.g. CEO, CFO

c—Date on which the member joined/left the Management Board, if in the financial year under consideration n (year under review) or $n-1$

d—Financial year under consideration n (year under review) or $n-1$

I—Benefits granted in financial year $n-1$

II—Benefits granted in financial year n (year under review)

III—Minimum value of granted compensation components that can be achieved in financial year n (year under review), e.g. Zero

IV—Maximum value of granted compensation components that can be achieved in financial year n (year under review)

1—Non-performance-based components, e.g. fixed salary, fixed annual one-off payments (amounts correspond to amounts in "Allocation" table); values in columns II, III and IV are identical

2—Non-performance-based components, e.g. benefits in kind and fringe benefits (amounts correspond to amounts in "Allocation" table); values in columns II, III and IV are identical

3—Total of non-performance-based components (1+2) (amounts correspond to amounts in "Allocation" table); values in columns II, III and IV are identical

4—One-year variable compensation, e.g. bonus, short-term incentive (STI), share in profits

5—Multi-year variable compensation (total of rows 5a-…), e.g. multi-year bonus, deferred components from one-year variable compensation, long-term incentive (LTI), subscription rights, other share-based compensation

5a-…—Multi-year variable compensation, broken down into plans and stating the period of time

6—Total of non-performance-related and variable components (1+2+4+5)

7—Service cost in accordance with IAS 19R form pension schemes and other benefits (amounts correspond to amounts in "Allocation" table); values in columns II, III and IV are identical

8—Total of non-performance-related and variable components and service cost (1+2+4+5+7)

Source: GCGC (2013:Appendix [19])

The model tables provided in the appendix shall be used to present this information."

Part 5 covers the tasks and responsibilities of the Supervisory Board, its Terms of Reference, its composition and remuneration as well as the formation of committees.

The first committee mentioned is the Audit Committee, introducing by the 2013 revision the term *"risk management system"*. The only other committee mentioned is the Nomination Committee.

Section 5.4.2 GCGC provides that *"[t]he Supervisory Board shall include what it considers an adequate number of independent members"*, whereas *"a Supervisory Board member is not to be considered independent in particular if he/she has personal or business relations with the company, its executive bodies, a controlling shareholder or an enterprise associated with the latter which may cause a substantial and not merely temporary conflict of interests"*.

Part 6, entitled *"Transparency"*, has suffered significant amendments during the 2013 review. Deletions from this part include insider information disclosure, disclosure of shareholding thresholds, communication media including internet and its use for company disclosures, as well as the recommendation to make English versions of publications available.

The sections which remained concern equal information of shareholders as well as international and domestic addressees, board members' shareholdings, and a *"financial calendar"*.

Part 7, finally, covers *"Reporting and Audit of the Annual Financial Statements"*.

We may conclude that the GCGC is relatively short and to the point, if compared to its Brazilian counterpart, for example, and as such comparable to the Portuguese version which however dedicates an own chapter to risk management (PCGC 2014:18)[5], while the GCGC only uses the word *"risk"* eight times, without defining its meaning or place within the corporate governance structure.

As most corporate governance codes, also the German code concentrates on listed companies. For unlisted companies in Europe, there is the *"Corporate Governance Guidance and Principles for Unlisted Companies in Europe"*, issued by the European Confederation of Directors Associations (ecoDa—www.ecoda.org).

Further guidance on corporate governance in Europe can be found in the 2011 Green Paper *"The EU corporate governance framework"*.[6]

3.2.3.6 Board Compensation

Regarding board compensation (cfr. section 2.1.12 above), section 87 AktG requires the supervisory board to ensure that management board's total compensation does not exceed *"usual remuneration"* without specific reason, referring to both market- and company-standards (Preen et al. 2014:101; cfr. Mülbert 2010:33).

---

[5]On corporate governance in Portugal, cfr. Pinto (2013); Esperança et al. (2011:141 ff.).
[6]http://ec.europa.eu/internal_market/company/docs/modern/com2011-164_en.pdf

The German Corporate Governance Code of May 13, 2013 specifies the relevant reference as *"the relation of board compensation to the compensation of senior management and the relevant staff in its totality"*, and recommends for the supervisory board to take this into account when fixing the compensation for each individual management board member (GCGC, Nr. 4.2.2). Thus, the GCGC specifies the legal requirement of a vertical appropriateness of Executive Board compensation, but leaves it to the supervisory board to define the relevant reference group(s). These turn out to be different for each company, depending on the corporate structure, level of internationalization, and form of organization. The GCGC thus allows for flexibility, but fails to provide clear guidance, as it doesn't even define the compensation, which therefore might be understood as base salary or total compensation.

Recent tendencies go towards giving the general assembly of shareholders a stronger *"say on pay"*, as also intended by the new German federal government coalition, but the initiative shall also in future rest with the supervisory board which established itself over a long term as a reliable element in the German corporate structure (Preen et al. 2014:102).

In January 2014 reports emerged according to which German banks, and in particular Deutsche Bank, had not respected limits introduced on executive bonuses, awarding rewards in excess of the base salary.

3.3 Risk Management Regulation

The International regulatory framework for banks, *"Basel III"*, provides for a concise banking supervision system, based on three pillars (cfr. Table 3.3):

- Pillar 1: Capital, risk coverage, containing leverage;
- Pillar 2: Risk management and supervision;
- Pillar 3: Market discipline.

With its "Basel III" rules, the Basel Committee for Banking Supervision launched a new version of banking regulation including rules for equity elements and ratios as well as for liquidity risk management. The European implementation was finalized in the summer of 2013 via the Capital-Requirements-Directive-(CRD-)IV-package. The transformation of the EU-directive into national law occurred through the CRD-IV-transformation law, whereby the obligation for the application of the new rules started as of January 1, 2014. The implementation of the increased capital requirements occurs step by step throughout a "phase-in". With regards to liquidity requirements, reporting duties have to be fulfilled via Liquidity Coverage Ratio (LCR) and Net Stable Funding Ratio (NSFR). Also these shall be made compulsory and be increased step by step following a monitoring period. The final layout of requirements however is still unclear as the Basel Commission plans further amendments.

Table 3.3 Basel III Overview

Basel Committee on Banking Supervision reforms - Basel III

Strengthens microprudential regulation and supervision, and adds a macroprudential overlay that includes capital buffers.

	Capital				Liquidity
	Pillar 1		Pillar 2	Pillar 3	
	Risk coverage	Containing leverage	Risk management and supervision	Market discipline	Global liquidity standard and supervisory monitoring
All Banks	**Quality and level of capital** Greater focus on common equity. The minimum will be raised to 4.5% of risk-weighted assets, after deductions. **Capital loss absorption at the point of non-viability** Contractual terms of capital instruments will include a clause that allows – at the discretion of the relevant authority – write-off or conversion to common shares if the bank is judged to be non-viable. This principle increases the contribution of the private sector to resolving future banking crises and thereby reduces moral hazard. **Capital conservation buffer** Comprising common equity of 2.5% of risk-weighted assets, bringing the total common equity standard to 7%. Constraint on a bank's discretionary distributions will be imposed when banks fall into the buffer range. **Countercyclical buffer** Imposed within a range of 0-2.5% comprising common equity, when authorities judge credit growth is resulting in an unacceptable build up of systematic risk.	**Securitisations** Strengthens the capital treatment for certain complex securitisations. Requires banks to conduct more rigorous credit analyses of externally rated securitisation exposures. **Trading book** Significantly higher capital for trading and derivatives activities, as well as complex securitisations held in the trading book. Introduction of a stressed value-at-risk framework to help mitigate procyclicality. A capital charge for incremental risk that estimates the default and migration risks of unsecuritised credit products and takes liquidity into account. **Counterparty credit risk** Substantial strengthening of the counterparty credit risk framework. Includes: more stringent requirements for measuring exposure; capital incentives for banks to use central counterparties for derivatives; and higher capital for inter-financial sector exposures. **Bank exposures to central counterparties (CCPs)** The Committee has proposed that trade exposures to a qualifying CCP will receive a 2% risk weight and default fund exposures to a qualifying CCP will be capitalised according to a risk-based method that consistently and simply estimates risk arising from such default fund.	**Leverage ratio** A non-risk-based leverage ratio that includes off-balance sheet exposures will serve as a backstop to the risk-based capital requirement. Also helps contain system wide build up of leverage.	**Supplemental Pillar 2 requirements.** Address firm-wide governance and risk management; capturing the risk of off-balance sheet exposures and securitisation activities; managing risk concentrations; providing incentives for banks to better manage risk and returns over the long term; sound compensation practices; valuation practices; stress testing; accounting standards for financial instruments; corporate governance; and supervisory colleges.	**Revised Pillar 3 disclosures requirements** The requirements introduced relate to securitisation exposures and sponsorship of off-balance sheet vehicles. Enhanced disclosures on the detail of the components of regulatory capital and their reconciliation to the reported accounts will be required, including a comprehensive explanation of how a bank calculates its regulatory capital ratios.	**Liquidity coverage ratio** The liquidity coverage ratio (LCR) will require banks to have sufficient high-quality liquid assets to withstand a 30-day stressed funding scenario that is specified by supervisors. **Net stable funding ratio** The net stable funding ratio (NSFR) is a longer-term structural ratio designed to address liquidity mismatches. It covers the entire balance sheet and provides incentives for banks to use stable sources of funding. **Principles for Sound Liquidity Risk Management and Supervision** The Committee's 2008 guidance *Principles for Sound Liquidity Risk Management and Supervision* takes account of lessons learned during the crisis and is based on a fundamental review of sound practices for managing liquidity risk in banking organisations. **Supervisory monitoring** The liquidity framework includes a common set of monitoring metrics to assist supervisors in identifying and analysing liquidity risk trends at both the bank and system-wide level.
SIFIs	In addition to meeting the Basel III requirements, global systemically important financial institutions (SIFIs) must have higher loss absorbency capacity to reflect the greater risks that they pose to the financial system. The Committee has developed a methodology that includes both quantitative indicators and qualitative elements to identify global systemically important banks (SIBs). The additional loss absorbency requirements are to be met with a progressive Common Equity Tier 1 (CET1) capital requirement ranging from 1% to 2.5%, depending on a bank's systemic importance. For banks facing the highest SIB surcharge, an additional loss absorbency of 1% could be applied as a disincentive to increase materially their global systemic importance in the future. A consultative document was published in cooperation with the Financial Stability Board, which is coordinating the overall set of measures to reduce the moral hazard posed by global SIFIs.				

Source: BIS.org (b)

3.3.1 Risk Management Regulation in Brazil

The Brazilian capital markets and financial systems are regulated and monitored by the National Monetary Council (*Conselho Monetário Nacional*—CMN), the Brazilian Central Bank (*Banco Central do Brasil*—BCB) and the Brazilian Securities and Exchanges Commission (*Comissão de Valores Mobiliários*—CVM).[7]

Regarding banks, the competent entity in the area of risk management is the Central Bank of Brazil (BCB), which in 2013 published a number of rules regarding risk management, including the Circular No. 3.678 dd. 31/10/2013, which provides information related to risk management, the assessment of the risk-weighted assets, and the assessment of Regulatory Capital (*"Património de Referência"*), in line with the new capital rules. It obliges banks in Brazil to publish a number of information as per 30 June and 31 December of each year and provides for relevant calculation formulae.

Other Circulars issued by BCB on 04/03/2013 regard the calculation of risk weighted assets, such as RWA_{CPAD} (Circular 3.644), RWA_{CIRB} (Circular 3.648), RWA_{JUR1-4} (Circulars 3.634 ff.), and RWA_{ACS} (Circular 3.645), RWA_{COM} (Circular 3.639), and RWA_{CAM} (Circular 3.641), RWA_{OPAD} (Circular 3.640), and RWA_{OAMA} (Circular 3.647).

Resolution 4.019 dd. 29/09/2011 issued by the National Monetary Council provides for prudential preventive measures aimed at ensuring the soundness, stability and the regular functioning of the National Financial System.

3.3.2 Risk Management Regulation in Germany

3.3.2.1 Regulatory Environment

A new EU-directive is under way to establish a framework for the recovery and liquidation of credit institutions and equity firms, the Banking Recovery and Resolution Directive. *"Recovery Plans"*, meant to prepare each entity for the event of a profound shock are being required since August 2013 from systemic relevant banks since the amendments made to KWG by the *"German Separate Banking Act"* (*"Deutsches Trennbankengesetz"*). Those are to be followed by *"Resolution Plans"* which shall establish and prepare for a wind-down scenario.

Apart from this, the European Union is discussing the 'Single Resolution Mechanism' (SRM). The Recovery Plan is to describe the potentials for recovery of an institution in a crisis and which specific means of turn-around should be used in different stress scenarios.

---

[7]http://www.bmfbovespa.com.br/en-us/international-investors/regulation-in-brazil/regulation-in-brazil.aspx?idioma=en-us

Based on the Liikanen Report of 2012 (http://ec.europa.eu/internal_market/bank/docs/high-level_expert_group/report_de.pdf) and the European Commission's proposal of *"new rules to stop the biggest and most complex banks from engaging in the risky activity of proprietary trading"* dated 29 January 2014 important measures are being put in place to prohibit or separate risky business *"from their deposit-taking business if the pursuit of such activities compromises financial stability"*. Accompanying measures were published to increase *"transparency of certain transactions in the shadow banking sector"*. Michel Barnier, Commissioner for internal market and services of the EC described those proposals as *"the final cogs in the wheel to complete the regulatory overhaul of the European banking system. This legislation deals with the small number of very large banks which otherwise might still be too-big-to-fail, too-costly-to save, too-complex-to-resolve."* (http://europa.eu/rapid/press-release_IP-14-85_en.htm)

That proposal shall *"apply only to the largest and most complex EU banks with significant trading activities. It will:*

1. *Ban proprietary trading in financial instruments and commodities, i.e. trading on own account for the sole purpose of making profit for the bank. This activity entails many risks but no tangible benefits for the bank's clients or the wider economy.*
2. *Grant supervisors the power and, in certain instances, the obligation to require the transfer of other high-risk trading activities (such as market-making, complex derivatives and securitisation operations) to separate legal trading entities within the group ("subsidiarisation"). This aims to avoid the risk that banks would get around the ban on the prohibition of certain trading activities by engaging in hidden proprietary trading activities which become too significant or highly leveraged and potentially put the whole bank and wider financial system at risk. Banks will have the possibility of not separating activities if they can show to the satisfaction of their supervisor that the risks generated are mitigated by other means.*
3. *Provide rules on the economic, legal, governance, and operational links between the separated trading entity and the rest of the banking group."*

(http://europa.eu/rapid/press-release_IP-14-85_en.htm)

In late 2014, the European Central Bank will take over full responsibility for banking supervision in Europe under the Single Supervisory Mechanism, following extensive review of big banks' balance sheets (Asset Quality Review, AQR) and systematic stress tests.

The Basel Committee on Banking Supervision established rules on risk data aggregation and internal risk reporting for banks and supervisory authorities in 2013 which refer to governance and infrastructure, risk data aggregation, and risk reporting. Its rules will be fully compulsory for global systemic relevant banks from 2016 onwards.

The Financial Stability Board (FSB) formed the Enhanced Disclosure Task Force in 2012 in order to improve risk disclosures in all areas of risk management. (http://www.financialstabilityboard.org/press/pr_130821.pdf)

It is apparent that regulatory and accounting requirements for banks have become ever more intense. This is so much so that some see the biggest danger in over-regulation rather than in economic changes: *"Changes in regulatory requirements and accounting standards, which have grown increasingly frequent and material in recent years, may have lasting implications for – and even threaten the survival of – the financial industry in general and Commerzbank's business model in particular."* (Commerzbank AR 2013:105)

3.3.2.2   KonTraG

The Law for Control and Transparency in Companies (Ge*setz zur Kontrolle und Transparenz im Unternehmensbereich*—KonTraG, of 1998) establishes several rules to include corporate governance and risk management as legal requirements and part of strategic planning. The law implies personal responsibility for managers, thus somewhat easing the principal-agent-conflict by imposing personal conse-quences on managers for the mismanagement of a corporation.

It also introduced Art. 91 par. 2 AktG (cfr. 3.2.3.1 above) and auditors are required to check the risk management systems in the companies they audit. As part of the rating systems required under the Basel frameworks, company-wide risk management systems are part of the review performed by banks on their customers (e.g. Management Risk Controlling (MRC)).

3.3.2.3   MaRisk

On December 14, 2012, German banking supervision authority BaFin published the fourth version of the Minimum Requirements for Risk Management (*Mindestanforderungen an das Risikomanagement*—MaRisk)[8] which came into effect on January 1, 2013 and had conformance periods generally until December 31, 2013. Its purpose is mainly to detail the requirements of section 25a of the German Banking Act (KWG) with regards to the risk management of credit institu-tions, given that the referred section does not define them.

The minimum canon of material risks is defined in section AT 2.2 of MaRisk:

(a) *"counterparty and credit risk (including country risk),*
(b) *market risk,*
(c) *liquidity risk, and*
(d) *operational risk."*

It further clarifies that apart from the size of an individual risk, there can be *"risk concentrations from a co-movement of risk positions within a risk type ("intra-risk concentrations") and from a co-movement of risk positions across different risk*

---

[8]English translation published on 15/08/2014:

types (due to common risk factors or interactions between various risk factors of different risk types – "inter-risk concentrations")". (BaFin[9])

Once again, the complexity of risk identification and assessment does not end at the first level. Regarding counterparty risk, for instance, Jorion (2009:929) observes: *"It is not enough to know your counterparty. You need to know your counterparty's counterparties, too."*

3.3.2.4   German Solvency Regulation (*Solvabilitätsverordnung*—SolvV)

Just as MaRisk, the German Solvency Regulation dd. 06/12/2013 is one of the main outflows of the German Banking Act (KWG). It establishes requirements for adequate capital provision and defines rules for the application of the Internal Ratings-Based (IRB), calculation of capital buffer requirements (sec. 33 ff.), and relevant risk positions (sec. 36). It also makes special reference to operational risk as the risk of losses resulting from inadequate or failed internal processes, systems, human error or external events and defines capital quotas (sec. 24 ff.).

Conglomerate-wide risk management system have to comply with the statutory requirements specified in section 25 (1) of the German Supervision of Financial Conglomerates Act (FKAG) in conjunction with section 25a KWG.

3.4   Brazilian Banks Under Analysis

Basis for our analysis of the five major banks in Brazil is the Brazilian Central Bank's ranking of banks by assets as of 31st December, 2013 (Table 3.4).

In general, banking—and bank lending in particular—has become much more important as a share of Brazilian GDP over the past 6 years, i.e. since the beginning of the financial crisis, than it had been in previous eras, as exemplified by Fig. 3.3.

Among the loan types, long-term loans, particularly for real estate, gain share against short-term lending. (Itaú AR 2013:A-10)

One main factor has been the relatively low and stable inflation rate in this traditionally high-inflation market, moving between 3% and 7% during the period under analysis, cfr. Fig. 3.4.

The recovery of the US economy strengthened the US dollar and led to lower asset prices in emerging markets. Accordingly, the Brazilian GDP growth in 2013 was below expectations, while unemployment maintained record-low levels. (Itaú AR 2013:A-10)

The following section is intended to give a brief description of the Brazilian banks under analysis with a special focus on their corporate governance and risk management systems.

---

[9]http://www.bafin.de/SharedDocs/Downloads/EN/Rundschreiben/dl_rs_1210_ba_marisk.pdf?__
blob=publicationFile

Table 3.4   Five largest Brazilian banks

31.12.2013		BRL/EUR:	3,2582		
Country	Bank	Total assets TBRL	Total TEUR	Employees	Branches
BR	Banco do Brasil	1,218,525,361	373,987,282	124,744	5,451
BR	Itaú Unibanco	1,027,324,008	315,304,158	118,251	3,924
BR	CAIXA ECONOMICA FEDERAL	858,475,356	263,481,479	126,098	3,289
BR	BRADESCO	776,724,294	238,390,613	97,413	4,684
BR	BNDES	762,953,109	234,163,989	2,896	1
Totals	5	4,644,002,128	1,425,327,521	469,402	17,349
Source:	Banco Central do Brasil	31.12.2013	BRL/EUR:	3,2582	(ECB)

Source: Banks' Annual Reports 12/31/2013; own presentation

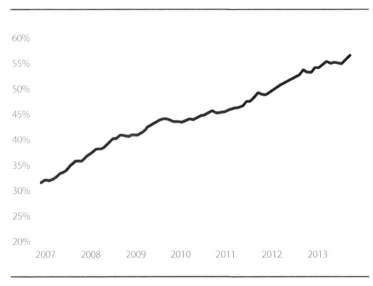

Bank Lending (as % of GDP)

Fig. 3.3   Bank Lending in Brazil (as % of GDP). Source: Itaú AR (2013:A-6)

3.4.1   Banco Do Brasil

Banco do Brasil (BB) was created by the Portuguese Prince Regent Dom João, following Dom João VI, shortly after he arrived in Brazil in 1808. In 1817, Banco do Brasil carried out its first public offering of shares in the Brazilian capital markets.

Today, BB is the largest financial institution in Latin America, with 58.6 million customers, 37.4 million checking accounts and 114,000 employees.

12-Month IPCA Inflation Rate

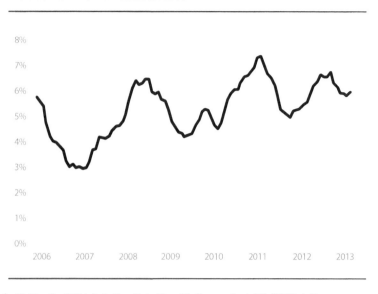

Fig. 3.4 12-Months IPCA Inflation Rate (Brazil). Source: Itaú AR (2013:A-7)

The bank provides solutions, services and products in the banking, investment, asset management, insurance, social security, premium bonds, payment systems, and others.

It has the largest service network in Brazil with 5,362 branches and 44,393 automated teller machines and operates a network of banking correspondents under the brand *"Mais BB"*, thus covering 5,425 Brazilian municipalities (97% of the total).

Outside of Brazil, Banco do Brasil operates in 24 countries—including Germany—through 49 branches and representative offices which can be found in four continents. Through 1124 correspondent financial institutions, BB covers another 139 countries. *"As a result, the organization is considered the Brazilian bank with the largest abroad service network, with its operations dedicated to existing Brazilian communities, the internationalization of Brazilian companies and the expansion of Brazil's trade relations with the world."* (BB AR 2012:2)

The company enjoys a strong brand and a strategic relationship with the Brazilian government at federal, state and local level, for example as the financial agent of the National Treasury, 16 states and 16 capital cities. (BB AR 2012:4)

The bank was awarded the ISO 20000 certification in technology and operates the BB-Caixa Datacenter Complex together with Caixa Econômica Federal to ensure capacity for further growth and the reduction of operational risks.

Furthermore, the bank highlights its dedication to corporate governance and sustainability, having adhered—in 2002—to the corporate governance practices required by the *Novo Mercado* segment of BM&FBovespa, of which it is part since 2006. (BB AR 2012:5)

3.4.1.1 Corporate Governance

Regarding Corporate governance, the bank states that *"Governance at Banco do Brasil (BB) defines an extensive view of the principles and practices that contribute to strengthening the transparency of its management process while enhancing its institutional value."*

In 2012, a Remuneration Committee was established and the number of members of the Board of Directors increased by one to eight (BB AR 2012:17).

Through the General Meeting, the global compensation amount of the bank's management is defined. For the Board of Directors, the remuneration is fixed in line with Law No. 9,292/96 and as such not linked to economic, social or environmental performance, while the Executive Board's remuneration consists of a fixed and a variable part, being the latter tied to the Bank's results (BB AR 2012:19).

The organizational structure of BB is shown in Fig. 3.5.

In 2006, the shares of BB had been listed for 100 years on the stock exchange, and the bank became part of the São Paulo Stock Exchange (Bovespa) *"Novo Mercado"*, undertaking to raise its free-float to 25%.

The result has been an improved performance of the shares, according to Mário Pierry, Director of Financial Sector Research for the Deutsche Bank as quoted in BB's Annual Report 2008: *"The market has made a better valuation on the Banco do Brasil shares over the past two years, due to many reasons. One of them is the fact that the bank's shares started being listed on the New Market, which increased the number of circulating shares and improved corporate governance. Another reason is the fact that BB has greatly improved its profitability, which now is comparable to the one from private competitors."* (BB AR 2008:42)

In 2008, in the middle of the global financial crisis, Banco do Brasil started to incorporate other entities, namely Banco do Estado de Santa Catarina (Besc), Banco

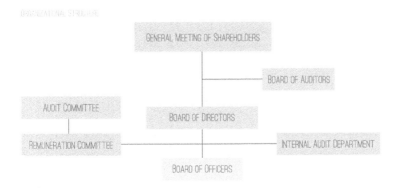

Fig. 3.5 Banco do Brasil Organizational Structure. Source: BB AR (2012:18)

Fig. 3.6 Banco do Brazil
ownership structure. Source:
http://www45.bb.com.br/
docs/ri/ra2013/eng/ra/02.
htm [17.09.2017]

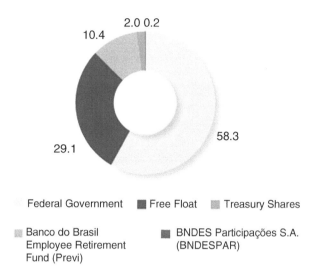

SHAREHOLDER BREAKDOWN (%)

Federal Government   ■ Free Float   Treasury Shares

Banco do Brasil   ■ BNDES Participações S.A.
Employee Retirement   (BNDESPAR)
Fund (Previ)

do Estado do Piauí (Bep) and Banco Nossa Caixa. In the following year, Banco do Brasil absorbed Banco Nossa Caixa and acquired 50% of the shares of Banco Votorantim and 51% of the shares of Banco Patagonia, in Argentina (BB AR 2010:7).

Today, Banco do Brasil is in essence still a state bank, with a free float of 29.1%, of which the majority is held by foreign investors as illustrated by Fig. 3.6.

Of the eight members of the Board of Directors, five are indicated by the State directly (by the Minister of Finance and the Minister of Planning, Budget and Management), including the CEO, one as their representative by the employees of Banco do Brasil S.A., and two get elected by the minority shareholders.

The Board of officers consists of the CEO and seven Vice-Presidents.

The bank has a strong focus on sustainable development which, jointly with human resources, constitutes one of the seven Vice-Presidencies of the Board of Directors, and *"has been cited, for the third year running, as one of the most sustainable financial institutions in the world, in The Sustainability Yearbook 2012, published by SAM—Sustainable Asset Management—the organization responsible for the selection process of the Dow Jones Sustainability Index on the New York Stock Exchange."* (BB AR 2011:11)

3.4.1.2   Risk Management

According to Fig. 3.7, Banco do Brasil understands risk management and corporate controls as a part of corporate governance:

Fig. 3.7 Banco do Brasil
Corporate Governance
structure. Source: BB AR
(2012:6)

CORPORATE GOVERNANCE

ORGANIZATIONAL STRUCTURE

RISK MANAGEMENT AND CORPORATE CONTROLS

BUSINESS STRATEGY

SOCIO-ENVIRONMENTAL RESPONSIBILITY

INTANGIBLE ASSETS

As principal risks, Banco do Brasil identifies market risk, credit risk, operational as well as liquidity risk, but also strategy risk, reputational risk and social-environmental risk. For each of these, specific policies, objectives, strategies, processes and systems are in place (BB AR 2012:25 ff.).

The Board of Directors defines the risk and credit policies, while risk governance is centralized within the Global Risk Committee (GRCo). The latter is made up by the Board of Officers, *"with responsibility for setting out the risk management strategies, the global risk exposure limits and the levels of compliance and capital allocation, depending on the risks"*. (BB AR 2012:25)

3.4.2   BNDES—Banco Nacional Do Desenvolvimento

The BNDES is a public bank, owned by the Federal Government and governed by private law. The bank depends on the Ministry of Development, Industry and Foreign Trade with the aim of implementing the Federal Government's investment policy by providing funding and support to projects which stimulate innovation, local and regional as well as socio-environmental development.

At the end of 2012, it had 2,853 employees and as per 31/12/2013 held assets of R $ 763 billion (c. € 234 billion).

BNDES is active in the whole of the Brazilian territory, trying to stimulate demand for financing in less-developed regions, in order to boost the economy and benefit society as a whole.

It finances all sectors of the economy, small to medium-large private companies, the public sector and the third sector (including NGOs) in areas such as infrastructure, agribusiness, the environment, social inclusion, culture, local and regional development, to name but a few.

The bank's financing operations are either direct or indirect. Indirect operations are realized through accredited financial institutions which forward them to the final client, while direct operations take place directly with the latter. (BNDES AR 2012:18)

A list of products and services is shown in Table 3.5.

Table 3.5 BNDES products and services

Products and services offered		
Type of operation	Product	Description
Direct	BNDES Finem	Financing undertaking with a minimum amount of R$ 10 million
	BNDES Credit limit	Credit for client in compliance with their obligations
	Subscription of securities	Purchasing minority shares or convertible debentures of a temporary nature, or investments through closed funds
	Project finances	Financing with the support of a project's cash flow
	BNDES Guarantees	Rendering guarantees to reduce the level of participation in the projects. Used in large-scale projects
	BNDES Bridge loan	Financing a project, granted in special cases to speed up investments via resources at the structuring stage of a long-term operation
	BNDES Exim post-shipment	Financing the commercialization of national goods and services abroad
Indirect	BNDES Automatic	Financing undertakings of up to R$ 20 million for micro, small, medium-sized, and medium-large companies, or up to R$ 10 million, if the client is a large company
	BNDES Finame	Financing production and commercialization of machinery and equipment
	BNDES Finame Leasing	Merchant leasing of machinery and equipment
	BNDES Exim Pre-Shipment	Financing national production of goods and services aimed at exports
	BNDES Exim	Financing national production aimed at exporting and commercializing goods and services abroad
	BNDES Card	Revolving pre-approved credit to acquire products, inputs and services

Source: BNDES AR 2012:19

3.4.2.1   Corporate Governance

Also BNDES's Board of Directors is composed of eight members, in cluding the president and the vice-president as well as six managing directors, all of whom are appointed by the President of the Republic. Specific decisions or general resolutions are taken in weekly meetings. The Board of Directors is being supported by the Advisory Board and the Internal Auditing Committee. The latter mediates dialog with external control and supervision entities, accompanies the independent auditor's activities as well as the compliance with internal and external regulation (BNDES AR 2012:19).

In 2007, a Risk Management Division was created: *"Control of activities and risk management were expanded and divided into the new Risk Management Area* (Área de Gestão de Riscos).*"* (BNDES AR 2007:8)

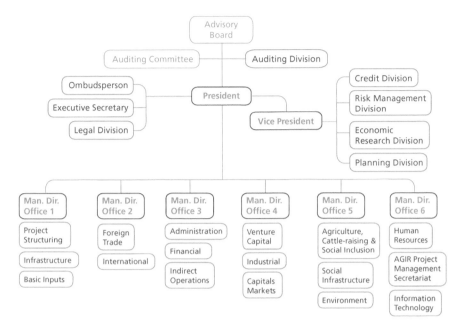

Fig. 3.8   BNDES organizational structure. Source: BNDES AR (2012:20)

The Risk Management Division, along with the Credit, Economic Research, and Planning Divisions report to the Vice President as per Fig. 3.8.

BNDES stresses *"managing ethics"* in a specific chapter at the same level as risk management, for instance, but consisting of only one paragraph. A *"BNDES System's Ethics Committee (CET/BNDES)"* exists and its Executive Secretariat is directly linked to the BNDES president's office, as established in the Code of Ethics for the BNDES System and in line with the applicable legislation, especially in Decree N°. 6,029/2007 and Resolution N°. 010/2008, of the Public Ethics Committee (CEP). Thus, while corporate governance does not seem to be a main topic at BNDES, ethics do occupy a prominent position in the organization. This appears to be due to its public nature and respective legislation and it remains unclear if this attitude goes beyond mere compliance with specific legislation.

3.4.2.2   Risk Management

Regarding risk management, BNDES states that *"One of the main goals in risk management at the BNDES is to contribute to the institution's financial sustainability, monitoring potential financial losses from credit risks, markets, liquidity and operational, from calculation of capital to take on risks, and assessment of adjustments in the institution's internal controls."* This passage shows a strong focus on financial risks and the only non-financial risk identified is operational risk (BNDES AR 2012:24).

3.4.3 Bradesco

Bradesco celebrated its 70th anniversary on March 10, 2013, and had 59,307 points of sale for 26.4 million account holders at the end of that year. Its profits increased by 5.5% to over R$ 12 billion, including its insurance business *"Bradesco Seguros"*.

It has been a listed stock company since 1946 and serves over 74 million clients in total.

The bank runs a foundation, *"Fundação Bradesco"*, which also provides 40 schools to over 100,000 pupils, granting quality education for free (Bradesco AR 2013:2).

It is part of the Dow Jones Sustainability Index and the Sustainability Index (ISE) of BM&FBovespa. Bradesco is a signatory of the UN Global Compact which is active in the areas of human rights, labor, the environment and anti-corruption (www.unglobalcompact.org) and in 2013 the strategic planning procedures for sustainability which had been adopted in 2011, entered the strategic planning process of the organization (Bradesco AR 2013:2).

"The Bank currently holds an AA+ rating (Excellent Corporate Governance Practices) from Austin Rating. Bradesco voluntarily adhered to the Code of Self-Regulation and Best Practices of Publicly-Held Companies (ABRASCA), adopting the "apply or explain" procedure, as part of its constant drive to improve its governance." (Bradesco AR 2012:36)

Bradesco offers the full range of an integrated banking services provider as shown by Fig. 3.9.

Its sustainability goals for 2013 included opening another 600,000 bank accounts for class D and E customers, as defined by Fundação Getúlio Vargas (FGV), being the two lower-income classes. This goal has been reduced to 400,000 for 2014 (Bradesco AR 2013:17).

Bradesco's capital structure and management are shown in Fig. 3.10.

3.4.3.1 Corporate Governance

According to its Annual Report, Bradesco's Management Board adheres to the best practices of *Instituto Brasileiro de Governança Corporativa* (IBGC) e da Securities and Exchange Commission (SEC). The board defines the responsibilities of top managers, thus improving the bank's accountability and transparency regarding information relevant to its stakeholders.

Fig. 3.11 shows its corporate governance structure, by which the Corporate Governance Committee depends on the Board of Executive Officers ("Diretoria Executiva") rather than on the Board of Directors ("Conselho de Administração") directly, where the Committee on Integrated Risk Management and Capital Allocation can be found (Fig. 3.11).

The bank also offers investment funds with socio-environmental criteria, including its *"FIC FIA Governança Corporativa"* which invests at least 67% of its net

OPERATIONS

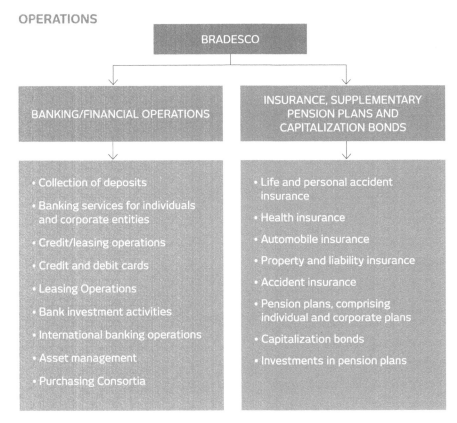

Fig. 3.9 Bradesco Product Portfolio. Source: Bradesco AR (2013:4)

assets in companies belonging to the Corporate Governance Index (IGC, *Índice de Governança Corporativa*) of BM&FBovespa (Bradesco AR 2013:48).

3.4.3.2 Risk Management

As per Fig. 3.12, Bradesco seems to understand corporate governance as part of risk management.

As mentioned before (3.4.3.1) however, corporate governance and risk management are organizationally ranking on the same level.

3.4.4 Caixa Econômica Federal

At the end of 2013, Caixa Econômica Federal (*"Caixa"*), the federal savings bank, had over R\$ 1.5 trillion of assets under management (+20.8% in 2013), of which R\$

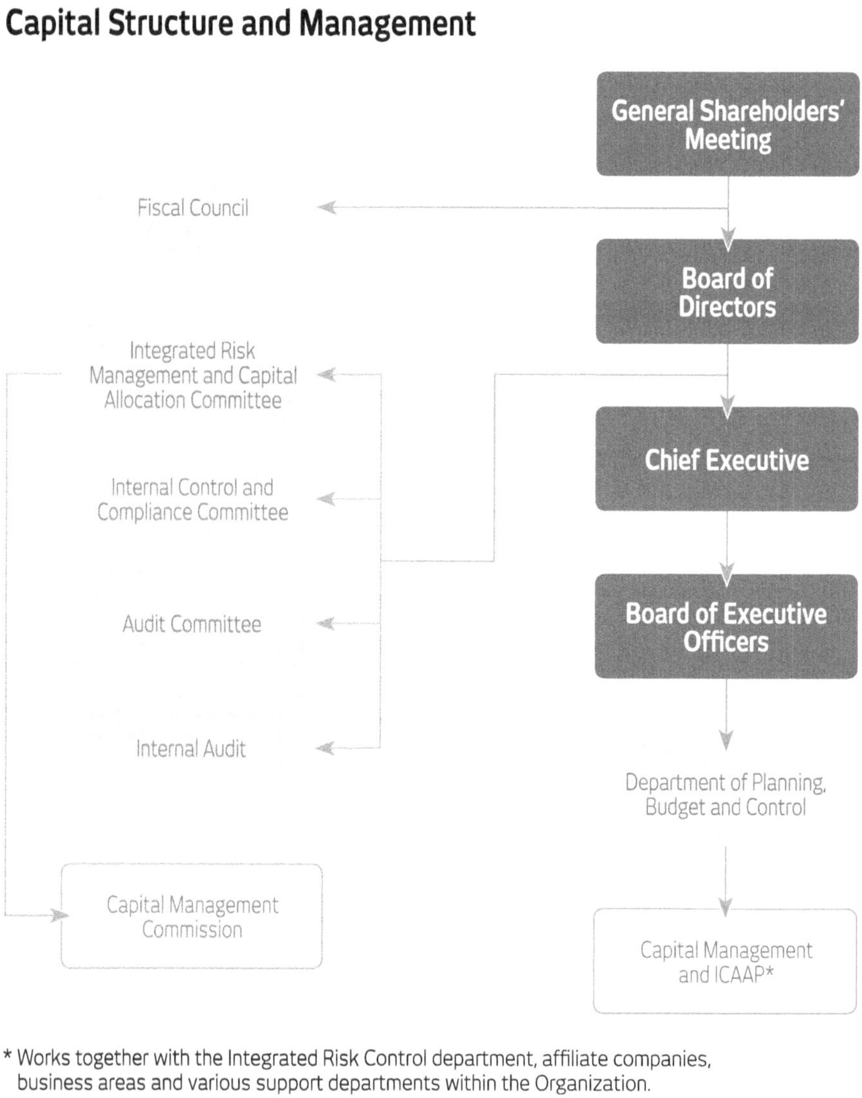

Capital Structure and Management

* Works together with the Integrated Risk Control department, affiliate companies, business areas and various support departments within the Organization.

Fig. 3.10 Bradesco Capital Structure and Management. Source: Bradesco AR (2012:18)

858.3 billion were its own assets. Net profits increased by 19.2% in 2013 to R$ 6.7 billion, with a medium return on average equity of 26.2%.

Caixa has been particularly strong in housing credits, which increased by 31.4% in 2013 to R$ 270.4 billion. This represents almost 55% of its R$ 494.2 billion loan portfolio and a 68.5% share of the Brazilian home loan market.

Its R$ 209.6 billion saving balance increased by 18.9% in 2013, representing a market share of 35%. Its branch network serves 71.7 million clients (+9.9% in 2013)

CORPORATE GOVERNANCE STRUCTURE

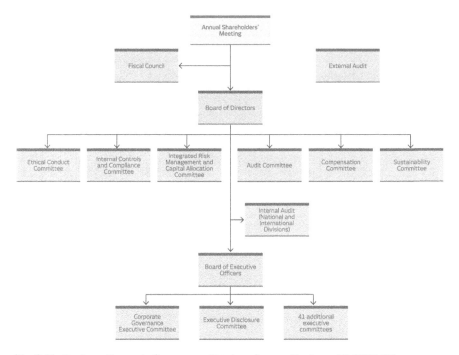

Fig. 3.11 Bradesco Corporate Governance Structure. Source: Bradesco AR (2013:54)

Fig. 3.12 Bradesco Risk Management. Source: Bradesco Risk Management Report Q4/2013:9

and consists of over 4000 branches and a total of around 67,500 service points, including the lottery network Caixa manages, 1 riverboat and 18 truck units. The bank plans to open another 2500 branches until 2015. Its client base consists mainly

Table 3.6 Caixa Financial Ratios and Items 2013

Ratios (%)	2011	2012	2013
Return on Average Assets	1.1	0.9	0.9
Return on Average Equity	29.6	25.9	26.2
BIS Ratio (or Basel II Index)	13.3	13.0	15.1
Public Sector Debt	31.0	29.0	24.7
Fee Income / Administrative Expenses (acum. 12m)	66.8	64.7	64.0
Fee Income / Personnel Expenses (acum. 12m)	108.6	105.6	102.6
Operating Efficiency Ratio (acum. 12m)	59.0	61.2	60.3
Items (R$ billion)	**2011**	**2012**	**2013**
Caixa's Asset	511	703	858
Amplified Loan Portfolio	253	361	494
Saving Deposits	150	176	210
Managed assets (Third party)	484	557	664

Source: Caixa MR 2013:6

of individual clients; while only 1.9 million of its customers are corporate, their number grew by 17.5% in 2013, i.e. at a stronger pace than that of private clients, which increased by 9.7%. (Caixa MR 2013:3 f.)

Caixa pays out social benefits, Family Allowance (*"bolsa família"*), social inclusion and financial emancipation support etc. and thus sees its role as one of *"financial institution and public policies agent"* (Caixa MR 2013:3), being also responsible for the *"minha casa, minha vida"* (My House, My Life) program.

While Caixa's own and third party assets, its loan portfolio, and saving deposits have grown constantly over the past years, its return on assets and equity have decreased somewhat. At the same time, its BIS ratio increased to over 15% (cfr. Table 3.6).

Through its insurance arm, Caixa Seguros Group, the company provides life, real estate and vehicle insurances. Its international presence however is limited to three representative offices in the US, Japan, and Venezuela. Yet it maintains a network of correspondent banks to allow international withdrawals and remittances (Caixa MR 2013:13 f.).

3.4.4.1 Corporate Governance

Regarding corporate governance, the entity states that *"CAIXA has a historic commitment and a contemporary corporate management, in line with the provisions of Decree No. 6.021/07"* (http://www14.caixa.gov.br/portal/idiomas/english/about_caixa/corporate_governance/governance) and continues to elaborate on the subject as follows: *"The year 2013 brought important advances related to corporate governance practices adopted by the Institution. A major milestone was the publication of Decree No. 7,973, of March 28, 2013, which approved the new Caixa Statute, bringing significant changes to the Company. The adjustments allowed the strengthening of Caixa's corporate government system, as well as providing the Board of Directors and the Board of Executive better management and monitoring of the implementation of the strategy Caixa."* (Caixa MR 2013:15).

Caixa first introduced a corporate governance section in its annual report in 2012.

3.4.4.2 Risk Management

Caixa's risk management is being described in its Management Report as compliant with the BCB-standards issued by the Central Bank of Brazil regarding the *"management of credit, operational, market, liquidity and other risks"* (Caixa MR 2013:17). The further description of its risk management organization is however quite generic, apart from the reference to a Capital Plan on normal and stress scenarios with a minimum 3 year time horizon (Caixa MR 2013:17).

3.4.5 Itaú

Itaú Unibanco (*"Itaú"*) is the largest Brazilian private bank with a full-service spectrum and the highest brand value in Brazil with an estimated brand value of R $ 19.3 billion, boasting the hightest number of facebook-fans (6.5 million) among banks worldwide (Itaú AR 2013:A-43).[10] It is the result of a merger between Unibanco, which started to operate in 1924 as Casa Bancária Moreira Salles, and Itaú which was established as Banco central de Crédito S.A. in 1944. The merger was announced on November 3rd, 2008 and followed by further acquisitions, mainly those of Redecard and Credicard in 2012 and 2013 respectively.

---

[10]Compare Commerzbank's mobile/online banking record under 3.5.1.

In 2013, Itaú issued its first consolidated annual report. In a note to the author dated 16/05/2014, Itaú's investor relations department stated as follows: *"Regarding the Consolidated Annual Report 2013, we launched this initiative—which is a first in Brazil—in order to provide for even more transparency and to facilitate communication with the different stakeholders, merging the annual report (with sustainability indicators following GRI), Form 20-F[11], and the prospectus for the issue of debt in just one document [...] being this a tendency of unification of our communication which we shall adopt over the coming years"*.

As its objective, Itaú mentions *"to be the leading bank in sustainable performance and client satisfaction"*. (Itaú AR 2013:A-40)

Itaú expresses its corporate culture by a set of ten principles called *"Nosso Jeito de Fazer ("Our Way of Making it Happen")"* which are:

- *"All for the client;*
- *Passion for performance;*
- *Ethical, responsible leadership;*
- *All-Stars who are team players;*
- *Focus on innovation and focused innovation;*
- *Processes serving people;*
- *Nimble and uncomplicated;*
- *Leave your stripes at the door;*
- *A sparkle in one's eyes; and*
- *Dream big." (Itaú AR 2013:A-41)*

3.4.5.1   Corporate Governance

Pedro Moreira Salles, Chairman of the Board of Directors, reports on corporate governance, while President and CEO, Roberto Setubal, covers risk management (Itaú AR 2012:8).

"Ethics, transparency and a focus on efficiency ensure the value of our bank and the creation of value for shareholders and society" (Itaú AR 2012:38)

Unibanco Asset Management began adopting the Principles for Responsible Investment (PRI) in July 2008, becoming the first major investment fund manager in Brazil to do so. Since 2006, *"the initiative seeks to incorporate social, environmental and corporate governance aspects in investment decision-making"* (Itaú AR 2008:85). CSR measures taken are shown in Table 3.7.

3.4.5.2   Risk Management

Itaú identifies main risk types as well as *"other risks"* as per Table 3.8.

In order to align incentives to its enterprise risk management, Itaú practices risk-adjusted compensation by *"attracting, retaining and compensating on merit its*

---

[11]As to be filed with the US Securities and Exchange Commission pursuant to section 13 or 15(d) of the Securiteis Exchange Act of 1934.

Table 3.7 Itaú measures of CSR

Selected Measures of Corporate Social Responsibility		2008	Goals 2009
Ratio of highest to lowest salary		n/a	n/a
Work-related accidents		n/a	n/a
Social and environmental projects were established by:		Executive Directors and Managers	Executive Directors and Managers
Standards of occupational safety and health were set by:		Executive Directors and Managers	Executive Directors and Managers
Regarding freedom to unionize, collective bargaining and internal worker representation among workers, the Company:		Follows ILO rules	Follows ILO rules
Private pension plans for:		All employees	All employees
Profit-sharing plans for:		All employees	All employees
Requirement that suppliers share Itaú's ethical and social/environmental responsibility standards:		Mandatory	Mandatory
For staff members to perform volunteer work, the company:		Organizes and encourages	Organizes and encourages
Value-added statement (DVA)			2008
Value added to be distributed (in R$) thousands			25,191,808
		%	in R$ thousands
Distribution of value-added	Taxes	34.43%	8,672,917
	Payroll	31.52%	7,941,480
	Stockholders	12.72%	3,205,181
	Reinvested Profits	19.31 %	4,598,302
	Third Parties	2.02%	507,539

Source: Itaú AR 2008:155

Table 3.8 Itaú main risk types

• Credit risk;	• Other risks:
• Market risk;	– Insurance risk;
• Operational risk;	– Strategic risk;
• Liquidity risk;	– Social and Environmental risk;
	– Reputational risk;
	– Model risk;
	– Regulatory risk.

Source: Itaú RMR 2014T1:2 ff

collaborators, encouraging prudent risk exposure levels in short-, medium- and long-term strategies, in line with the interests of its shareholders, regulatory authorities and the organization's culture. The governance structure of compensation and incentive to the prudent risk taking has been consolidating in line with the best international compensation and governance practices". (Itaú RMR 2014T1:44).

Table 3.9 Five largest German banks

Country	Bank	Total TEUR	Employees	Branches
DE	Deutsche Bank	1.611.400.000	98.254	2.907
DE	Commerzbank	549.661.000	52.944	0
DE	KfW	464.800.000	5.374	1
DE	DZ Bank	386.978.000	28.962	15
DE	Unicredit	290.018.000	19.092	933
Totals	5	3.302.857.000	204.626	3.856

Source: Banks' Annual Reports 12/31/2013; own presentation

3.4.6   Summary

The Brazilian banks under analysis are quite heterogeneous, given their private and public backgrounds as well as different objectives and business models. As we shall see however, the same can be said about the five major banks in Germany.

Most of the banks mentioned above await a court ruling on their handling of account adjustments made under anti-inflation laws enacted between 1987 and 1991. Depositors are suing several banks for a total which may reach R$150 billion (US $62 billion), a move opposed not only by banks but also by politicians.[12] (*The Economist*, February 8th, 2014:61).

3.5   German Banks Under Analysis

Given that the German Central Bank (*"Bundesbank"*) does not issue figures for individual institutions, there is no ranking comparable to that of the Brazilian Central Bank. We therefore compiled data from the Annual Reviews as per 31st December 2013. The resulting ranking is also based on total assets, and as such comparable to that of BCB, cfr. Table 3.9.

3.5.1   Commerzbank

Commerzbank was founded in 1870 as Commerz- und Disconto-Bank in Hamburg. Until the 1930s, it grew through a number of acquisitions. During the German Banking Crisis of 1931, also Commerzbank ran into difficulties and was finally merged by the German government in 1932 with the Barmer Bankverein. As a consequence of a related share issuance, the German state held a majority in the bank until 1937 when the issues were sold to private investors. Following the Second World War, the institution was split and only reunited in 1958. In 1990,

---

[12]In this context, Pedro Malan, a former finance minister has been quoted as saying that "*In Brazil, even the past is unpredictable*". (The Economist, February 8th, 2014:61)

Commerzbank moved its headquarters back from Düsseldorf to Frankfurt and acquired, in 2006 the remaining shares in specialized real estate lender Eurohypo from Allianz and Deutsche Bank. In its current form and logo, Commerzbank is the product of the acquisition of Dresdner Bank in 2009. This deal went through a number of changes as it was agreed prior to the Lehman Brothers collapse and then subject to subsequent changes to prices and timing. The integration process was concluded in May 2011, and the repayment of the tranches of state aid directly repayable by Commerzbank occurred in 2013 (Commerzbank AR 2013:9), however the Federal State, represented by SoFFin, still held 13% of Commerzbank's stock as of 12/31/2013.

During the financial crisis, and due also to uncovered risks in relation to Dresdner Bank business, Commerzbank had to tap the state fund for financial market stabilization (Sonderfonds Finanzmarktstabilisierung—SoFFin). The conditions of that financial support had to be re-negotiated in order to be acceptable to the European Commission and included a reduction of management salaries, exclusions or special conditions for dividends and an obligation to grant additional loans to the German *"Mittelstand"*, i.e. medium-sized enterprises regarded as the backbone of the German economy. Over 40% of German companies are clients of Commerzbank (Commerzbank AR 2013:4).

Today, its main markets are Germany and Poland. Relative to its size it is thus a very 'local' bank, although 14% of Eurozone's international trade are being processed through Commerzbank (Commerzbank AR 2013:4).

Still owing to the financial crisis are the three strategic focus areas, (i) *"investment into the profitability of the core business"*, (ii) *"consistent cost management"*, and (iii) *"optimization of capital endowment"* (Commerzbank AR 2013:8). These clearly point towards a strategy of consolidation rather than growth, even following a stronger financial year 2012. This includes the value-conscious (*"wertschonend"*) wind-down of (international) commercial real estate finance and ship finance activities, as well as a reduction of personnel by 5200 until 2016 and even translated into the reduction from nine to seven members of the board of directors.

In stark contrast stands the 2007 Commerzbank's annual report title which read *"Focus on growth and efficiency"*, despite of the subprime crisis (cfr. Commerzbank AR 2007:98 ff.) while the main facts and figures consisted of the following:

- *"Group net income reached a record €1.92bn, roughly one fifth more than in 2006*
- *A proposal will be put to the AGM to raise the dividend per share one third to €1.00*
- *Commerzbank Group's balance-sheet total rose moderately by 1.3% to €616.5bn*
- *Capital ratios are within the defined range and thus at a sound level"*

In 2013, Commerzbank's Polish operations have been re-branded as mBank and received several distinctions as world leader in mobile and online banking (Commerzbank AR 2013:9).[13]

---

[13]Compare Itaú's facebook-record under 3.4.5.

3.5.1.1   Corporate Governance

Commerzbank's stock is included in the ECPI Ethical Indices (cfr. Fig. 3.13), which select the 150 top capitalized companies in the European and EMU markets respectively which are eligible investments under the ECPI SRI Screening Methodology and Controversial Sectors Screening (http://www.ecpigroup.com/wp-content/uploads/2014/05/ECPI_EMU_ETHICAL_EQUITY.pdf).

Commerzbank's Annual Report (2013) attributes one section to *"corporate responsibility"* (p. 23–46) and another one covers the group risk report (p. 97–132).

Corporate governance is described as *"responsible and transparent management and its control aiming at sustainable creation of value"* with reference to and support of the German Corporate Governance Code (Commerzbank AR 2013:25). Commerzbank's responsible person for corporate governance is the board member heading the legal area.

In line with the GCGC, Commerzbank reports on the recommendations of the GCGC it does not comply with (*"comply or explain"*). These refer to section 4.2.1 GCGC, given that the attribution of board members' responsibilities is done by the managing board itself rather than the supervisory board. Other topics are executive compensation and women in management positions. (Commerzbank AR 2013:25–27).

The compensation report (Commerzbank AR 2013:28 ff.) reports on the fixed salary which was approved by the general assembly in line with section 120 par. 4 AktG, as well as short- and long term incentives (STI/LTI), with a term of one and 4 years, respectively.

3.5.1.2   Risk Management

The Group Risk Report (Commerzbank AR 2013:97 ff.) shows and categorizes Commerzbank's risks and risk management structures (Figs. 3.14 and 3.15).

The 2013 focus had been on the reduction of non-core assets particularly in ship and commercial real estate finance (Commerzbank AR 2013:111).

Indices containing the Commerzbank share
Blue chip indices
DAX
EURO STOXX Banks
Sustainability indices
ECPI Ethical EMU Equity
ECPI Ethical Euro Equity

Fig. 3.13 Indices including Commerzbank. Source: Commerzbank AR (2013:20)

Fig. 3.14 Commerzbank's risk management structure. Source: Commerzbank AR (2013:100)

Fig. 3.15 Commerzbank's Risk Committee. Source: Commerzbank AR (2013:100)

3.5.2 Deutsche Bank

Deutsche Bank (DB) is still by far the biggest bank in Germany by total assets, although those have decreased from EUR 2022 billion to EUR 1,611 billion between the end of 2012 and 31/12/2013. Its total assets are thus almost three times those of its closest rival, Commerzbank, and 4.3 times of Brazilian's largest, Banco do Brasil.

Internationally, Deutsche Bank describes itself as one of the leading global universal banks with a wide variety of business segments ranging from capital markets to private and corporate clients and asset management. Apart from its top position in Germany, Deutsche Bank has a strong position in Europe, North America and important emerging markets, especially in Asia. This is reflected by its main hubs which are Frankfurt am Main, London, New York, São Paulo, Dubai, Singapore, and Hong Kong (DB AR 2013:22).

Following the retirement of DB's longstanding CEO, Josef Ackermann, two Co-CEOs with equal rights, Jürgen Fitschen and Anshu Jain have been heading Deutsche Bank since June 1st, 2012. The Executive Board is responsible for controlling the group, strategic steering, the allocation of resources, financial reporting and risk management. It is noteworthy that the control of the group is expressly noted as part of the Management Board's duties. Due to the size and complexity of the organization, a wider, additional body of management has been in place: The board members as well as senior managers from DB's regions, sections and infrastructure functions make up the Group Executive Committee (GEC) which has the role of coordination and steering global business sections and regions (cfr. Fig. 3.16). Its tasks include the continuous information of the Board about business development and significant transactions, as well as advising the Board on strategic questions and the preparation of board decisions (DB AR 2013:19 f.).

Management structure

Fig. 3.16 Deutsche Bank Management Structure. Source: DB AR (2013:20)

Deutsche Bank continues to practice and support the *"universal banking model"* (*"Universalbankmodell"*) which according to its AR 2013 *"best meets the increasingly complex requirements of its clients"* (DB AR 2013:21). This stands in contrast to the separate banking system (*"Trennbankensystem"*) being promoted by several supervisory authorities, particularly in the United States of America.[14]

In September 2012, Deutsche Bank launched a program called Strategy 2015+ *"to address the current challenges and to successfully position itself in a changed environment characterized by macroeconomic uncertainties, increasing regulation, historically low interest rates, growing margin pressure and, not least, a critical public perception of the financial industry"*. (DB AR 2013:21) This program is also meant to save costs of € 4.5 billion per year (DB AR 2013:19 ff.).

3.5.2.1 Corporate Governance

DB's system of corporate governance is based on the German Stock Corporation Act and the German Corporate Governance Code, and consists of five key elements:

- effective decision-making on the basis of appropriate information;
- good relations with shareholders;
- effective cooperation between the Management Board and Supervisory Board;

---

[14]The US Banking Act of 1933—also known as Glass-Steagall Act—limited commercial bank activities, also by restrictions on affiliations between commercial banks and securities firms. These restrictions were repealed in 1999 by the Gramm-Leach-Bliley Act which was later blamed for contributing to the 2007–2009 financial crisis, while others argued that the ability of commercial banks to acquire securities firms as well as the latter's ability to convert into bank holding companies helped mitigate the crisis.

- a performance-based compensation system with a sustainable and long-term focus;
- transparent and timely reporting.

(DB AR 2013:24)

In 2013, Deutsche Bank established a *"Compensation Control Committee"* as well as an *"Integrity Committee"* to monitor compliance with acceptable business conduct. Thus the total number of Supervisory Board Committees increased to seven.

In April 2013, Management Board compensation at Deutsche Bank was reformed *"following the completion of an independent review of the bank's compensation systems commissioned by the Supervisory Board"*, placing a stronger focus on qualitative aspects *"so that variable compensation is determined not just on the basis of financial targets, but also on "how" performance is achieved"*. (DB AR 2013:25) Determination of annual variable compensation depends on Group-wide and individual performances which are linked to a *"sustainable development of earnings"*; the relevant components consist of a *"Culture and Client Factor"* and at least 50% of variable compensation is equity-based and most of the bonus is deferred.

In its annual declaration of conformity pursuant to section 161 of the German Stock Corporation Act, DB confirmed its compliance with the German Corporate Governance Code with two exceptions regarding the targeted pension level and the nomination committee.

As for the definition of its stakeholders, Deutsche Bank puts its shareholders— 50% of which are German, while 79% are institutional investors including banks (Fig. 3.17)—first, followed by clients, staff, and society.

Also its Non-Core Operations Unit (NCOU, Figs. 3.18 and 3.19) is listed as a stakeholder, following clients. While it does not become clear in which way this unit acts as a stakeholder, its purpose is rather important for the bank's risk management strategy and shall therefore be briefly discussed here, too.

The NCOU was established in the fourth quarter of 2012 in order to reduce risks from non-core assets and business activities, apparently a *"bad bank"* within DB. Its initial risk-weighted asset (RWA, pro-forma Basel III) amounted to € 141 billion and total adjusted assets (TAAs) to € 120 billion (Fig. 3.20).

Most of the assets in the NCOU relate to Corporate Banking & Securities, followed by Corporate Investments. Provisions for credit losses increased by 29%

Structural Data

		2013	2012	2011
Number of shareholders		566,979	610,964	660,389
Shareholders by type in % of share capital¹	Institutional (including banks)	79	75	74
	Private	21	25	26
Regional breakdown in % of share capital¹	Germany	50	45	52
	European Union (excluding Germany)	26	33	26
	Switzerland	6	6	6
	USA	15	13	13
	Other	4	2	3

Fig. 3.17 Deutsche Bank Shareholder Structure. Source: DB AR (2013:30)

in € m.	2013	2012
Net revenues	867	1,054
Total provision for credit losses	818	634
Noninterest expenses	3,358	3,312
Income before income taxes	**(3,306)**	(2,923)
Risk-weighted assets	48,483	80,317
Assets	54,224	97,451

Fig. 3.18 DB-NCOU reporting 2013 (excerpt). Source: DB AR (2013:60)

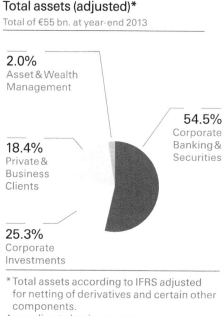

Total assets (adjusted)*
Total of €55 bn. at year-end 2013

2.0%
Asset & Wealth
Management

54.5%
Corporate
Banking &
Securities

18.4%
Private &
Business
Clients

25.3%
Corporate
Investments

* Total assets according to IFRS adjusted
  for netting of derivatives and certain other
  components.
According to business areas assets were
transferred from in 2012.
Figures rounded

Fig. 3.19 DB-NCOU asset breakdown. Source: DB AR (2013:60)

in 2013 *"mainly due to specific credit events across portfolios including exposure to European commercial real estate"* (DB AR 2013:60).

The aim of the NCOU is to reduce the balance sheet by selling assets to third-party investors, *"unwinding complex structures by working with multiple parties including other dealers, investors and financial institutions."* (DB AR 2013:60).

As the NCOU business wind down proceeded, DB reallocated economic capital for operational risk in an amount of € 892 million to its Core Bank in the third quarter of 2013. (DB MR 2013:60 [148]).

Fig. 3.20 DB RWA 2012-
2013. Source: DB AR
(2013:61)

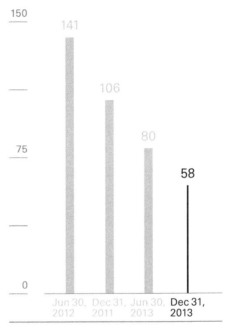

Accelerated de-risking
Risk-weighted asset equivalents in € bn.*

150

141

106

80

58

75

0

Jun 30,   Dec 31,   Jun 30,   **Dec 31,**
2012   2011   2013   **2013**

* Risk-weighted assets plus equivalents
of capital deduction items; based on CRD IV

3.5.2.2   Risk Management

In general, DB's risk profile is characterized by a high diversity dictated by its broad
spectrum of products and markets. Key risks are being measured by DB using the
"undiversified Total Economic Capital metric", thus showing each business division's risk profile individually, before taking cross-risk effects on Group level into
account. The high level of diversification leads to a significant benefit in all five
business divisions as illustrated by Table 3.10.

Between end-2012 and end-2013, Deutsche Bank's loan book decreased by 5%
to € 382 billion—mainly due to NCOU—while maximum exposure to credit risk
decreased by 20% to € 1.6 trillion. Regional credit risk exposure was evenly spread
over DB's key markets but provisions for credit losses increased by 20% to € 2.1
billion. The single largest industry category loan book was residential mortgages
with € 148 billion, of which 78% are attributable to the solid German market.

Market risk decreased, generally speaking, for DB during 2013, while its operational risk profile increased as measured by economic capital usage.

Table 3.10 Deutsche Bank Risk Profile 2013

Risk profile of our corporate divisions as measured by total economic capital

In % (unless slated otherwise)	Corporate Banking & Securities	Global Transaction Banking	Deutsche Asset & Wealth Management	Private & Business Clients	Non-Core Operations Unit	Consolidation & Adjustments	Total in € m	Total
Dec 31, 2013								
Credit Risk	17	7	1	14	5	0	12,013	44
Market Risk	18	1	6	11	5	7	12,738	47
Operational Risk	9	0	2	3	5	0	5,253	19
Diversification Benefit	(7)	(1)	(2)	(3)	(3)	0	(4,515)	(17)
Business Risk	5	0	0	0	1	0	1,682	6
Total EC in € m in %	11,398 / 42	2,033 / 7	2,010 / 7	6,671 / 25	3,349 / 12	1,710 / 6	27,171 / 100	100 / 0
Dec 31, 2012								
Credit Risk	16	6	1	13	8	0	12,574	44
Market Risk	14	1	5	11	10	5	13,185	46
Operational Risk	7	0	2	1	7	0	5,018	17
Diversification Benefit	(5)	0	(2)	(2)	(6)	0	(4,435)	(15)
Business Risk	7	0	0	0	1	0	2,399	8
Total EC in € m in %	11,118 / 39	1,781 / 6	2,009 / 7	6,720 / 23	5,782 / 20	1,331 / 5	28,741 / 100	100 / 0

Source: DB MR 2013:59 [147]

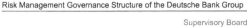

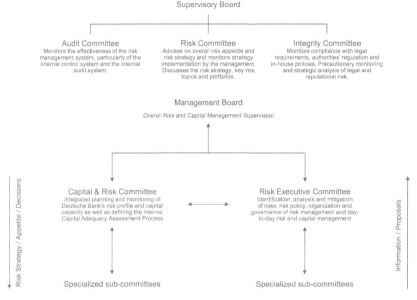

Fig. 3.21 DB Risk Management Governance Structure. Source: DB MR (2013:64 [152])

Liquidity reserves as of end-2013 amounted to € 196 billion and the Common Equity Tier 1 capital ratio (formerly: Core Tier 1 capital) increased from 11.4% to 12.8% under Basel 2.5. (DB MR 2013:60 ff. [148 ff.])

Figure 3.21 shows the structure of Deutsche Bank Group's Risk Management Governance Structure.

3.5.3   DZ Bank

DZ BANK AG Deutsche Zentral-Genossenschaftsbank, Frankfurt am Main (DZ BANK—DZB), as the parent company in the DZ BANK Group, acts on the one hand as a central institution for over 900 cooperative banks and their c. 12,000 branch offices and on the other hand as a corporate bank. DZ Bank Group is an integral part of the German Volksbanken Raiffeisenbanken cooperative financial network, which includes around 1100 local cooperative banks. The group comprises a number of specialized institutions as shown in Fig. 3.22.

COMPANY BRANDS

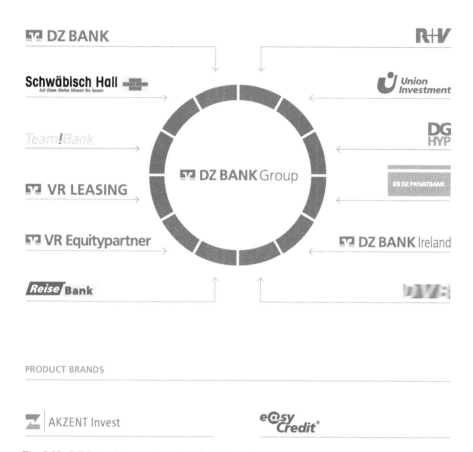

Fig. 3.22 DZ Bank Group. Source: DZB AR 2013:3 (cover)

3.5.3.1 Risk Management

Contrary to the habit of most of its peers, DZ Bank calls its risk report *"opportunity and risk report"*, thus adopting the *"Yin & Yang"* approach described above under 2.2.1.

DZ BANK Group defines *"opportunities as unexpected positive variances from the forecast financial performance for the coming year"*. Accordingly, risks are understood to be *"adverse developments affecting financial position or financial performance, and essentially comprise the risk of future losses or insolvency"*. The annual report continues to expand that *"[t]he risk management system is more detailed than the system for the management of opportunities because risk management is subject to comprehensive statutory requirements and is also of critical importance to the continued existence of the DZ BANK Group as a going concern.*

The management of opportunities is based on a qualitative approach and is tightly integrated into the strategic planning process." (DZB AR 2013:74). The definition for risk used by this entity clearly stresses the financial aspects of business, seemingly neglecting non-financial risks. This impression is largely confirmed by the typology of risks used with two of the three main types covering financial risks and only the third, *"business-performance"* risk being a non-financial risk group, including operational, business, and reputational risk as shown in more detail by Table 3.11.

DZB management units have to take *"conscious decisions"* regarding the assumption or avoidance of risks, observing *"guidelines and risk limits specified by the head office"*. Furthermore, *"divisions responsible for risk management are separated both in terms of organization and function from downstream divisions"*. (DZB AR 2013:79).

3.5.3.2 Corporate Governance

Not much can be found in its annual report about corporate governance but the plan *"to enhance corporate governance in the DZ BANK Group with the aim of integrating the local cooperative banks even more closely."* (DZB AR 2013:88).

As a matter of fact, corporate governance is being dealt with inside the opportunities and risks report under the sub-title *"risk-oriented corporate governance"* and described as a system *"based on three pillars that are interlinked and well established in the monitoring and control environment. The DZ BANK Group thereby has a governance structure that complies with MaRisk requirements, sets out the operational framework for risk management, and fosters the development of an appropriate group-wide risk culture"*. (DZB AR 2013:88).

The *"governance structure of risk management"* of DZ Bank Group is pictured in Fig. 3.23.

3.5.4 KfW

Among the three largest financial institutions in Germany, DZ Bank is the only public entity. According to section 2 par. 1 Nr. 2 KWG it does not qualify as financial institution under that law, but has nonetheless been applying its main rules (KfW AR 2013:152). Its name *"Kreditanstalt für Wiederaufbau"* (Credit Entity for Reconstruction) is somewhat outdated as it refers to the post-World War II era. Its main purpose has however remained much the same given that it nowadays finances change by supporting public, corporate and private investors in the areas of employment, education, energy, environment, and health as well as internationalization and developing countries. The bank was also a strong contributor to the reunification of Germany over the past 25 years.

In the public interest, KfW promotes developments in line with three mega-trends:

Table 3.11 DZ Bank Risk Typology[1]

	Risk type	Definition	Risk factors
Core financial sector risks	**Credit risk** – Traditional credit risk – Issuer risk – Replacement risk	Risk of losses arising from the default of counterparties (borrowers, issuers, other counterparties)	– Concentration of loans with a longer term to maturity and a non-investment-grade credit rating – Deterioration in the credit quality of public-sector bonds – Increased requirement for allowances for loans on losses and advances
	Equity risk	Risk of losses arising from negative changes in the fair value of that portion of the long-term equity investments portfolio in which the risks are not included in other types of risk	Increased requirement for the recognition of impairment losses on the carrying amounts of investments
	Market risk – Interest-rate risk – Spread risk – Equity price risk – Currency risk – Commodity risk – Market liquidity risk	– Risk of losses on financial instruments or other assets arising from changes in market prices or in the parameters that influence prices (market risk in the narrow sense of the term) – Risk of losses arising from adverse changes in market liquidity (market liquidity risk)	– Widening of credit spreads on European government bonds – Shortages of market liquidity
	Liquidity risk	Risk that cash and cash equivalents will not be available in sufficient amounts to ensure that payment obligations can be met (insolvency risk)	– Funding structure for lending business – Uncertainty surrounding tied-up liquidity – Changes in the volume of deposits and loans – Funding potential in money markets and capital markets – Fluctuations in fair value, marketability of securities, and the eligibility of such securities for use in collateralized funding arrangements – Exercise of liquidity options – An obligation on the DZ BANK Group to pledge its own collateral
Specialist financial sector risks	**Technical risk of a home savings and loan company**[2] – New business risk	– Risk of a negative impact from possible variances compared with the planned new business volume (new business risk) – Risk of a negative impact that could arise from variances	– Decline in new business – Changed customer behavior (unrelated to changes in interest rates)

(continued)

Table 3.11   (continued)

	Risk type	Definition	Risk factors
	– Collective risk	between the actual and forecast performance of the collective building society business caused by significant long-term changes in customer behavior unrelated to changes in interest rates (collective risk)	
	Actuarial risk – Biometric risk – Interest-rate guarantee risk – Premium and claim risk – Reserve risk – Cost risk – Lapse risk	Risk that the actual cost of claims and benefits deviates from the expected cost as a result of chance, error or change	– In the case of products with long-term guarantees, calculation assumptions vary over the term of the contracts compared with the assumptions at the time the contracts were signed – The actual impact of losses exceeds the forecast impact
Business-performance risk	**Operational risk**	Risk of losses from human behavior, technological failure, weaknesses in process or project management, or external events	– Business interruptions – Insufficient availability of employees – Malfunctions or breakdowns in data processing systems – Disruptions to outsourced processes and services – Inaccurate external financial reporting – Impact of market manipulation and accounting or tax fraud – Failure to recognize violations of legal provisions
	Business risk	Risk of losses arising from earnings volatility which, for a given business strategy, is caused by changes in external conditions or parameters	– Fiercer competition based on pricing and terms – Insufficiently competitive electronic trading platforms
	Reputational risk	Risk of losses from events that damage the confidence of customers, investors, the labor market, or the general public in DZ BANK Group entities or in the products and services they offer	Worsening of the reputation of the banking sector as a result of the financial crisis and the sovereign debt crisis

[1] A part from spread risk, migration risk on securities, and migration risk on traditional loans, which are covered by the capital buffer
[2] Including the business risk and reputational risk of BSH
Source: DZB AR 2013:76.

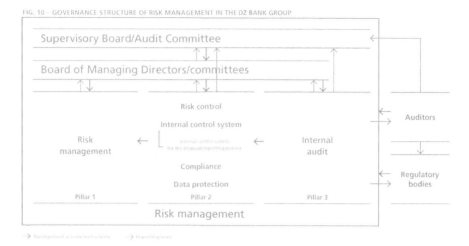

Fig. 3.23 DZ Bank's Risk Management Governance Structure. Source: DZB AR (2013:79)

- Use of natural resources (environmental protection and climate change), which accounts for approx. 40% of KfW's financing;
- Demographic development (both in developed and developing countries);
- Globalization (including ensuring the competitiveness of the national economy).

KfW defines sustainability, the *"aim of our daily work"* (KfW AR 2013:7), as targeting an ecologically sound, socially just, and economically powerful development.

3.5.4.1   Risk Management

The risk management section in KfW's 2013 Annual Report is quite brief, only defining it as a central task of overall bank steering and referring to an *"adequate risk profile"* to allow the bank to *"perform its tasks sustainably and over the long term"*. The board of directors is informed about the risk profile of the bank on a monthly basis, the supervisory board at least quarterly (KfW AR 2013:152).

As a case in point, KfW transferred EUR 319 million to Lehman Brothers on September 15, 2008, despite of previous signs of bankruptcy and thus found itself unexpectedly in the center of a scandal as Lehman filed for Chapter 11 bankruptcy protection a few hours after the transfer was made by KfW. A subsequent PwC-report identified a number of issues regarding the internal organization of KfW and reportedly identified seven recommendations as to how procedures at KfW should be improved in order to avoid another error as this one. Of particular public concern was the fact that the German Central Bank had halted the transaction for lack of funding on the relevant KfW account, but notwithstanding information about the difficult situation of Lehman Brothers gathered by KfW staff and discussed in an emergency meeting, KfW transferred funds to that account in order to enable

the transfer still on that Monday morning. (SZ 17/05/2010, http://www.
sueddeutsche.de/geld/nach-lehman-ueberweisung-peinliche-details-zur-kfw-panne-
1.537637).

In its 2008 Annual Report, KfW also referred to this mishap in the following way:

*"During the course of the financial crisis, and after the payment mistakenly made
to Lehman Brothers, KfW systematically reviewed its risk management and control
workflows to assess whether structural action was required. This process focused on
further developing group-wide control processes (e.g. for securities and operational
risks), and expanding the real-time decision-orientated reporting system. In addition, the Group is working on increasing its investment control and further developing its early risk warning system. It is also reviewing methods of valuing
structured products. Activities with regard to these topics started as projects during
the reporting year, and will be continued and implemented in 2009." (KfW AR
2008:18).*

3.5.4.2   Corporate Governance

Due to its nature as a public entity which reports directly to the Ministry of Finance,
KfW is bound to the Federal Public Corporate Governance Code (*Public Corporate
Governance Kodex—PCGK*), the corporate governance code of the federal republic.
A declaration of conformity was first signed by KfW on 06/04/2011. (KfW AR
2013:150) In 2008, the Supervisory Board and the Managing Board of KfW had
issued a declaration of intent regarding the *PCGK* in which they recognize the
principles of the code and seek to implement them at KfW as soon as possible.
For the financial year 2010 a corporate governance section was first introduced and
the Managing Board and the Board of Supervisory Directors for the first time issued
a declaration of compliance with the recommendations which shall be renewed
annually, and disclose and detail any deviations for the code principles in a corporate
governance report, according to KfW's 2009 Annual Report. (KfW AR 2009:19).

Regarding executive remuneration, two points appear noteworthy:

1. None of the board members except for the CEO received a variable compensation
   for the years 2012 and 2013, while in 2012, they received bonuses (*"recognition
   premiums"*) for the financial year 2011 of only EUR 20,000 (in one case, EUR
   5000 *pro rata*).
2. Base salary was reduced between 2012 and 2013 from an already moderate
   c. EUR 600,000 to c. EUR 500,000, by which all board members but the CEO
   suffered partly severe salary cuts, cfr. Table 3.12.

The Annual Report does not give an explicit explanation for the reduction of base
salary, the abolition of bonuses for ordinary board members from 2011 onwards, or
the increase of base salary of the CEO, but mentions that the CEO's remuneration is
linked to his performance. (KfW AR 2013:153 ff.)

Table 3.12 Reumeration Table for KfW 2013

Jahresvergütung des Vorstands und Zuführung zu den Pensionsrückstellungen in den Jahren 2013 und 2012 in TEUR

	Gehalt		Variable Vergütung		Sonstige Bezüge		Gesamt		Zuführung zu den Pensions-rückstellungen	
	2013 TEUR	2012 TEUR	2013 TEUR	2012 TEUR	2013 TEUR	2012 TEUR	2013 TEUR	2012 TEUR	2013 TEUR	2012 TEUR
Dr. Ulrich Schröder (Vorstandsvorsitzender)	698,6	680,3	260,0	250,0	81,9	97,9	1.040,5	1.028,2	421,7	794,2
Dr. Günther Bräunig	518,8	632,6	0,0	0,0	30,2	31,3	549,0	663,9	477,7	1.026,9
Dr. Norbert Kloppenburg	518,8	668,4	0,0	0,0	42,3	52,7	561,1	721,1	479,8	1.032,7
Dr. Edeltraud Leibrock	518,8	510,2	0,0	0,0	51,4	50,4	570,2	560,6	293,2	276,5
Bernd Loewen	508,1	514,8	0,0	0,0	46,0	46,0	554,1	560,8	392,0	382,6
Dr. Axel Nawrath	491,5	498,3	0,0	0,0	100,4	107,0	591,9	605,3	553,8	678,5
Gesamt	**3.254,6**	**3.504,6**	**260,0**	**250,0**	**352,2**	**385,3**	**3.866,8**	**4.139,9**	**2.618,2**	**4.191,4**

[1] Aus rechnerischen Gründen können in der Tabelle Rundungsdifferenzen auftreten.

[2] Die Gehälter von Dr. Günther Bräunig, Dr. Norbert Kloppenburg, Bernd Loewen und Dr. Axel Nawrath enthielten 2012 eine Anerkennungsprämie für das Geschäftsjahr 2011 in Höhe von 20 TEUR, bei Dr. Edeltraud Leibrock anteilig 5 TEUR.

Source: KfW AR 2013:153

3.5.5   HypoVereinsbank: UniCredit Bank AG

In 1998 the two big Bavarian banks, Bayerische Hypotheken- und Wechsel-Bank and Bayerische Vereinsbank merged and became Bayerische Hypo- und Vereinsbank Aktiengesellschaft (HVB). Its eldest predecessor, Hochfürstlich-Brandenburg-Anspach-Bayreuthische Hofbanco, had been founded in 1780 by Margrave Karl Alexander von Brandenburg-Ansbach.

Following the 1998 merger, the bank pursued various acquisitions to expand its international business—particularly in the CEE region—while practicing a regional approach in Germany.

In 2003, HVB's commercial real estate financing division was spun off and listed as Hypo Real Estate. This specialized real estate lender was nationalized following an unsuccessful merger with Depfa bank and re-branded as pbb Deutsche Pfandbriefbank in 2009.

HVB itself was acquired in 2005 by the Italian bank Unicredit S.p.A. and subsequently continued its strategy of growth via an M&A strategy by merging with Vereins- und Westbank Hamburg, acquiring a corporate loan portfolio from Westfalenbank AG, etc. At the same time however, some participations were divested, including that in Bank Austria which was sold in 2006 without a tender process to HVB's parent company Unicredit, leading to a number of shareholder claims.

Since 2008, HVB has been using the corporate design of UniCredit Group, but continues to use the name HypoVereinsbank, while the name UniCredit is becoming more and more commonly used, internally and externally.

As announced in the 2012 annual report, HVB introduced a new business model and reorganized the structure of HVB Group, consisting since the beginning of 2013 of the following sections:

* Commercial Banking (CB);
* Corporate & Investment Banking (CIB);
* Asset Gathering;
* Other/consolidation.

Profits in 2013 decreased significantly, particularly in HVB's commercial banking section, while the corporate & investment banking section, despite generating almost the same income as commercial banking, proved much more profitable.

HVB's Annual Report has remained much the same since 2007 both in size and structure, however the risk report section has increased in volume and thus its relative weight over that period, while the corporate governance chapter kept its length although its structure changed, including now a *"Women's Council"* section. (HVB AR 2013:3 ff., 215 ff.; HVB AR 2007:251 ff.)

3.5.5.1   Risk Management

"In the course of our business activities, risks are identified, quantified, assessed, monitored and actively managed. We therefore regard it as one of our core objectives to apply these considerations in order to integrate risk management, risk-controlling and risk-monitoring processes in all segments and functions." (HVB AR 2013:52)

Table 3.13 HVB Risk Typology

• Credit risk;	• Other risks:
• Market risk;	– Business risk;
• Liquidity risk;	– Strategic risk;
• Operational risk;	– Reputational risk;
	– Real estate risk;
	– Financial investment risk;
	– Pension risk.

Source: HVB AR 2013:52 f

HVB Group companies included in its consolidated financial statements are part of the risk management program of HVB Group. Various criteria, e.g. size, portfolio structure, and risk content are applied to classify them according to the Internal Capital Adequacy Assessment Process (ICAAP). Measurement of the economic capital is performed differently for the individual risk types. All other companies are subject to a simplified approach to calculate economic capital.

HVB's risk typology is as shown in Table 3.13.

Operational risk is understood by HVB as *"the risk of losses resulting from inadequate or failed internal processes, systems, human error or external events. This definition includes legal risk but not strategic risk or reputational risk. Legal risk includes, but is not limited to, fines, penalties and damages resulting from regulatory measures and settlements paid to private individuals."*

HVB's risk management program is *"built around the business strategy adopted by the Management Board, the Bank's risk appetite and the corresponding risk strategy. Implementation of the risk strategy is a task for the Bank as a whole, with key support from the Chief Risk Officer (CRO) organisation."* (HVB AR 2013:53).

3.5.5.2 Corporate Governance

In relation to its de-listing in 2008, HVB's Management and Supervisory Boards decided that the bank would voluntarily comply with the rules of the German Corporate Governance Code *"to the extent that these provisions can be applied to an unlisted Company with just one shareholder".* (HVB AR 2013:260).

HVB's Management Board consists of eight members which have, since January 2013, responsibilities according to the new organizational structure of the bank.

Members of the management board receive a base salary paid monthly plus a variable, performance-related compensation which also takes into account *"the changed economic environment and the requirements of the regulators and strengthens the importance of sustainable company success"* (HVB AR 2013:271) and includes a bonus paid out over a five year period according to the following plan (HVB AR 2013:271):

- Year 1: 20% of the bonus disbursed in cash
- Year 2: 20% of the bonus disbursed in cash
- Year 3: 20% of the bonus disbursed in UniCredit S.p.A. stock

- Year 4: 20% of the bonus disbursed in UniCredit S.p.A. stock and 10% in cash
- Year 5: 10 % of the bonus disbursed in UniCredit S.p.A. stock

The corporate governance report provides a summary of the five supervisory board meetings which took place in 2013 and describes the work of the two supervisory board committees: the remuneration & nomination committee and the audit committee.

HVB was the first bank in Germany to form its own Women's Council in December 2009, *"with which it has a new tone in the German banking world ever since. Besides dealing with feedback and comments and regularly discussing economic and social issues relating to women, the Council looks at ways of improving the position of women in the financial sector [...]"*. The Council, consisting of around 30 *"outstanding entrepreneurs and managers"* meets for plenary sessions at least twice a year and is specifically empowered by HVB's Management Board to make recommendations and launch its own initiatives. (HVB AR 2013:255).

3.6   Summary

3.6.1   Banking Regulation

Given that banks in Brazil and Germany adhere to the rules of the Basel Committee, rules are in the end quite comparable. Local differences remain however, especially due to the unequal structure of its financial (supervisory) system as well as cultural aspects.

3.6.2   Corporate Governance Frameworks

The corporate governance frameworks, mainly consisting of the corporate governance codes, are different in appearance and detail, but quite comparable in terms of practical implementation. Compensation committees are becoming the norm, and Familiy Councils and/or Advisory Boards on a larger scale, and in both countries, would be welcome.

3.6.3   Risk Management Regulation

Risk management regulation in general is still quite different, and a further approximation between the countries, and internationally might be wished for. Notwithstanding, particularly banks do historically have a strong risk management mentality, thus do not differ much between the entities under analysis.

3.6.4 Banks Under Analysis

The Brazilian and German banks under analysis are quite different, both in a national comparison and individually. Notwithstanding, they are, respectively, the five largest banks in their home economies while globally, only Germany's Deutsche Bank is among the ten largest in the world (rank 10 by total assets). Commerzbank holds position 40 worldwide, and Banco do Brasil ranks 54th (http://www.relbanks.com/worlds-top-banks/assets-2013).

The comparison was helped by the fact that for all banks, the financial year corresponds to the calendar year, all publish their accounts online in English, while this had not occurred for the year 2013 for all institutions as of cut-off date for our analysis.

Both countries show a high proportion of public banks in their top-5 and based on the above analysis, the following *"pairs"* of comparable banks can be identified:

Banco do Brasil—Deutsche Bank (e.g. for their dominant size)
Itaú—Commerzbank (i.a. for their online record)
Bradesco—Unicredit HVB (e.g. for its strong consumer brand)
BNDES—KfW (both development banks)
Caixa—DZ Bank (comparable not least for their (quasi-)public nature)

Interestingly, most banks understand risk management as part of corporate governance (bank names), while some see them as separate topics, and only in one instance (Bradesco) corporate governance appears to be a part of risk management.

Regarding the grouping of countries into market-based, bank-based and *"other"* countries (cfr. 2.1.22 above), we may conclude that Brazil falls into the third category, together with countries such as France and Italy (which may also, and independently, be considered culturally close to each other), given their relatively independent position regarding corporations and as such may also be able to exercise an active role in the further development and implementation of corporate governance best practices in Brazilian companies of different sizes and industries.

Chapter 4
Research Design

4.1 Introduction

"Theorists, policy-makers, and practitioners share the intuition that corporate governance reflects national culture." (Licht et al. 2005:231; cfr. Bebchuk and Roe 1999:168)

It is difficult however to employ culture in economic studies for its *"soft"* characteristics which do not easily fit into the usual framework of economic analysis. Therefore, culture was often dealt with in an anecdotal way or as a *"black box"*. One possible proxy for culture used in order to circumvent this difficulty in assessing or categorizing national culture is religion (Stulz and Williamson 2003; Beck et al. 2003; cfr. Landes 2000). While religion has indeed been shaping national culture over the past ca. 2000 years, it is difficult to operationalize it to this end, given the differences, lack of comparability and different denominations on both a national and international level. Particularly in our case, comparing Brazil and Germany, one would be faced with one culture still dominated by Roman Catholicism [although, over the past 40 years, its share in the population has dropped from well over 90% to 'only' 64.6% in 2010 (IBGE 2010:92)] and another almost evenly split between the latter (30.15%), Protestantism (29.23%) and those unaffiliated with any religion (33.06%) (BPB 2013). This significant difference is certainly not eased by the fact that *"Brazilian Catholicism"* is in fact strongly influenced by local customs and mixed with earlier religions and/or customs, as well as many different denominations of Christian belief.

Licht et al. (2005:231) therefore reformulate the question into *"in what way do the laws on the books in different societies reflect the culture that prevails in those societies? Put another way: are meaningful, measurable elements of the culture found in different countries manifest in the statutory legal rules of those countries?"*

La Porta et al. (1998, 2002) introduced an integrated approach to law and finance and thus redefined the analytical framework for comparative research on corporate governance. By the operationalization of investors' legal rights and legal origins they provide statistical tools which correlate with several important economic factors, leading to the desire to enhance investors' rights through legislative reforms. The *"legal approach"* later presented became *"the preferred way to understand corporate governance"* (Licht et al. 2005:230). Based on a classification of legal origins, this system has also been used as a proxy for colonial impact on social institutions, leading to the notion that in general, common law origin predicts a better economic performance.

At the same time, failures in the attempt to implement *"western"* legal systems in formerly soviet states lead to the view that the simple codification of investor rights is insufficient to achieve the desired aims, such as transparency and accountability.

Therefore, Pistor et al. (2000) stressed the the importance of legality understood as law enforcement and the mode of legal transplantation. (Licht et al. 2005:230).

Another approach is to test the perception of professionals working in the area to evaluate their understanding of changes. This is the approach to be adopted in what follows.

4.2 Methodology

To test the first 10 hypotheses, self-completion questionnaires (Bryman and Bell 2011:230 ff.). have been be used in order to obtain data on the sentiment of respondents vis-à-vis the questions.

Regarding the last two hypotheses, a content analysis (Bryman and Bell 2011:288 ff.) was carried out regarding the contents of annual reports of the five largest banks in each of the two countries under analysis.

This study is a *"bounded system"* that is limited by a defined time frame and a certain number of institutions (2×5) and countries (2) (cfr. Creswell 1998:37). The research took place in a time period of 5 months, starting in January 2014 and ending in May 2014. During this period, document analysis and the survey were performed. The survey was completed predominantly by respondents from Brazil and Germany.

Content analysis shall be carried out to obtain a solid and clear background about the studied banks and their specific attitude towards corporate governance and risk management topics.

4.3 Data

Due to the nature of the hypothesis to be tested this study, qualitative data—such as risk management quality or corporate governance importance—have been used, as for example individual thoughts on corporate governance developments. These were then translated into numerical values for statistical evaluation. Whenever possible, quantitative data—such as word counts—were used to analyse and confirm hypotheses on a more objective basis.

The relevant units of analysis shall be:

1. Corporate governance in the selected jurisdictions;
2. Risk management in the selected jurisdictions;
3. Selected financial institutions in the selected jurisdictions.

4.4 Identification of Variables

4.4.1 Independent Variables

Independent variables used in this study are:

a. Country;
b. Year;
c. Financial Institutions;
d. Non-Financial Institutions

4.4.2 Dependent Variables

Dependent variables used in this study are:

a. Risk management quality;
b. Risk management regulation;
c. Risk management importance;
d. Corporate governance quality;
e. Corporate governance regulation;
f. Corporate governance importance.

   With regards to Brazill and Germany:

g. Comparability of corporate governance;
h. Comparability of risk management;
i. Comparability of financial institutions;
j. Executive remuneration.

   With regards to Annual Reports:

k. Word count;
l. Topic highlights;
m. Introduction of specific sections.

4.5 Overview of Research Design

In order to receive comparable and meaningful data against which the hypotheses could be tested, two main sources have been identified:

1. A specific online survey carried out mainly amongst financial professionals in Germany and Brazil;
2. The Annual Reports of the five largest banks in each country.

We assume that there is a strong difference between Brazil and Germany regarding corporate governance and risk management. Furthermore we assume that significant changes have occurred since the beginning of the latest financial crisis regarding corporate governance and risk management, both in Brazil and Germany. In order to analyse the obtained data objectively, statistical analysis shall be applied to establish whether there is any correlation between the variables:

- Significance of difference between variables;
- General applicability of obtained conclusions.

4.6 Sample and Data Collection Procedures

4.6.1 Survey

The survey was prepared and tested using the survey tools of *"surveymonkey.com"*. The questionnaire was prepared in English and translated into German and Portuguese to allow respondents (mainly from Brazil and Germany, but also from Portugal, Austria and Switzerland) to answer in their mother tongue. The different language versions have been available following below-mentioned links since February 2014 and responses for this study were collected until end of March, 2014:

- English: http://surveymonkey.com/s/CGRMEN
- German: http://surveymonkey.com/s/CGRMDE
- Portuguese: http://surveymonkey.com/s/CGRMPT

Those links (or any combination of them or individually, according to the receiver (s)) were then distributed among several institutions, companies, lawfirms, individuals and organizations linked to corporate governance and risk management by email. Those addressees either responded themselves and/or forwarded the link (s) to their members, partners, colleagues, acquaintances or friends. Among the addressees were:

- Direct contacts from the personal address book of the author, including lawfirms and consultancies in Europe and Brazil;
- LinkedIn contacts;

- Several universities in Brazil, Germany, and Portugal (UAL, Nova School of Business and Economics, USP, University of Frankfurt; etc.);
- Surveymonkey Audience;
- The Brazilian Corporate Governance Institute (IBGC);
- The Commission of the German Corporate Governance Code;
- The German foundation Hans Böckler Stiftung;
- The Global Association of Risk Professionals (GARP);
- The International Corporate Governance Network (ICGN);
- The Portuguese Corporate Governance Institute (IPCG/cgov);
- Xing contacts.

The full survey in its three language versions is attached as Annex I–III to this document. It is split into the following parts:

4.6.1.1   Questions on the Respondent

Questions 1 to 4 deal with the professional situation and experience of the respondent, including their job function, industry, permanence in the current line of work and the country they have been working for. Questions 5 and 6 regard specific experience of the participant in the survey regarding risk management and corporate governance.

The reason for this is to establish the qualification of respondents to answer the subsequent, specific questions related to corporate governance, risk management, and financial institutions in both, Brazil and Germany.

4.6.1.2   Question Regarding Corporate Governance and Risk Management Changes

Questions 7 and 8 regard the perceived changes of corporate governance and risk management. In line with the subjective nature of the topic and structure of the survey, questions for the respondents' opinion were asked (*"How would you say..."*). The questions were sub-divided into nine specific areas for each by combining sets of three topics (quality, regulation and importance of risk management or corporate governance) with three area-specific questions (the respondent's organization, their region(s), and the topic in general).

4.6.1.3   Questions on the Comparability of Corporate Governance and Risk Management in Brazil and Germany

Questions 9 and 10 inquire about the respondent's opinion (*"Do you think..."*) regarding comparability of Brazil and Germany when it comes to corporate governance and risk management with nominally scaled multiple choice options (*yes/no/don't know*[1]).

The reason behind these binary response format questions is to be able to establish whether respondents think that the countries are comparable with regards to the general topics, before going into detail. This allows determining later, based on answers to specific questions, whether there is a difference between the perceived general comparability and specific comparison of individual, specific aspects of those general topics.

4.6.1.4   Questions Regarding Corporate Governance and Risk Management Differences and Similarities Between the Two Countries

Questions 11 to 16 request a comparison between Brazil and Germany for differences and similarities regarding risk management, corporate governance and financial institutions, giving the ordinarily scaled choices of *major similarity/minor similarity/no similarity* for the following six categories:

- Institutional background;
- Regulatory background;
- Business environment;
- Political environment;
- Economic environment;
- Social environment;
- Other (please specify).

4.6.1.5   Questions Regarding Remuneration in (Non-)financial Institutions

The last three questions of the survey do not regard differences between Brazil and Germany, but are rather covering specific aspects of risk management and corporate governance regarding financial institutions, non-financial companies, and in general. They are structured as closed questions with responses in the form of a modified Likert scale (Bryman and Bell 2011:239f.)

Questions 17 and 18 ask respondents in six (sub-)questions regarding financial institutions (question 17) and non-financial institutions (question 18) whether they *strongly agree/somewhat agree/somewhat disagree/strongly disagree* with the following statements on executive remuneration, with the option to select *"no opinion"*:

---

[1]For a discussion on whether or not to offer "don't know" answers, cfr. Bryman and Bell (2011:260).

- Executive remuneration in financial institutions (total package) is now more closely linked to a prudent risk management than before the latest financial crisis;
- This is particularly true for bonuses;
- This is particularly true for share options;
- This is particularly true for other benefits;
- Executive remuneration in financial institutions (total package) is now more often subject to a cap/limit than before the latest financial crisis.

4.6.1.6 Questions on the Importance and Interrelation of Corporate Governance and Risk Management

On a metrical scale, question 19 allows the respondent to *strongly agree/somewhat agree/somewhat disagree/strongly disagree* with the following statements on the importance and interrelation of corporate governance and risk management, with the option to select *"no opinion"*:

- Risk management has become more important since the beginning of the financial crisis;
- Corporate governance has become more important since the beginning of the financial crisis;
- Risk management is more important in financial institutions than in other businesses.
- Risk management is part of corporate governance;
- Corporate governance is more important in financial institutions than in other businesses.

4.6.1.7 Summary

In total, the 19 questions with their sub-questions add up to 135 questions asking respondents to give information about themselves, the geographic areas they work in as well as their opinion on corporate governance, risk management, and financial institutions-related topics in Brazil and Germany. The high number of (partly similar) detailed questions and cross-checks against opposite questions (e.g. similarities/differences) imply an intrinsic test of validity and allow for a detailed comparative analysis.

4.6.2 Annual Reports

In order to analyze the development of corporate governance and risk management within the reporting in banks, and thus the influence the latest financial crisis has had on them, we analyzed the annual reports as the main reporting tool of corporations and the ultimate summary of their activities and performance over the respective year, for the five largest banks by assets for Brazil and Germany.

Those were collected in their English.pdf-versions for the period 2007 until 2013, if available. Whenever those were not available, the local language version was used (in seven instances), and in three cases (Banco do Brasil, BNDES, and Caixa) the respective 2013 annual reports were not yet available as of the date of analysis (April 2014) and therefore couldn't be considered for this study. Consequently, the overall comparability within the year 2013 and with respect to the preceding years is limited, particularly among the Brazilian banks under analysis.

4.7   Analysis Procedures

4.7.1   Survey

A total of 282 surveys were filled by respondents online until cut-off, of which 47 were excluded from the analysis for not having responded to 30 or more of the 135 questions. Of the remaining sample of 235, 104 showed relevant professional experience in Germany, 103 in Brazil, four in both afore-mentioned countries and 24 in other countries. Given the low number of respondents which were not experienced in either Brazil or Germany (including those with professional experience in both countries), their answers were not taken into account when it came to the comparison of those two countries, but did count regarding hypotheses which do not include such direct comparison.

Question 1 asked respondents to select the area which best describes their job function. The result shows that 45.6% of respondents work directly with risk management, corporate governance or financial services. The remainder includes Consulting, Management, and Research. The distribution of activities is presented in Fig. 4.1.

The principal industries of participant's organizations (Question 3) are more diverse than their field of work—as one may expect—but still over 60% work in the finance industry including insurance. These are distributed as shown in Fig. 4.2.

Almost 60% of respondents have been in their current line of work for over 5 years (Question 2), indicating a high level of seniority and work experience, thus granting an enhanced level of quality for responses, as illustrated by Fig. 4.3.

Regarding geography, almost 90% of participants in our survey are or were working for the Brazilian or German market (Question 4), warranting a deep regional knowledge and cultural understanding, cfr. Fig. 4.4.

Asked specifically about the countries covered by respondents with regards to risk management (Question 5), the distribution looks as shown in Fig. 4.5.

The same question regarding corporate governance (Question 6) produced the outcome shown in Fig. 4.6.

The two figures on jurisdictions for specific activity in the areas of risk management and corporate governance show that more than half (64%/57%) of the

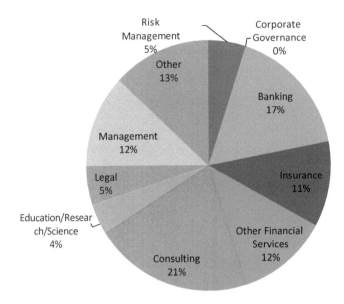

Fig. 4.1 Participants by job function. Source: own presentation

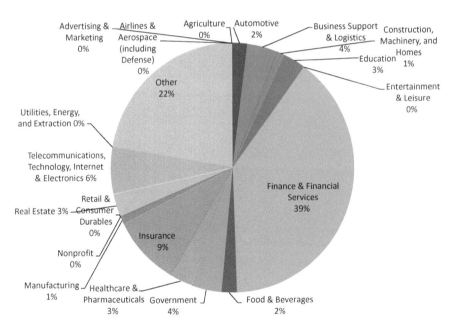

Fig. 4.2 Participants' industries. Source: own presentation

Fig. 4.3 Respondents'
work experience in years.
Source: own presentation

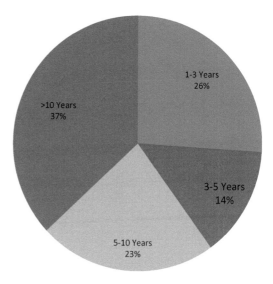

Fig. 4.4 Respondents'
geography of activity.
Source: own presentation

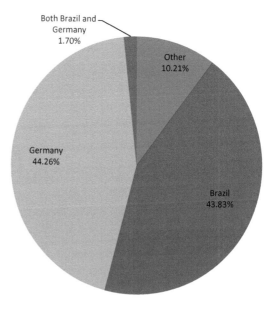

respondents do work directly with those topics or have done so before and are as such particularly knowledgeable. This shows once more the high level of insight of respondents into the topics at hand. The higher granularity of the structure of answers as compared to Fig. 4.4 would make grouping of answers for analysis by this measure more complex and the results less focused, thus leading us to use the answers from respondents who identified themselves with Brazil or Germany under question 4 as basis for our comparative analysis, as described above.

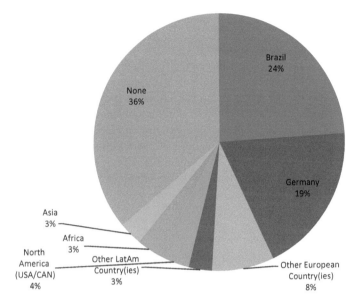

Fig. 4.5 Respondents' risk management jurisdictions. Source: own presentation

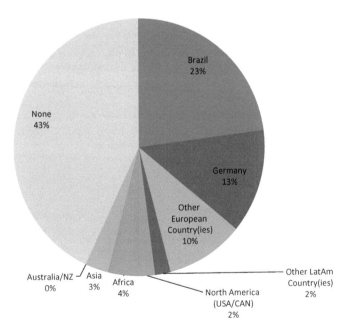

Fig. 4.6 Respondents' corporate governance jurisdictions. Source: own presentation

The results of the surveys have been transferred from the surveymonkey.com site and converted into SPSS format. SPSS has been used to analyze the data in order to receive dependable results for the testing of the hypotheses. To this end, variance testing using the Levene's test for equality of variances and t-tests for equality of means were applied to ordinal variables. For questions 17 and 18 of our survey, for instance, a modified Likert scale was used from *"I strongly agree"* to *"I strongly disagree"* with the alternative option *"I have no opinion"* instead of the usual *"Undecided"* as an opt-out option. (Cfr. Bryman and Bell 2011:254).

For categorical variables, chi-square tests were performed, as for example in questions 9 ff. where the answer options consisted of *"YES"*, *"NO"*, and *"DON'T KNOW"* or else *"Major difference"*, *"Minor difference"*, and *"No difference"*.

4.7.2   Annual Reports

Given the lack of three documents within the scope of 10 entities over a period of 7 years, 67 annual reports were analyzed with a total of over 16,000 pages (cfr. Annex IV). Each report was tested for the existence of an own section for corporate governance and a separate one for risk management. Whenever this was the case, the value *"1"* was attributed. In cases where one of the topics constitutes a sub-section of the report, the value *"0.5"* was given. All other cases were coded with value *"0"*.

Subsequently, we checked whether or not risk management was part of corporate governance within the structure of each report. In all confirmative cases, value *"1"* was given, *"-1"* for cases in which corporate governance was described as part of risk management and *"0"* in all other cases.

Furthermore, the documents were submitted to a word count regarding the following key words, using the search function in different pdf-viewers:

- Crisis/crises;
- Corporate Governance;
- Risk Management;
- Risk; and
- Corporate Social Responsibility.

Depending on the language version of the report, the following expressions were used:

- Crisis, crise(s), Krise(n) for crisis;
- Corporate Governance, governança corporativa for corporate governance;
- Risk management, gestão de risco(s), gerênciamento de risco(s), gestão integrada de risco(s), Risikomanagement for risk management;
- Risk, risco, Risiko for risk; and
- (corporate) social responsibility, CSR, (corporate) social governance, sustainability, socio(-)environmental responsibility, responsabilidade social, responsabilidade

socio(-)ambiental, RSC, sustentabilidade; (soziale) Verantwortung for corporate social responsibility.

Those counts were then manually checked and corrected for cases in which they had been used outside of the context of this study. The numerical result of those counts was entered into a list.

Finally, the initial pages of each report were manually searched for highlighted topics which appear on the following list:

- Corporate Governance;
- Risk Management;
- Corporate Social Responsibility; and
- Crisis.

Whenever one of the above topics was highlighted, the value *"1"* was attributed, else *"0"*, unless in a case where the reference was stressed but not really highlighted in comparison to those which received value *"1"*. For the latter, the value *"0.5"* was attributed.

This way, a list of over 54,000 scores was obtained which were then analyzed over time and between countries.

The 67 annual reports have been analyzed by country of origin of the financial institutions as well as by year. Even when corrected for the three missing reports, the Brazilian reports account only for 34.8% of the volume as expressed in pages, while reports from German banks make up 65.2% of the pages.

The analysis shows that only 46.2% of the analyzed reports from Brazil include corporate governance as a main section Regarding risk management/risk control/risk report, only 47.8% show these topics as a main section. For Germany, the equivalent figures stand at 53.8% and 52.2%, respectively, and thus significantly higher.

In contrast to this, 6 Brazilian reports (75%) highlight corporate governance and 88.2% do so for corporate social responsibility, while the German values amount to a mere 2 (25%) and 11.8% respectively.

Risk management and the financial crisis received even less attention: the former was highlighted once in Brazil and twice in Germany, while only one report in Germany paid special attention to the crisis (none in Brazil).

Interestingly, 70% of the Brazilian reports include risk management as part of corporate governance in their structure, while in Germany, only 30% do so.

The evolution of references (i.e. times, key words were mentioned) to our focus key words crisis, corporate governance (CG), risk management (RM) and corporate social responsibility (CSR) can be illustrated as in Fig. 4.7.

When analyzing the numbers from both, Brazil and Germany, *"crisis"* had a peak of references in 2008 reports and while still high in 2009, the numbers decreased over time, with another upswing in 2011.

"Corporate governance" has seen a stable evolution on a relatively low level, while *"risk management"*'s rate of increase between 2007 and 2011 went almost in parallel, albeit on a higher level, but has been increasing significantly from 2011 to 2013.

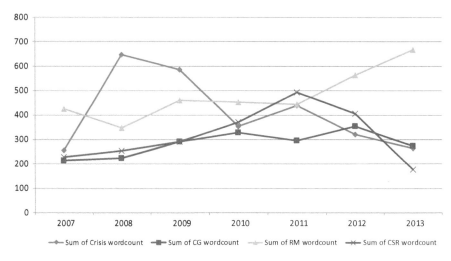

Fig. 4.7 Word count evolution, Brazil and Germany. Source: own presentation

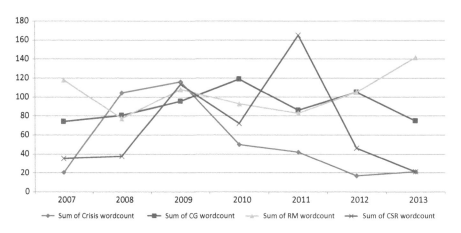

Fig. 4.8 Word count evolution, Brazil. Source: own presentation

In contrast to this, *"CSR"* figures increased constantly until 2011 but then were the only ones to contract to a level below that of 2007.

Generally, it should be noted that those four indices move all in a relatively close range between c. 200 and 700 words in total and are thus comparable.

In the case of Brazil, the word count for *"crisis"* reached its highest value in 2009, rather than 2008, after it had already increased roughly fivefold from 2007 to 2008. After 2009, however, the decline has been uninterrupted (Fig. 4.8).

"Corporate governance" figures have been stable, although on a much higher level than in Germany, relative to the other sets of data for Brazil. Similarly, *"risk management"* has been increasing notably since 2011.

Regarding *"CSR"* word count figures, we find a steep increase between 2010 and 2011, followed by a sharp decline. As with the other numbers for Brazil, the higher variance compared to the German sample can be explained by the relatively low totals, in a range between c. 20 and 165 words.

The case of Brazil stresses the *"decoupling"* of *"corporate governance"* and *"risk management"* which have been very close to one another between 2008 and 2012, before moving in opposite directions in 2013. It remains to be seen whether this is a real trend or if they will merge again as has happened in 2008 when they came from different directions.

In general, the German figures (Fig. 4.9) show a lower level of variance than the Brazilian results. The absolute numbers are much higher, in a range of c. 140–540 words per data set. This is still disproportional compared to Brazilian numbers when corrected for the volume of reports (as measured in number of pages), which is roughly twice as high in Germany as in Brazil.

The same is true with regards to the *"risk"* word count—which includes combinations such as *"risk management"*—as exemplified by Fig. 4.10.

The absolute numbers for Germany are on average and corrected for the higher volume of Geman reports, 3.3 times higher than the Brazilian ones.

Regarding the question under scrutiny, the results show that the evolution of times the word *"risk"* was used in Brazilian annual reports was basically flat over the period under analysis until they increased in 2013.

In a stark contrast to the Brazilian case, the use of the word *"risk"* has increased constantly in Germany over the period under review, from around 4000 in 2007/2008 to almost exactly 7000, which represents a growth of 83.8% over the period.

The increase in Brazil from 815 in 2007 to 1694 in 2013—and which was actually even lower than the effective increase between 2012 and 2013 (109.7%)—stood at 107.9%. As noted before, the year 2013 figures in the Brazilian case are disturbed by the fact that three of the five reports were not available. This would lead to a decrease

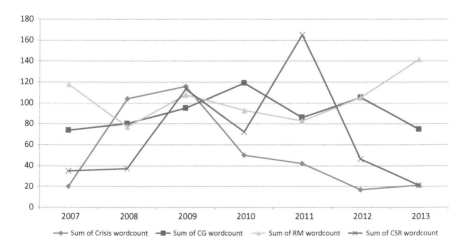

Fig. 4.9 Word count evolution, Germany. Source: own presentation

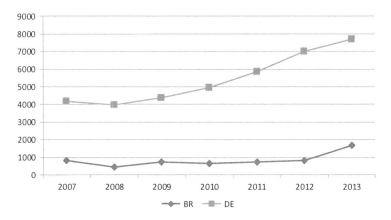

Fig. 4.10 Word count evolution *"risk"*, Brazil and Germany. Source: own presentation

of the total figure, if those were not over-compensated by the fact that Itaú for the first time issued a consolidated annual report in 2013 with 3.5 times as many pages and 4.1 times as many references to *"risk"*.

4.8   Summary

4.8.1   Survey

The questionnaires were answered by a relatively high number of respondents, given the limited population dealing with the topics under analysis in two specific jurisdictions. The answering and evaluation of questions was relatively straight-forward as mostly closed questions were used, partly in the format of a modified Likert scale and coded accordingly, thus being directly comparable and easy for respondents to understand. (Cfr. Bryman and Bell 2011:250 ff.) In order to mitigate the disadvantage of this method, namely to exclude exhaustive and detailed answers, almost each answer had a Comment/Other section. The possibility to comment was however barely ever used and thus disregarded completely, as were answers from those who did not answer 30 or more of the 135 questions. The respondent's professional background and field of expertise warrant a deep understanding of the issues at hand.

As such, the overall quality of questionnaire responses may be considered as high.

4.8.2 Annual Reports

The content analysis (Bryman and Bell 2011:288 ff.) performed on the annual reports of the years 2007–2013 from the ten banks under analysis was logically limited by the relatively small amount of documents, given the limited number of institutions and the restricted time frame (which, however, could only have been extended into the past and thus into a period before the onset of the financial crisis). Still, and more in the word count section than with regards to highlighting, for instance, high individual and total values allow for some comparison of development over time and between countries.

In line with recent history, the numbers from both countries, Brazil and Germany, indicate that the term *"crisis"* had a peak of references in 2008 (primarily in Germany) and 2009 (particularly in Brazil) after which the numbers decreased over time, with another upswing in 2011 in the German data set which can be explained by the European sovereign debt crisis. The peak in the same year of Brazilian CSR figures is much more difficult to explain, it might have to be related to political factors such as the change in the presidency and social unrest.

"Corporate governance" and *"risk management"* have both seen a relatively stable evolution until 2011, when *"risk management"* word count increased from an already higher level in comparison to *"corporate governance"*.

In contrast to this, *"CSR"* figures increased constantly until 2011 but then were the only ones to contract to a level below that of 2007.

Towards the end of our time line, all variables/indices decrease back to 2007 levels, except for *"risk"* (including *"risk management"*), which has almost doubled since its low point in 2008.

Chapter 5
Discussion and Conclusion

Germany and Brazil are clearly different in many aspects, but surprisingly similar when it comes to certain aspects of corporate governance and risk management in financial institutions. On a macro-economic level, they are indeed comparable. Both are among the biggest countries in terms of their economies, and Brazil at times shows stronger data. For instance, market capitalization reaches only 43.4% of GDP in Germany, but 54.6% in Brazil, while these ratios in countries such as the US (114.9%) and the UK (122.0%) are more than twice as high. (Worldbank.org, 2012 data)

Given that this study has focused on the period since 2007, and thus on the global financial and European debt crises, many of the similarities found herein might be attributed to the fact that both countries have fared relatively well during that period, which on the other hand makes them rather comparable despite their obvious differences.

Those differences reside in per-head output, (in)equality of income distribution, an almost opposite socio-regional environment and, obviously, different cultures. All of those are certainly factors which made most respondents to our questionnaires state that the objects of analysis were not comparable for both countries.

The fact that yet most corporate governance and risk management indicators as perceived by the same respondents yielded similar results for Brazil and Germany may be attributable to a relative cultural proximity when it comes to finance, and to banking in particular.

Where significant differences between those two countries could be verified, especially with regards to corporate governance (including remuneration), these occurred mainly in Brazil which may be explained by the fact that Brazil had more potential for improvement in this area, while risk management has been on a relatively high level in (large) financial institutions of both countries for quite some time now.

As such, it shall be interesting to see to what extend these tendencies continue to materialize going forward or whether they separate, possibly due to a higher risk

R. C. Gericke, *Corporate Governance and Risk Management in Financial Institutions*, Contributions to Management Science, https://doi.org/10.1007/978-3-319-67311-0_5

appetite by lenders in Brazil than in Germany and/or the consequences of a lack of experience some—and particularly the first-time—borrowers have in Brazil.

Both, the Brazilian and German Corporate Governance Codes should in our view include a section on the meaning and place of risk management within the corporate governance structure, as does, for example the Portuguese Corporate Governance Code (PCGC).

5.1 Conclusions

In this monograph, we have discussed various aspects of corporate governance and risk management from an international viewpoint and with a special focus on Brazil and Germany as well as banking, taking into account the developments since the beginning of the latest financial crisis in 2007/2008.

Clearly, Brazil and Germany are quite different countries—culturally and economically. Still, there are some similarities, for example regarding total market capitalization or the Open Budget Index.

In terms of corporate governance we could confirm that the general impression is still that of very clear differences, but when looking deeper into the different topics, we found that differences are diminishing as Brazil is improving in these areas, while Germany appears to progress quite slowly.

With regards to risk management, differences are perceived to be strong overall, but appear to be muted in the area of financial services, certainly due to strict and similar or even identical regulation (e.g. Basel III).

Our analysis of data from surveys used for this study shows that there have been moderate increases in quality, regulation and perceived importance of both, risk management and corporate governance. This is largely true for both countries, still we found that especially regarding corporate governance, such increases have been lower or even non-existent in Germany as compared to Brazil.

The hypotheses that corporate governance and risk management had become more important over the 2007–2013 period could however not be fully confirmed as results of the analysis of annual reports did not produce consistent results.

The reason might be that the Brazilian society feels a stronger necessity to improve in those areas than that of Germany, which might have started from a higher level. Still, the crises (financial and European souvereign) have had more impact—although still moderate—on Germany than on Brazil, which only showed a very weak performance in 2009.

Agreement existed amongst participants in the survey that risk management is a part of corporate governance, although also here, affirmation from participants covering Germany was weaker than that from respondents working in Brazil.

Consequently, we believe that risk management should be included as a section in its own right in corporate governance codes, given that, still today, "risk management is typically not covered, or is insufficiently covered, by existing corporate governance standards or codes" (OECD 2009:9). This would also help to further strengthen the conceptual integration of risk management as part of corporate governance and might support the advancement of both.

Furthermore, the establishment of risk-, advisory- and remuneration-committess (where not already in place) and Family Councils for family-owned businesses might be helpful to instill more discipline and achieve a higher internal independence.

In summary, no major changes have been perceived to have taken place in the areas of risk management and corporate governance, while it is evident that a number of (regulatory) developments have occurred during that period. They may however have been relatively constant and were therefore, subjectively, less noted, or expectations were higher so that the actions taken appear weaker in the perception of our respondents.

5.2 Limitations

This study is clearly limited by its scope of investigation. As such, all the restrictions used to define its limits are at the same time limiting its results.

Such factors include firstly the restriction on ten banks. The study of banks other than the top five, different types of financial institutions, or other types of companies—including smaller entities—would certainly yield different results—which would then be interesting to compare to the conclusions drawn in this paper.

Another limitation is the time window chosen. Although it ends at a very recent point in time—and therefore cannot immediately be pushed out into following periods—the starting point in 2007 only allows to study recent developments, rather than those over decades, for instance.

Yet another limitation is the regional one. While some comparison has been made to other jurisdictions, Brazil and Germany have been—in line with its purpose—the immediate focus of this study.

This work is further limited by the concept, basis, and realization of its empirical analysis: Whilst a relatively high and comparable number of respondents from both focus countries participated, respondents from other areas were too few to provide for significant insight into differences between the *"inside"* and an *"outside"* perspective.

5.3 Suggestions for Further Investigation

In order to fill the gaps left by this study, further investigation could be carried out on the evolution of corporate governance and risk management in other sectors, other financial institutions, and other countries. Particularly those geographies should be subject to a comparable analysis which have suffered more during the financial crisis than the two focus countries in this study actually have.

Furthermore, the time horizon of analysis could be extended both forward as time passes, and backward to get a long-term perspective, while due to the emergence of corporate governance in the 1990s, a time extension into the past beyond that period would hardly generate meaningful results.

Finally, other aspects of governance, such as equity and debt governance[1] could be analysed in conjunction with questions dealt with in this study.

---

[1]Cfr. Foos (2012).

Bibliography

Abell P, Samuels J, Cranna M (1994) Mergers, motivation and directors' remuneration. Centre for Economic Performance. Discussion Paper No. 199, July 1994

Acemoglu D, Johnson S, Robinson J, Thaicharoen Y (2003) Institutional causes, macroeconomic symptoms: volatility, crises and growth. J Monet Econ 50:49–123

Adiloglu B, Vuran B (2012) The relationship between the financial ratios and transparency levels of financial information disclosures within the scope of corporate governance: evidence from Turkey. J Appl Bus Res 28(4): ABI/INFORM Global, p 543ff

Aguilera RV, Desender KA, Kabbach de Castro LR (2011) Perspectives on comparative corporate governance. In: The SAGE handbook of corporate governance, p 379 ff. Electronic copy available from http://ssrn.com/abstract=1797142

Altman EI, Saunders A (1998) Credit risk measurement: developments over the last 20 years. J Bank Financ 21(1998):1721–1742

Anderson, Richard C & Associates. Risk management & corporate governance. OECD 2009. www.oecd.org/dataoecd/29/4/42670210.pdf

Aoki M (1994) The Japanese firm as a system of attributes. In: Aoki M, Dore R (eds) The Japanese firm: sources of competitive strength. Oxford University Press, Oxford, pp 11–40

Archer EC (2003) How governance concerns are reshaping executive and director compensation. Inst Invest J 2003(2):80–83

Armstrong M, Thompson P, Brown D, Cotton C (2006) Reward management. Chartered Institute of Personnel and Development

Ballou B, Heitger DL (2008) Integrating governance, risk, and reporting to create long-term value. Strateg Financ I 2008:36–41

BB.com. http://www.bb.com.br/portalbb/page3,136,3595,0,0,2,8.bb?codigoMenu=1308&codigoNoticia=11382& codigoRet=3322&bread=5

BCBS – Basel Committee on Banking Supervision, Enhancing corporate governance for banking organizations, February 2006. Available from http://www.bis.org/publ/bcbs122.pdf

BCGC – Brazilian Corporate Governance Code – Código das Melhores Práticas de Governança Corporativa, IBGC, São Paulo, 2010

Bebchuk LA, Roe MJ (1999) A theory of path dependence in corporate governance and ownership. Stanford Law Rev 52:127, 168

Beblo M, Wolf E, Zwick T (2005) Erfolgsabhängige Vergütung: Welche Faktoren führen zu einer Motivationssteigerung bei Topmanagern? zfo 74(2):78–84

Beck T, Demirguc-Kunt A, Levine R (2003) Law, endowments, and finance. J Financ Econ 70:137

© Springer International Publishing AG, part of Springer Nature 2018
R. C. Gericke, *Corporate Governance and Risk Management in Financial Institutions*, Contributions to Management Science,
https://doi.org/10.1007/978-3-319-67311-0

Bengtsson E (2012) The political economy of banking regulation – does the Basel 3 accord imply
    change? (January 24, 2012)
Bengtsson E (2013) The political economy of banking regulation – does the Basel 3 accord imply a
    change? Credit and Capital Markets – Kredit und Kapital 46(3):303–329
Berens W, Schmitting W (2004) Zum Verhältnis von Controlling, Interner Revision und
    Früherkennung vor dem Hintergrund der Corporate Governance. Corporate Govern Control
    51–75
BIS.org (a). http://www.bis.org/bcbs/basel3/basel3_phase_in_arrangements.pdf [05.03.2017]
BIS.org (b). http://www.bis.org/bcbs/basel3/b3summarytable.pdf [05.03.2017]
Black BS, de Carvalho AG, Sampaio JO (2014) The evolution of corporate governance in Brazil.
    Emerging Markets Review. Available from http://papers.ssrn.com/sol3/papers.cfm?abstract_
    id=2181039
Black F, Scholes M (1974) The pricing of options and corporate liabilities. J Polit Econ 81:637–654
Blume D, Alonso F (2007) Institutional investors and corporate governance in Latin America:
    challenges, promising practices and recommendations. In: Financial Market Trends (Nov 2007),
    p 93 ff. Available from http://www.keepeek.com/Digital-Asset-Management/oecd/finance-and-
    investment/institutional-investors-and-corporate-governance-in-latin-america_fmt-v2007-art15-en
Blume ME (1968) The assessment of portfolio performance: an application of portfolio theory. Ph.
    D. dissertation, Univ. Chicago
Blundell-Wignall A, Wehinger G, Slovik P (2009) The elephant in the room: the need to deal with
    what banks do. OECD J Financ Mark Trends 2009(2):11–35
Bhimani A (2009) Risk management, corporate governance and management accounting: emerging
    interdependencies, editorial. Manag Account Res 20:2–5
Bobirca A, Miclaus PG (2007) Extensiveness and effectiveness of corporate governance regulations
    in South-Eastern Europe. World Acad Sci Eng Technol 30:7–12
Bodie Z, Merton R (1995) A conceptual framework of analyzing the financial environment. In:
    Crane DB, Bodie Z, Froot KA, Perold AF, Merton RC (eds) The global financial system: a
    functional perspective. Harvard Business School Press, Boston
Borchert J (2010) Ambition and opportunity in federal systems: the political sociology of political
    career patterns in Brazil, Germany, and the United States, Leuven. http://soc.kuleuven.be/web/
    files/11/72/W02-33.pdf [27.05.2010]
Bordean O-N, Pop ZC (2012) A comparative study of corporate governance issues: the case of
    Germany and Romania. IUP J Corp Gov XI(1):20
Bovespa. http://ri.bmfbovespa.com.br/-banco de dados [03.09.2014]
BPB. Soziale Situation in Deutschland – Religionszugehörigkeit. http://www.bpb.de/nachschlagen/
    zahlen-und-fakten/soziale-situation-in-deutschland/145148/religionszugehoerigkeit, 27/09/2013
Brown I, Steen A, Foreman J (2009) Risk management in corporate governance: a review and
    proposal. Corp Gov 17(5):546–558
Brühwiler B (2009a) Die Norm ISO 31000. In: MQ Management und Qualität 1–2/2009. http://
    www.saq.ch/fileadmin/user_upload/mq/downloads/mq_2009_01_bruehwiler.pdf [15.01.2017]
Brühwiler B (2009b) Prozess und Methoden. In: MQ Management und Qualität 3/2009. http://
    www.saq.ch/fileadmin/user_upload/mq/downloads/mq_2009_03_bruehwiler.pdf [15.01.2017]
Brühwiler B (2009c) Die Risikomanagement-Politik. In: MQ Management und Qualität 4/2009.
    http://www.saq.ch/fileadmin/user_upload/mq/downloads/mq_2009_04_bruehwiler.pdf
    [15.01.2017]
Brühwiler B (2009d) KMU: schlanke Prozesse nutzen. In: MQ Management und Qualität 5/2009.
    http://www.saq.ch/fileadmin/user_upload/mq/downloads/mq_2009_05_bruehwiler.pdf
    [15.01.2017]
Brühwiler B (2009e) Der Beruf des Risikomanagers. In: MQ Management und Qualität 7–8/2009.
    http://www.saq.ch/fileadmin/user_upload/mq/downloads/mq_2009_07_bruehwiler.pdf
    [15.01.2017]
Bryman A, Bell E (2011) Business research methods. Oxford University Press, Oxford

Buhleier C, Splinter S (2013) Aufsichtsrat und Risikomanagement. Deloitte Corporate-Governance-Forum, S. 2 ff

Burghof H-P, Hunger A (2003) Access to stock markets for small and medium sized growth firms: the temporary success and ultimate failure of Germany's *Neuer Markt*.http://www.ipo-underpricing.de/Downloads/Hunger/Hunger_Access.pdf

Burt BA (2001) Definitions of risk. University of Michigan, Ann Arbor

Byers SS, Paige Fields L, Fraser DR (2008) Are corporate governance and bank monitoring substitutes: evidence from the perceived value of bank loans. J Corp Finan 14(2008):475–483

Cadbury A (1992) Report of the committee on the financial aspects of corporate governance (The Cadbury Report), London

Campos NF, Iootty M (2007) Institutional barriers to firm entry and exit: case-study evidence from the Brazilian textiles and electronics industries. Econ Syst 31(4):346–363

Carroll AB, Buchholtz AK (2012) Business and society: ethics, sustainability, and stakeholder management. South-Western Cengage Learning, Mason, OH

Carvalhal da Silva AL, Leal RPC (2006) Ownership, control, valuation and performance of Brazilian corporations. Corp Ownersh Control 4:300–308

GCGC – Government Commission, German Corporate Governance Code, May 13, 2013. http://www.dcgk.de//files/dcgk/usercontent/en/download/code/D_CorGov_final_2013.pdf

Cheng AT (2014) Danger in the shadows. In: Insititutional Investor, 38–41

Chernenko S, Fritz Foley C, Greenwood R (2012) Agency costs, mispricing, and ownership structure, March 2012. Available from http://www.people.hbs.edu/ffoley/pubsub.pdf

Chhabra AB (Summer 2008) Executive stock options – moral hazard or just compensation? J Wealth Manag 11(1):20–35

Claessens S, Feijen E, Laeven L (2008) Political connections and preferential access to finance: the role of campaign contributions. J Financ Econ 88:554–580

Claessens S, Yurtoglu B (2012) Corporate governance in emerging markets: a survey. Available from http://ssrn.com/abstract=1988880, January 15, 2012, p 1 ff

Cremers KJM, Nair VB. Governance mechanisms and equity prices, August 2003. Available from http://www1.fee.uva.nl/fm/PAPERS/Cremers.pdf

Creswell JW (1998) Qualitative inquiry and research design: choosing among five approaches. Sage, Thousand Oaks, CA

Dallas LL (2012) Short-termism, the financial crisis, and corporate governance. J Corp Law 37(2):265

Dalton DR, Daily CM, Johnson JL, Ellstrand AE (1999) Number of directors and financial performance: a meta-analysis. Acad Manag J 42(6):674–686

De Carvalho AG, Pennacchi G (2012) Can a stock exchange improve corporate behavior? Evidence from firms' migration to premium listings in Brazil. J Corp Finan 18(4):883–903

De Soto H (1989) The other path: the invisible revolution in the Third World. Harper and Row, London

Deutsche Börse AG (2001) Rules and regulations Neuer Markt, Frankfurt, 18.10.2001

Djankov S, La Porta R, Lopez-de-Silanes F, Shleifer A (2002) The regulation of entry. Q J Econ 117:1–35

Docherty PT (2008) Basel II and the political economy of banking. Int J Polit Econ 37(2):82–106

Donker H, Zahir S (2008) Takeovers, corporate control, and return to target shareholders. Int J Corp Gov 1(1):106–134

Drennan LT, Beck M (2001) Corporate governance: a mandate for risk management? www.nottingham.ac.uk/business/cris/ukec/2001paper4.doc

Dyck A, Zingales L (2004) Private benefits of control: an international comparison. J Financ 59:537–600

Eckstein H (2002) Case study and theory in political science. In: Gomm R, Hammersley M, Foster P (eds) Case study method: key issues. Key Texts, London, pp 119–163

Eichenwald K (2005) Conspiracy of fools. Broadway Books

Elkington J (1997) Cannibals with forks: the triple bottom line of 21st century business. Wiley, San Francisco

Emeseh E, Ako RT, Okonmah P, Obokoh LO (2009) Corporations, CSR and self regulation: what lessons from the global financial crisis? German Law J 11(2):230–259

Ernst & Young (2013) Marktkapitalisierung 2011–2013. Schweizer Konzerne im internationalen Vergleich, 19.12.2013

Esperança P, Sousa A, Pereira I, Soares E (2011) Corporate governance no Espaço Lusófono. Texto Editores

Estrin S, Prevezer M (2010) A survey on institutions and new firm entry: how and why do entry rates differ in emerging markets? Econ Syst 34(3). Available from https://ssrn.com/abstract=1898717

Estrin S, Prevezer M (2011) The role of informal institutions in corporate governance: Brazil, Russia, India, and China compared. Asia Pac J Manag 28:41. http://link.springer.com/article/10.1007/s10490-010-9229-1/fulltext.html [14.01.2017]

European Commission (2001) Promoting a European framework for corporate social responsibility, Brussels, 18.7.2001

European Commission (2011) A renewed EU strategy 2011–14 for corporate social responsibility, Brussels, 25.10.2011

Faccio M, Lang LHP (2002) The ultimate ownership of western European corporations. J Financ Econ 65:365–395

Fama EF (1971) Risk, return, and equilibrium. J Polit Econ 79(1):30–55

Filatotchev I, Toms S, Wright M (2006) The firm's strategic dynamics and corporate governance lifecycle. Int J Manage Financ 2(4):256–279

FMT – Financial Market Trends [Anonymous] (1995) Financial markets and corporate governance. Financial Market Trends; Nov 1995; 62; ABI/INFORM Global, p 13 ff

Foos D (2012) Equity and debt governance: the impact on bank risk. Available from http://www.virtusinterpress.org/IMG/pdf/Helsinki_conference_paper_17.pdf

Freeman RE (1984) Strategic management: a stakeholder approach. Boston

Friedland J (2009) The subprime and financial crises. Int J Discl Gov 6(1):40–57

Friedman M (1962) Capitalsim and freedom (Reissued with new Preface 1982)

Friedman M (1970) The social responsibility of business is to increase its Profits. New York Times Magazine, September 13, 1970

Frye MB, Nelling E, Webb E (2006) Executive compensation in socially responsible firms. Corp Gov Int Rev 14(5):446–455

Froot KA, Scharfstein DS, Stein JC (1993) Risk management: coordinating corporate investment and financing policies. J Finan 48(5):1629–1658

Fuchs E, Jerabek R (2009) Korruption und Amtsmissbrauch, 2. Auflage, Wien 2009

Gadhoum Y, Lang LHP, Young L (2005) Who controls US? Eur Financ Manag 11(3):339–363

GCGC (2013) Appendix [19]. http://www.dcgk.de/en/code/archive.html?file=files/dcgk/usercontent/en/download/code/D_CorGov_final_2013.pdf [05.03.2017]

Gebauer et al (2008) (cit Goldmann et al 2010:189)

Gerlach ML (1992) Alliance capitalism: the social organization of Japanese business. University of California Press, Berkeley

Gilboa I, Lieberman O, Schmeidler D (2008) On the definition of objective probabilities by empirical similarity. Available from http://www.tau.ac.il/~igilboa/pdf/GLS_Definition_Objective_Probabilities.pdf

Globerman S, Shapiro D (2003) Governance infrastructure and US foreign direct investment. J Int Bus Stud 33(1):19–39

Goergen M, Renneboog L, Zhang C (2008) Do UK institutional shareholders monitor their investee firms? CentER Discussion Paper Series No. 2008-38; ECGI – Finance Working Paper No. 208/2008 (April 2008)

Goldmann G, Grothe A, Madruga K, Odebrecht C (2010) Nachhaltigkeit im Vergleich: Deutschland und Brasilien: Stand, interkulturelle Unterschiede und Perspektiven

Golub BW, Crum CC (2010) Risk management lessons worth remembering from the credit crisis of 2007–2009. J Portfolio Manag, Spring 2010:21–44

Gompers PA, Ishii JL, Metrick A (2003) Corporate governance and equity prices. Q J Econ 118 (1):107–155

GRI – Global Reporting Initiative, Reporting Principles and Standard Disclosures (2013) Available from https://www.globalreporting.org/resourcelibrary/GRIG4-Part1-Reporting-Principles-and-Standard-Disclosures.pdf

Grothe A. CSR und unternehmerische Nachhaltigkeit. In: Goldmann et al 2010

Gyomlay K, Moser S (2005) The market value of reputation. In: Streiff T (ed) 6th International sustainability leadership symposium. The Sustainability Forum Zürich, Zürich

Hall RB (ed) (2002) The emergence of private authority in global governance. Cambridge University Press, Cambridge

Hart SL (2007) Capitalism at the crossroads: aligning commerce, earth and humanity, 2nd edn. Wharton School Publishing, New Jersey

Hastings DF (2006) Banking – gestão de ativos, passivos e resultados em instituições financeiras

Helmke G, Levitsky S (2003) Informal institutions and comparative politics: a research agenda. Working paper no. 307, Kellogg Institute for International Studies, University of Notre Dame, Notre Dame, Indiana

Henderson MT, Bainbridge S (2013) Boards-R-Us: reconceptualizing corporate boards. Coase-Sandor Institute for Law and Economics Working Paper No. 646

Hirschman AO (1970) Exit, voice, and loyality – responses to decline in firms, organizations and states. Harvard University Press, Cambridge/London

Hofstede. http://geert-hofstede.com/brazil.html [07.01.2017]

Hollister HT (2005) 'Shock therapy' for Aktiengesellschaften: can the Sarbanes-Oxley certification requirements transform German corporate culture, practice and prospects? NW J Int Law Bus 25:453–484

Hull JC (2010) Risk management and financial institutions, 2nd edn. Pearson

Hunger A (2002) Market segmentation and IPO-underpricing: the German experience, working paper. University of Munich

IBGE (2010) Censo Demográfico, Rio de Janeiro, pp 1–215

Igalens J, Roussel P (1999) A study of the relationships between compensation package, work motivation and job satisfaction. J Org Behav 20(7):1003–1025

IIF (2014) Report on governance for strengthened risk management, 2012. Available from http://www.iif.com/download.php?id=PTVGcYdhz8I [04.09.2014]

ISO.org (2017) http://www.iso.org/iso/sr_schematic-overview.pdf [05.03.2017]

Jacob CK (2012) The impact of financial crisis on corporate social responsibility and its implications for reputation risk management. J Manag Sustain 2(2):259

Jorion P (2009) Risk management lessons from the credit crisis. Eur Financ Manag 15(5):923–933

Kaplan S, John Garrick B (1981) On the quantitative definition of risk. Risk Anal I(I):11–27

Keitsch D (2007) Risikomanagement. Schäffer-Poeschel Verlag Stuttgart

Khan S, Vanwynsberghe R (2008) Cultivating the under-mined: cross-case analysis as knowledge mobilization. Qual Soc Res 14(5)

Kindleberger CP, Aliber RZ (2011) Manias, panics, and crashes – a history of financial crises. Palgrave, New York

Kirchhoff KR. Good Company Ranking 2013 – Corporate Social Responsibility-Wettbewerb der 70 größten Konzerne Europas. Available from http://www.kirchhoff.de/fileadmin/20_Download/2013-Highlights/Studie_Good_Company_Ranking_2013.pdf

Kirkpatrick G (2009) Corporate governance lessons from the financial crisis. OECD J Financ Trends, Volume 2009 – Issue 1

Klapper LF, Love I. Corporate governance, investor protection, and performance in emerging markets. The World Bank, Policy Research Working Paper 2812, April 2002

Kleinfeld Belton R (2005) Competing definitions of the rule of law – implications for practitioners. Carnegie Papers, Number 55, January 2005

Klonoski R (2012) Adopting a global code of business ethics: a comparative analysis of German and U.S. attitudes toward universal guidelines. J Law Soc Sci 1(1):102–111

Kooiman J (2003) Governing as governance, London

Krieg H-J (2010) Reizwort Bonus – Sinn oder Unsinn variabler Vergütung. Available from http://www. symposion.de/kapitel33640101_WERK7001006.html@ fi3ce32455e7da40ec1063ba2c822b0908

Landes D (2000) Culture makes almost all of the difference. In: Harrison LE, Huntington SP (eds) Culture matters 2

Ladipo D, Nestor S, Risser D (2008) Board profile, structure and practice in large european banks: a comparative corporate governance study. Nextor Advisors, London

Ladipo D, Nestor S (2009) Bank boards and the financial crisis – A corporate governance study of the 25 largest European banks. Nextor Advisors, London

La Porta R, Lopez-de-Silanes F, Shleifer A, Vishny RW (1998) Law and finance. J Polit Econ 106:1113, originally appeared as NBER Working Paper No. 5661 (1996)

La Porta R, Lopez-de-Silanes F, Shleifer A (2002) Government ownership of banks. J Financ LVII (1):265–301

Leitschuh H (2008) CSR ist gut, nachhaltiges Wirtschaften ist besser. uwf, Jg. 1/08, Heidelberg

Levy H (2010) The CAPM is alive and well: a review and synthesis. Eur Financ Manag 16 (1):43–71

Licht AN, Goldschmidt C, Schwartz SH (2005) Culture, law, and corporate governance. Int Rev Law Econ 25(2):229–255

Lipton M, Neff DA, Brownstein AR, Rosenblum SA, Emmerich AO, Fain SL (Wachtell, Lipton, Rosen, & Katz) (2011) Risk management and the board of directors. In: Bank and Corporate Governance Law Reporter 45(6):793–799

Lister M (2010) Wege aus der Finanzkrise – Anpassungsbedarf im Risikomanagement der Finanzinstitute. In: Frank Keuper/Fritz Neumann (Hrsg) Corporate governance, risk management und compliance – Innovative Konzepte und Strategien, pp 293–309

Litzcke S, Linssen R, Maffenbeier S, Schilling J (2012) Korruption: Risikofaktor Mensch – Wahrnehmung, Rechtfertigung, Meldeverhalten. Wiesbaden

Loew T, Ankele K, Braun S, Clausen J (2004) Bedeutung der internationalen CSR-Diskussion für Nachhaltigkeit und die sich daraus ergebenden Anforderungen an Unternehmen mit Fokus Berichterstattung, Münster und Berlin

Lorson P, Peters S, Fuhrmann C (2014a) Nachhaltige Unternehmensführung: Sustainability versus Corporates Social Responsibility und ähnliche Konzepte: Abgrenzung und Vergleich auf der Basis aktueller Studien. In: Zeitschrift für Corporate Governance (ZCG) 2014:11 ff

Lorson P, S Peters, Fuhrmann C (2014b) Nachhaltigkeit versus Konzepte unternehmerischer Verantwortung. In: Zeitschrift für Corporate Governance (ZCG), 2014:53 ff

Lubrano M. Corporate Governance in Brazil: Observations on 2000-2007 and comparisons with other Latin American and BRIC markets. Washington: IFC/Word Bank Corporate Governance Department

Mahoney LS, Thorn L (2006) An examination of the structure of executive compensation and corporate social responsibility: a Canadian investigation. J Bus Ethics 69:149–162

Maier KM (2007) Risikomanagement im Immobilien- und Finanzwesen – Ein Leitfaden für Theorie und Praxis

Markowitz H (1952) Portfolio selection. J Financ 7:77–91

Markowitz H (1959) Portfolio selection: efficient diversification of investments. Wiley, New York

Martin DX (2013) A seat and at voice at the table. In: Institutional Investor, May 2013

Maslow AH (1943) A theory of human motivation. Psychol Rev 50(4):370–396

Meehl P (2003) Clinical versus statistical prediction: a theoretical analysis and a review of the evidence. Echo Point Books & Media, Brattleboro, VT

Merton RK (1957) Social theory and social structure. Free Press, New York

Middelhoff T (2007) Was ist Corporate Governance? In: Compliance-Magazin.de (http://www. compliancemagazin.de/corporategovernance/anforderungen/karstadtquelle020507.html), 02.05.2007

Milgrom P, Roberts J (1990) The economics of modern manufacturing: technology, strategy and organization. Am Econ Rev 80:511–528

Moerke A, Dolles H (2004) Corporate governance in multinational organizations during turbulent times: cases from the automotive industry. Working Paper No. 04/3. Deutsches Institut für Japanstudien, Tokio, pp 1–33

Monks RAG, Nell M (2004) Corporate governance

Montiel I (2008) Corporate social responsibility and corporate sustainability – separate pasts, common futures. Org Environ 21:245–269

Morck R (2005) The history of corporate governance around the world: family business groups to professional advisors. University of Chicago Press, Chicago

Mülbert PO (2010) Corporate governance of banks after the financial crisis – theory, evidence, reforms, law. Working Paper N°.130/2009, April 2010, http://ssrn.com/abstract=1448118

Nenova T (2003) The value of corporate voting rights and control: a cross-country analysis. J Financ Econ 68:325–351

Neßler C, Lis B (2014) Corporate Governance – Eine unternehmens-kulturelle Frage, in ZCG3/2014:106 ff

Nicoletti G, Scarpetta S (2003) Regulation, productivity, and growth: OECD evidence. World Bank Policy Research Working Paper 2944, January 2003. http://library1.nida.ac.th/worldbankf/fulltext/wps02944.pdf

Norman W, MacDonald C (2004) Getting to the Bottom of *"Triple Bottom Line"*. Bus Ethics Q 14 (2):243–262

Normenkontrollrat, Nationaler (2007) Anwendung des Standardkosten-Modells im europäischen Vergleich. Available from http://www.bundesregierung.de/Content/DE/StatischeSeiten/Breg/Anlagen/2007-01-00-skm-in-europa.html?nn=437032

North DC (1994) Economic performance through time. Am Econ Rev 84(June):359–368

Nwogugu M (2005) Corporate governance, legal reasoning, credit risk and corporate strategy – The Case of Encompass Services Inc. Managerial Law 2005; 47, 1/2; ABI/INFORM Global

OECD (1999) OECD principles for corporate governance: standards and guidelines for shareholder rights and other governance issues

OECD (2004) OECD principles for corporate governance. Available from http://www.oecd.org/daf/ca/corporategovernanceprinciples/31557724.pdf

OECD (2009) Corporate governance and the financial crisis – key findings and main messages, June 2009

Oliva EC, de Albuquerque LG (2006) Filosofia e Modelo dos Programas de Remuneração das Empresas que aderiram aos níveis diferenciados de Governança Corporativa da BOVESPA. Revista de Gestão USP, São Paulo 13(2):79–96, abril/junho 2006

O'Neill J (2001) Building Better Global Conomic BRICs. Global Economics Paper No: 66, 30th November 2001

Oord F (2013) Corporate governance: hidden cracks still remain. http://www.executiveboard.com/blogs/corporate-governance-hidden-cracks-still-remain/?business_line=legal-risk-compliance. 16/09/2013

Pava M (2007) A response to 'Getting to the bottom of "Triple Bottom Line"'. Bus Ethics Q 17 (1):105–110

PCGC – Portuguese Corporate Governance Code – Código de Governo das Sociedades, IPCG (2014) http://www.cgov.pt/images/stories/ficheiros/codigo_de_governo_das_sociedades_do_ipcg.pdf

Peng MW (2001) How entrepreneurs create wealth in transition economies. Acad Manag Exec 15 (1):95–108

Peng MW, Heath P (1996) The growth of the firm in planned economies in transition: institutions, organizations and strategic choice. Acad Manag Rev 21(2):492–528

Pinto JC (coord) (2013) A Emergência e o Futuro do Corporate Governance em Portugal – Volume comemorativo do X aniversário do Instituto Português de Corporate Governance, December 2013

Pistor K, Raiser M, Gelfer S (2000) Law and Finance in Transition Economies, EBRD Working Paper No. 48

Plamper H (2010) Governance, risk management und compliance – Was benötigt der Staat zur Krisenbewältigung? Frank Keuper/Fritz Neumann (Hrsg.): corporate governance, risk management und compliance – Innovative Konzepte und Strategien, pp 121–140

Porter ME, Kramer MR (2006) Strategy & society, the link between competitive advantage and corporate social responsibility. Harv Bus Rev 84(12):76–93

Preen A, Raible K-F, Pacher S, Wagner R (2014) Zur Angemessenheit von Vorstandsbezügen – Ein Plädoyer für eine Versachlichung der Diskussion. ZCG 3/14, pp 101–105

Quaresma A (2011) Modelos de Corporate Governance: Sua influência na gestão do risco e consequente desempenho financeiro das organizações, Lisboa

Ragin C (1993) Introduction to qualitative comparative analysis. In: Janoski T, Hicks A (eds) The comparative political economy of the welfare state. Cambridge University Press, New York, pp 299–319

Ramalho R (2003) The effects of an anti-corruption campaign: evidence from the 1992 presidential impeachment in brazil, MIT WP

Regalli M, Soana M-G (2012) Corporate governance quality and cost of equity in financial companies. Int J Bus Admin 3(2); March 2012, p 2 ff., doi:https://doi.org/10.5430/ijba.v3n2p2

Renn O (2005) Risk governance – towards an integrative approach, Geneva, September 2005

Ricardo D (1817) On the principles of political economy and taxation

Rodrigues J (2009) Corporate Governance – Retomar a confiança perdida, Escolar Editora

Ross S (1976) The arbitrage theory of capital asset pricing. J Econ Theory 13(3):341–360

Rossi C (2012a) Incentives, behaviors and cognitive bias in the risk function. Risk Professional, April 2012, p 32 ff

Rossi C (2012b) Incentives, behaviors and cognitive bias in the risk function. http://blogs.rhsmith.umd.edu/cliffordrossi/files/2012/02/OFRRiskGovernanceCVR11111112.pdf [14.04.2017]

Rott R (2009) A systemic evaluation of the German corporate governance code: the battle between inconsistency and persistence. In: López-Iturriaga FJ (ed) Codes of good governance around the world. Nova Publishers, Hauppauge, pp 187–214

Rudder CE (2008) Private governance as public policy: a paradigmatic shift. J Polit 70(4):899–913

Safetyrisk.net. http://www.safetyrisk.net/new-risk-management-standard-asnzs-iso-31000/ [03.09.2014]

Schaller S. The democratic legitimacy of private governance. an analysis of the ethical trading initiative. Institute for Development and Peace, University of Duisburg-Essen, Duisburg (INEF Report, 91/2007)

Savage GT, Nix TW, Whitehead CJ, Blair JD (1991) Strategies for assessing and managing organizational stakeholders. Acad Manag Exec 5(2):61–75

Schaupensteiner W (2004) Korruption in Deutschland. Lagebild. Maßnahmen und Gefahren. In: Schilling A, Dolata U (Hrsg) Korruption im Wirtschaftssystem Deutschland. Jeder Mensch hat seinen Preis, pp 117–136

Scheffner J (2012) IKS im Wandel – Vom Risikomanagement zur Performancesteigerung. Haufe Online Redaktion. 26.04.2012. http://www.haufe.de/controlling/controllerpraxis/ICS-im-wandel-vom-risikomanagement-zur-performancesteigerung_112_89896.html

Schmalhardt H (2010) Korruption als unternehmerisches Risiko. In: Frank Keuper/Fritz Neumann (Hrsg) Corporate Governance, Risk Management und Compliance – Innovative Konzepte und Strategien, pp 143–162

Schuch E (2011) Welche Möglichkeiten bietet Corporate Social Responsibility für die Entwicklung in Schwellenländern? Untersuchung anhand Brasiliens

Schulte J (2001) Von der Börse zum Wertpapiermarktorganisator. Ebs-Forschung, DUV: Wirtschaftswissenschaft Volume 30

Schumpeter JA (1911) The theory of economic development. Cambridge, MA

Schütte M (2009) Eckpunkte für die Vergütung von Managern, 62. Jahrgang – ifo Schnelldienst 11/2009

Sharma R (2014) BIITS and ballots – how elections this year in five emerging markets could boost – or hurt – reform. Time, January 20, 2014

Sharma T, Narwal M (2006) Managing business crisis: the CSR perspective. Soc Respons J 2 (2):124–130

Shinkman M, Herd D (2014) A SMART risk approach – how to use key risk indicators to make more intelligent, risk-informed decisions. http://www.garp.org/risk-news-and-resources/ 2014/march/a-smart-risk-approach.aspx?utm_source=Newsletter&utm_medium=Email& utm_campaign=WeekInRisk_March21_2014, 19/03/2014 [03.09.2014]

Shleifer A, Vishny RW (1997) A survey of corporate governance. J Financ 52:737–783

Silveira ADM, Leal RPC, Carvalhal-da-Silva AL, Barros LABC (2007) Evolution and determinants of firm-level corporate governance quality in Brazil. In: Paper presented at the International Research Conference on Corporate Governance in Emerging Markets, Istanbul, 15–18 November 2007

Silveira ADM (2010) Governança Corporativa no Brasil e no Mundo. Elsevier

Smith A (1776) An inquiry into the nature and causes of the wealth of nations

Sobel PJ, Reding KF (2004) Aligning corporate governance with enterprise risk management. Manag Account Q 5(2):29–37

Standke F (2010) Unternehmensweiter Ansatz zu einer Governance-, Risk- und Compliance-Lösung. In: Frank Keuper/Fritz Neumann (Hrsg) Corporate Governance, Risk Management und Compliance – Innovative Konzepte und Strategien, pp 267–291

Stigler GJ (1971) Theory of economic regulation. http://www.ppge.ufrgs.br/GIACOMO/arquivos/ regulacao2/stigler-1971.pdf

Stulz RM, Williamson R (2003) Culture, openness, and finance. J Financ Econ 70(3):313–349

Transparency.org. http://media.transparency.org/maps/cpi2013-940.html [03.09.2014]

Valukas AR, Lehman Brothers Holdings, Inc. et al. Debtors Report, March 11, 2010. Excerpts available from http://web.stanford.edu/~johntayl/Examiner%20on%20Lehman%20Weekend.pdf

Viviers S, Bosch JK, Smit E, Buijis A (2008) Is responsible investment ethical? S Afr J Bus Manag 39(1):15–25

Weber M (1988) Politik als Beruf, in: Gesammelte Politische Schriften, hrsg. von J. Winckelmann, 5. Auflage Mohr Siebeck, Tübingen

Weisman A (2013) In-flight adjustment. Institutional Investor, May 2013:44 ff

Wieser C (2005) "Corporate Social Responsibility" – Ethik, Kosmetik oder Strategie? – Über die Relevanz der sozialen Verantwortung in der Strategischen Unternehmensführung

Williamson OE (1985) The economic insitutions of capitalism: firms, markets, relational contracting. Macmillan, New York

Wolf A (2009) Aufbau und Eignung unterschiedlicher Vergütungsmodelle als Anreizsystem – Vergütung und Motivation in Kreditinstituten, Grin Verlag, 1. Auflage 2009

World Bank (2013) Doing Business 2014 – Understanding regulations for small and medium-size enterprises, Washington. http://www.doingbusiness.org/~/media/GIAWB/Doing%20Business/ Documents/Annual-reports/English/DB14-Full-Report.pdf

Yeoh P (2007) Corporate governance models: is there a right one for transition economies in Central and Eastern Europe? Manag Law 49(3):57–75

Zingales L (1998) Corporate governance. Available from http://papers.ssrn.com/sol3/papers.cfm? abstract_id=46906

Printed by Printforce, the Netherlands